Microsoft® Office
Access 2003

Alison Balter

Teach
Yourself

Sams Publishing, 800 East 96th Street, Indianapolis, Indiana 46240 USA

Microsoft® Office Access 2003 in a Snap

Copyright © 2005 by Sams Publishing

International Standard Book Number: 0-672-32544-6

Library of Congress Catalog Card Number: 2004094055

Printed in the United States of America

First Printing: August 2004

07   06   05   04   4   3   2   1

Trademarks

Warning and Disclaimer

Bulk Sales

Sams Publishing offers excellent discounts on this book when ordered in quantity for bulk purchases or special sales. For more information, please contact

U.S. Corporate and Government Sales

1-800-382-3419

corpsales@pearsontechgroup.com

For sales outside of the U.S., please contact

International Sales

1-317-428-3341

international@pearsontechgroup.com

Associate Publisher
Michael Stephens

Acquisitions Editor
Loretta Yates

Development Editor
Audrey Doyle

Managing Editor
Charlotte Clapp

Project Editor
Elizabeth Finney

Production Editor
Benjamin Berg

Indexer
Mandie Frank

Proofreader
Cindy Long

Technical Editor
Jon Price

Publishing Coordinator
Cindy Teeters

Book Designer
Gary Adair

About the Author

Alison Balter is the president of InfoTechnology Partners, Inc., a computer consulting firm based in Camarillo, California. Alison is a highly experienced independent trainer and consultant specializing in Windows applications training and development. During her 20 years in the computer industry, she has trained and consulted with many corporations and government agencies. Since Alison founded InfoTechnology Partners, Inc. (formerly Marina Consulting Group) in 1990, its client base has expanded to include major corporations and government agencies such as Shell Oil, Accenture, AIG Insurance, Northrop, the Drug Enforcement Administration, Prudential Insurance, Transamerica Insurance, Fox Broadcasting, the United States Navy, and others.

InfoTechnology Partners, Inc. is a Microsoft Certified Partner, and Alison is a Microsoft Certified Professional. Alison was one of the first professionals in the computer industry to become a Microsoft Certified Solutions Developer (MCSD).

Alison is the author of more than 300 internationally marketed computer training videos, including 18 Access 2000 videos, 35 Access 2002 videos, and 15 Access 2003 videos. These videos are available by contacting Alison's company, InfoTechnology Partners, Inc. Alison travels throughout North America giving training seminars in Microsoft Access, Visual Studio .NET, Microsoft SQL Server, Visual Basic, and Visual Basic for Applications. She is also featured in several live satellite television broadcasts for National Technological University.

Alison is a regular contributing columnist for *Access/Office/VB Advisor* as well as other computer publications. She is also a regular on the Access, Visual Studio .NET, SQL Server, and Visual Basic national speaker circuits. She was one of four speakers on the Visual Basic 4.0 and 5.0 World Tours seminar series co-sponsored by Application Developers Training Company and Microsoft.

Alison is also author of six other books published by Sams Publishing: *Alison Balter's Mastering Access 95 Development*, *Alison Balter's Mastering Access 97 Development*, *Alison Balter's Mastering Access 2000 Development*, *Alison Balter's Mastering Access 2002 Desktop Development*, *Alison Balter's Mastering Access 2002 Enterprise Development,* and *Teach Yourself Microsoft Office Access 2003 in 24 Hours*. Alison is a co-author of three Access books published by Sams Publishing: *Essential Access 95*, *Access 95 Unleashed*, and *Access 97 Unleashed*.

An active participant in many user groups and other organizations, Alison is a past president of the Independent Computer Consultants Association of Los Angeles and of the Los Angeles Clipper Users' Group. She is currently vice president of the Ventura County Professional Women's Network, and will be the president of the group next year.

On a personal note, Alison keeps herself busy horseback riding, skiing, ice skating, running, lifting weights, hiking, traveling, and dancing. She most enjoys spending time with her husband, Dan, their daughter Alexis, their son Brendan, and their Golden Retriever, Brandy.

Alison's firm, InfoTechnology Partners, Inc., is available for consulting work and onsite training in Microsoft Access, Visual Studio .NET, Visual Basic, and SQL Server, as well as for Windows Server 2003, Windows 2000, Windows NT, Windows 98, Windows XP, PC networking, and Microsoft Exchange Server. Contact Alison by electronic mail at Alison@InfoTechnologyPartners.com, or visit InfoTechnology Partners' Web site at www.InfoTechnologyPartners.com.

Dedication

*I dedicate this book to my husband Dan, my daughter Alexis, my son
Brendan, my parents Charlotte and Bob, and to my real father, Herman.
Dan, you are my partner in life and the wind beneath my wings. You are a
true partner in every sense of the word. I am so lucky to be traveling the path
of life with such a spectacular person. Alexis, you are the sweet little girl that
I always dreamed of. You are everything that I could have ever wanted and
so very much more. You make every one of my days a happy one! Brendan,
you are the one who keeps me on my toes. There is never a dull moment with
you around. I wish I had just a small portion of your energy. I thank you for
the endless laughter that you bring to our family and for reminding me
about all of the important things in life. Mom and Dad, without all that you
do to help out with life's chores, the completion of this book could never have
been possible. Words cannot express my gratitude!*

*To my real father, Herman, I credit my ability to soar in such a technical
field to you. I hope that I inherited just a small part of your intelligence, wit,
and fortitude. I am sorry that you did not live to see this accomplishment. I
hope that you can see my work and that you are proud of it. I also hope that
in some way you share in the joy that Dan, Alexis, and Brendan bring to me.*

*Finally, I want to thank God for giving me the gift of gab, a wonderful career,
an incredible husband, two beautiful children, a very special home, and an
awesome life. Through your grace, I am truly blessed.*

Acknowledgments

Writing a book is a monumental task. Without the support and understanding of those close to
me, my dreams for this book would have never come to fruition. Special thanks go to the following
special people who helped to make this book possible:

Dan Balter (my incredible husband) for his ongoing support, love, encouragement, friendship,
and for, as usual, being patient with me while I wrote this book. Dan, words cannot adequately
express the love and appreciation that I feel for all that you are and all that you do for me. You
treat me like a princess! Thank you for being the phenomenal person you are. I enjoy sharing not
only our career successes, but even more I enjoy sharing the life of our beautiful children, Alexis
and Brendan. I look forward to continuing to reach highs we never dreamed of. There is no one I'd
rather spend forever with than you.

Alexis Balter (my precious daughter) for giving life a special meaning. Your intelligence,
compassion, caring, and perceptiveness are far beyond your years. Alexis, you make all my hard

work worth it. No matter how bad my day, when I look at you, sunshine fills my life. You are the most special gift that anyone has ever given me.

Brendan Balter (my adorable son) for showing me the power of persistence. Brendan, you are small, but boy are you mighty! I have never seen such tenacity and fortitude in such a little person. Your imagination and creativity are amazing! Thank you for your sweetness, your sensitivity, and your unconditional love. Most of all, thank you for reminding me how important it is to have a sense of humor.

Charlotte and Bob Roman (Mom & Dad) for believing in me and sharing in both the good times and the bad. Mom and Dad, without your special love and support, I never would have become who I am today. Without all your help, I could never get everything done. Words can never express how much I appreciate all that you do!

Al Ludington for helping me to slow down and experience the shades of gray in the world. You somehow walk the fine line between being there and setting limits, between comforting me and confronting me. Words cannot express how much your unconditional love and friendship means to me. Thanks for showing me that a beautiful mind is not such a bad thing after all.

Sue Terry for being the most wonderful best friend anyone could possibly have. You inspire me with your music, your love, your friendship, and your faith in God. Whenever I am having a bad day, I picture you singing "Dear God" or "Love Thy Neighbor Blues," and suddenly my day gets better. Thank you for the gift of friendship.

Roz, Ron, and Charlie Carriere for supporting my endeavors and for encouraging me to pursue my writing. It means a lot to know that you guys are proud of me for what I do. I enjoy our times together as a family. Charlie, have a great time at Yale.

Steven Chait for being a special brother. I want you to know how much you mean to me. When I was a little girl, I was told about your gift to write. You may not know this, but my desire to write started as a little girl wanting to be like her big brother.

Sonia Aguilar for being the best nanny that anyone could ever dream of having. You are a person far too special to describe in words. I can't tell you how much it means to know that Alexis and Brendan have someone so loving and caring with whom to spend their days. You are an amazing model of love, kindness, and charity. Te amo muchisimo y Dios te bendiga!

Doug and Karen Sylvester for being wonderful friends. You are loads of fun to be with and are always there when we need you. We are so glad you are such an integral part of our lives.

Anita Srinivasa for being a wonderful friend, doctor, and confidante. You've been there in both the good times and the bad, and have known when to step in and when not to. You are a very special person, and I hope that you are always a part of our lives.

Anne Weidenweber for being a great friend and walking partner. I am so glad that our relationship is developing far beyond a business relationship. I love our walks and the time we spend together. You are an inspiring, uplifting, and motivating influence in my life.

Greggory Peck from Blast Through Learning for his contribution to my success in this industry. I believe that the opportunities you gave me early on have helped me reach a level in this industry that would have been much more difficult for me to reach on my own.

Edie Swanson for being a great assistant. Thanks for making my day-to-day work life easier.

Diane Dennis, Shell Forman, Joyce Milner, Scott Barker, Ron Henderson, Norbert Foigelman, Chris Sabihon, and all of the other wonderful friends that I have in my life. Diane, you have been my soul mate in life since we were four! Shell, my special "sister," I am lucky to have such a special friend as you. Joyce, miles can't keep our hearts apart. I only wish that we could see more of each other. Scott, you have always been a great business and personal support. Ron, you started out as a client, but have a *very* special place in my heart. Norbert, you are a very special friend to me, and to my family. Chris, not only are you a special friend, but you have had an important impact on my spiritual path in life!

Ellen McCrea, Chuck Hinkle, Bob Hess, Herb Schmidt, Eli Facuseh, and all of the other special clients and work associates that I have in my life. Although all of you started out as work associates, I feel that our relationship goes much deeper than that. I am *very* lucky to have people in my work life like you. Thank you all for your patience with my schedule as I wrote this book.

Kim Spilker, Loretta Yates, Audrey Doyle, Elizabeth Finney, Charlotte Clapp, Benjamin Berg, and Jon Price for making my experience with Sams a positive one. I know that you all worked very hard to ensure that this book came out on time and with the best quality possible. Without you, this book wouldn't have happened. I have *really* enjoyed working with *all* of you over these past several years. I appreciate your thoughtfulness and your sensitivity to my schedule and commitments outside of this book. It is nice to work with people who appreciate me as a person, not just as an author.

We Want to Hear from You!

As the reader of this book, *you* are our most important critic and commentator. We value your opinion and want to know what we're doing right, what we could do better, what areas you'd like to see us publish in, and any other words of wisdom you're willing to pass our way.

As an associate publisher for Sams Publishing, I welcome your comments. You can email or write me directly to let me know what you did or didn't like about this book—as well as what we can do to make our books better.

Please note that I cannot help you with technical problems related to the topic of this book. We do have a User Services group, however, where I will forward specific technical questions related to the book.

When you write, please be sure to include this book's title and author as well as your name, email address, and phone number. I will carefully review your comments and share them with the author and editors who worked on the book.

Email: feedback@samspublishing.com

Mail: Michael Stephens
            Associate Publisher
            Sams Publishing
            800 East 96th Street
            Indianapolis, IN 46240 USA

For more information about this book or another Sams Publishing title, visit our Web site at www.samspublishing.com Type the ISBN (0672325446) or the title of a book in the Search field to find the page you're looking for.

PART I

Introduction to Relational Databases and Access 2003

1

✔ Start Here

Microsoft Access is an extremely powerful product. It is the perfect product for storing and working with database information. Many people store database information in Word documents or Excel spreadsheets. Although Excel has limited database capabilities, it is not a robust database product. Microsoft Access is the perfect product for storing customer information, mailing lists, wine lists, recipes, or any other types of data that you need to keep track of. Once you have entered data into Microsoft Access, it is easy to retrieve just the data that you want whenever you want it. This book shows you how to harness the power of this marvelous product, taking advantage of all that it has to offer.

What Is a Relational Database?

The term *database* means different things to different people. For many years, in the world of xBase (that is, dBASE, FoxPro, CA-Clipper), database was used to describe a collection of fields and records. (Access refers to this type of collection as a table.) In a client/server environment, database refers to all the data, schema, indexes, rules, triggers, and stored procedures associated with a system. In Access terms, a database is a collection of all the tables, queries, forms, data access pages, reports, macros, and modules that compose a complete system. *Relational* refers to the fact that the tables that comprise the database relate to one another.

What Types of Things Can I Do with Microsoft Access?

I often find myself explaining exactly what types of applications you can build with Microsoft Access. Access offers a variety of features for different database needs. You can use it to develop six general types of applications:

- Personal applications
- Small-business applications
- Departmental applications
- Corporationwide applications
- Front-end applications for enterprisewide client/server databases
- Intranet/Internet applications

Access As a Development Platform for Personal Applications

You can use Access to automate everything from your wine collections to your home finances. Using Access's built-in wizards, you can create application switchboards that allow you to easily navigate around the application, data-entry screens, and reports, as well as the underlying tables that support them.

If you're an end user and don't want to spend too much time learning the intricacies of Access, you'll be satisfied with Access as long as you're happy with a wizard-generated personal application. After reading this text, you can make minor modifications, and no problems should occur. It's when you want to substantially customize a personal application without the proper knowledge base that problems can occur.

Access As a Development Platform for Small-Business Applications

Access is an excellent platform for developing an application that can run a small business. Its wizards let you quickly and easily build the application's foundation. The ability to build code modules allows power users and developers to create code libraries of reusable functions, and the ability to add code behind forms and reports allows them to create powerful custom forms and reports.

The main limitation of using Access for developing a custom small-business application is the time and money involved in the development process. Many people use Access wizards to begin the development process but find they need to customize their applications in ways they can't accomplish on their own. Small-business owners often experience this problem on an even greater scale than personal users. The demands of a small-business application are usually much higher than those of a personal application. Many doctors, attorneys, and other professionals have called me in after they reached a dead end in the development process. They're always dismayed at how much money it will cost to make their application usable. An example is a doctor who built a series of forms and reports to automate her office. All went well until it came time to produce patient billings, enter payments, and generate product receivable reports. Although at first glance these processes seemed simple, upon further examination, the doctor realized that the wizard-produced reports and forms did not provide the sophistication necessary for her billing process. Unfortunately, the doctor did not have the time or programming skills to add the necessary features. So, in using Access as a tool to develop small-business applications, it is important that you be realistic about the time and money involved in developing anything but the simplest of applications.

Access As a Development Platform for Departmental Applications

Access is perfect for developing applications for departments in large corporations. Most departments in large corporations have the development budgets to produce well-designed applications.

Most departments have some local talent on hand that can help to develop the forms and reports necessary for the application. If complex design or coding is necessary, large corporations usually have on-site resources that can complete the development process. If on-site developers are unavailable, most corporations are willing to outsource to obtain the necessary expertise.

Access As a Development Platform for Corporationwide Applications

Although Access might be best suited for departmental applications, you can also use it to produce applications that you distribute throughout an organization. How successful this endeavor is depends on the corporation. There's a limit to the number of users who can concurrently share an Access application while maintaining acceptable performance, and there's also a limit to the number of records that each table can contain without a significant performance drop. These numbers vary depending on factors such as the following:

- How much traffic already exists on the network.

- How much RAM and how many processors the server has.

- How the server is already being used. For example, are applications such as Microsoft Office being loaded from the server or from local workstations?

- What types of tasks the users of the application are performing. For example, are they querying, entering data, running reports, and so on?

- Where Access and Access applications are run from (the server or the workstation).

- What network operating system is in place.

My general rule of thumb for an Access application that's not client/server based is that poor performance generally results with more than 10–15 concurrent users and more than 100,000 records. Remember that these numbers vary immensely depending on the factors mentioned, as well as on what you and the users define as acceptable performance. If you go beyond these limits, you should consider using Access as a front end to a client/server database such as Microsoft SQL Server—that is, you can use Access to create forms and reports while storing tables and possibly queries on the database server.

Access As a Front End for Enterprisewide Client/Server Applications

A client/server database, such as Microsoft SQL Server or Oracle, processes queries on the server machine and returns results to the workstation.

The server software itself can't display data to the user, so this is where Access comes to the rescue. Acting as a front end, Access can display the data retrieved from the database server in reports, datasheets, or forms. If the user updates the data in an Access form, the workstation sends the update to the back-end database. You can accomplish this process either by linking to these external databases so that they appear to both you and the user as Access tables or by using techniques to access client/server data directly.

Access As a Development Platform for Intranet/Internet Applications

By using data access pages, intranet and Internet users can update application data from within a browser. *Data access pages* are Hypertext Markup Language (HTML) documents that are bound directly to data in a database. Although Access stores data access pages outside a database, you use them just as you do standard Access forms except that Microsoft designed them to run in Microsoft Internet Explorer 5.5 or higher, rather than in Microsoft Access. Data access pages use dynamic HTML in order to accomplish their work. Because they are supported only in Internet Explorer 5.5 or higher, data access pages are much more appropriate as an intranet solution than as an Internet solution.

In addition to using data access pages, you can also publish database objects as either static or dynamic HTML pages. *Static HTML pages* are standard HTML pages that you can view in any browser. You can publish database objects either dynamically to the HTX/IDC file format or to the ASP (Active Server Pages) file format. *Dynamic HTML pages* are pages that are published by the Web server each time that they are rendered. The Web server publishes HTX/IDC files dynamically, and these files are therefore browser independent. The Web server also dynamically publishes ASP files published by Microsoft Access, but the published ASP pages require Internet Explorer 4.0 or higher on the client machine.

Access 2002 introduced the ability to create Extensible Markup Language (XML) data and schema documents from Jet or SQL Server structures and data. You can also import data and data structures into Access from XML documents. You can accomplish this either using code or via the user interface.

NOTE

Alison Balter's *Mastering Access 2002 Enterprise Development*, published by Sams, covers the details of developing client/server applications with Microsoft Access.

KEY TERMS

Data access pages—Hypertext Markup Language (HTML) documents that are bound directly to data in a database.

Static HTML pages—Standard HTML pages that you can view in any browser.

Dynamic HTML pages—Pages that are published by the Web server each time that they are rendered.

Starting Microsoft Access

The first step in getting started is to launch Microsoft Access. You launch Microsoft Access from the Start menu or from a desktop shortcut.

To start Access from the **Start** menu, you select **Start**, **Programs**, **Microsoft Office**, **Microsoft Office Access 2003**. The **Access Desktop** with the **Getting Started** window appears, as shown in the following figure. Here you can get help, open an existing database, or create a new database.

The Getting Started window in Microsoft Access is where you can get help, open an existing database, or create a new database.

 TIP

When you first launch Access, a special window, called the *task pane*, appears on the right side of the screen. From the **task pane**, you can easily open a recently used database, create a new database of any type, or navigate to any database stored locally or on a network drive.

 **KEY TERM**

Task pane—A special window from which you can easily open a recently used database, create a new database, or navigate to any database stored locally or on a network drive.

To start Access from a desktop shortcut, with the Windows desktop active, simply double-click the **Access** desktop shortcut. Access launches.

Opening an Existing Database

After you have started Access, you can create a new database or open an existing database. A database is a single file that contains objects such as tables, queries, forms, and reports. A database is stored as a file on your computer or on a network computer. To work with the objects in a database, you must open the database file.

To open an existing database from the **Getting Started** window, follow these steps:

1. Click **More** under the **Open** options. The **Open** dialog box appears, as shown in the following figure.

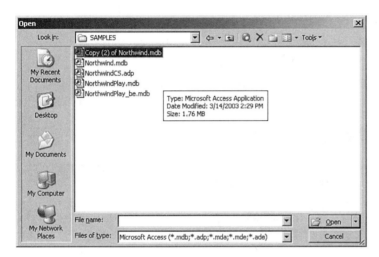

The Open dialog box appears when you click More under the Open options.

2. If necessary, open the **Look In** drop-down list box to select another drive or directory.

3. Click to select the filename of the database you want to open.

4. Click **Open**. Access opens the database.

To open a recently used database from the **Getting Started** window, follow these steps:

1. Locate the database in the list of files in the **Getting Started** window.

2. Click the link to the desired database. Access opens the database.

To open an existing database from the **File** menu, follow these steps:

1. Choose **File**, **Open**. The **Open** dialog box appears.

2. If necessary, open the **Look In** drop-down list box to select another drive or directory.

3. Click to select the filename of the database you want to open.

4. Click **Open**. Access opens the database.

To open a recently used database from the **File** menu, follow these steps:

1. Open the **File** menu.

2. Locate the desired database in the list of recently used files at the bottom of the **File** menu.

3. Click to select the desired file. Access opens the database.

The Access Desktop

The Access **Desktop** contains a title bar, a menu bar, one or more toolbars, and the **Database** window, as shown in the following figure.

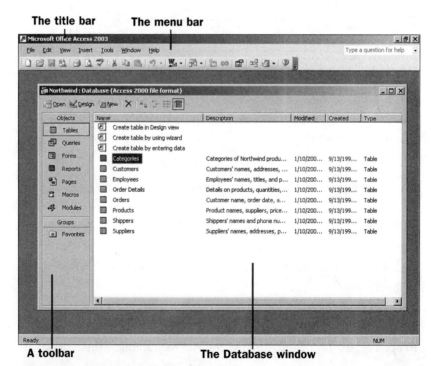

The title bar   The menu bar

A toolbar   The Database window

The Access Desktop.

Menu bars and toolbars change, depending on the view you are in at any given time. For example, when you look at a table object, there are tools on the toolbar that are appropriate when working with tables. When you are in **Design** view for a form, you see tools appropriate for designing a form.

The Database Window

When you open a database, the **Database** window, shown in the following figure, appears within the Access desktop window. The **Database** window allows you to select any of the **Objects** tabs. The **Database** window contains its own buttons and objects that are not found in its parent window, the Access desktop window. The table that follows describes these buttons and objects and what they do. The objects are discussed in more detail in the sections that follow.

The Buttons and Objects in the Database Window

Button/Object	Description
Open	Opens the object you have selected.
Design	Allows you to modify the design of the selected object.
New	Opens a new object based on the type of object selected.
Tables	Lists the tables in the database. Each table contains data about a particular subject.
Queries	Lists the queries in the database. Each query is a stored question about data in the database.
Forms	Lists the forms in the database. Each form allows you to view, add, edit, and delete data.
Reports	Lists the reports for the database. Each report allows you to send table data to the printer or screen in a format that you define.
Pages	Lists the data access pages. This allows viewing of and working with data from the Internet or an intranet.
Macros	Lists the macros created to automate the way you work with data.
Modules	Lists the modules of programming code created for the database.
Groups/Favorites	Allows you to create your own groups of favorite objects that you frequently work with (forms, reports, and so on). An example would be sales reports.

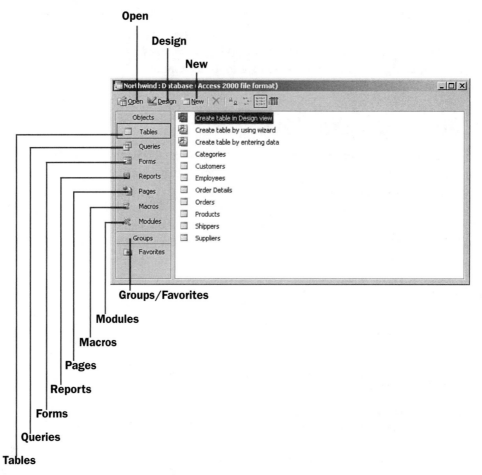

The Database Window.

A Preview of the Database Components

As mentioned previously, tables, queries, forms, reports, data access pages, macros, and modules combine to comprise an Access database. Each of these objects has a special function. The following sections take you on a tour of the objects that make up an Access database.

Tables: A Repository for Data

Tables are the starting point for an application. Whether data is stored in an Access database or you are referencing external data by using linked tables, all the other objects in a database either directly or indirectly reference tables.

To view all the tables that are contained in an open database, you click the **Tables** icon in the **Objects** list. (Note that you don't see any hidden tables unless you have checked the **Hidden Objects** check box in the **Options** dialog box's **View** page.) If you want to view the data in a table, you double-click the name of the table you want to view. (You can also select the table and then click the **Open** button.) Access displays the table's data in a datasheet that includes all the table's fields and records, as shown in the following figure. You can modify many of the datasheet's attributes and even search for and filter data from within the datasheet. If the table is related to another table (such as the Northwind Customers and Orders tables), you can also expand and collapse the subdatasheet to view data stored in child tables.

NOTE

The Northwind database ships with Microsoft Access. If you did not do a complete install of Microsoft Access, this file might not be available to you. In that case, you must reinstall and designate that you wish to install the sample files.

Customer ID	Company Name	Contact Name	Contact Title	
ALFKI	Alfreds Futterkiste	Maria Anders	Sales Representative	Obere
ANATR	Ana Trujillo Emparedados y helados	Ana Trujillo	Owner	Avda.
ANTON	Antonio Moreno Taquería	Antonio Moreno	Owner	Matad
AROUT	Around the Horn	Thomas Hardy	Sales Representative	120 Ha
BERGS	Berglunds snabbköp	Christina Berglund	Order Administrator	Berguv
BLAUS	Blauer See Delikatessen	Hanna Moos	Sales Representative	Forste
BLONP	Blondel père et fils	Frédérique Citeaux	Marketing Manager	24, pla
BOLID	Bólido Comidas preparadas	Martín Sommer	Owner	C/ Ara
BONAP	Bon app'	Laurence Lebihan	Owner	12, rue
BOTTM	Bottom-Dollar Markets	Elizabeth Lincoln	Accounting Manager	23 Tsa
BSBEV	B's Beverages	Victoria Ashworth	Sales Representative	Fauntl
CACTU	Cactus Comidas para llevar	Patricio Simpson	Sales Agent	Cerrito
CENTC	Centro comercial Moctezuma	Francisco Chang	Marketing Manager	Sierras
CHOPS	Chop-suey Chinese	Yang Wang	Owner	Haupts
COMMI	Comércio Mineiro	Pedro Afonso	Sales Associate	Av. do
CONSH	Consolidated Holdings	Elizabeth Brown	Sales Representative	Berkel
DRACD	Drachenblut Delikatessen	Sven Ottlieb	Order Administrator	Walse
DUMON	Du monde entier	Janine Labrune	Owner	67, rue
EASTC	Eastern Connection	Ann Devon	Sales Agent	35 Kin
ERNSH	Ernst Handel	Roland Mendel	Sales Manager	Kirchg
FAMIA	Familia Arquibaldo	Aria Cruz	Marketing Assistant	Rua O
FISSA	FISSA Fabrica Inter. Salchichas S.A.	Diego Roel	Accounting Manager	C/ Mor

Record: 1 ▶ ▶I ▶* of 91

The Datasheet view of the Customers table in the Northwind database includes all the table's fields and records.

As an Access power user or developer, you will often want to view the table's design, which is the blueprint or template for the table. To view a table's design, click the **Design** icon with the table selected. In **Design** view, shown in the following figure, you can view or modify all the field names, data types, and field and table properties. Access gives you the power and flexibility you need to customize the design of tables.

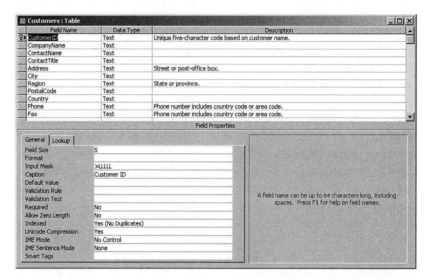

The design of the Customers table, which you can customize if you want.

Relationships: Tying the Tables Together

A relationship between two tables indicates how those tables are related to one another. To properly maintain data integrity and ease the process of working with other objects in a database, you must define relationships among the tables in a database. You accomplish this by using the **Relationships** window. To view the **Relationships** window, with the **Database** window active, you select **Tools**, **Relationships** or you click **Relationships** on the toolbar. In this window, you can view and maintain the relationships in the database. If you or a fellow user or developer have set up some relationships, but you don't see any in the **Relationships** window, you can select **Relationships**, **Show All** to unhide any hidden tables and relationships (you might need to click to expand the menu for this option to appear).

Notice in the figure that many of the relationships have join lines between tables and show a number 1 on one side of the join and an infinity symbol on the other. This indicates a one-to-many relationship between the tables. In a one-to-many relationship, a record in one table can have many related records in another table. If you double-click a join line, the **Edit Relationships** dialog box opens. In this dialog box, you can specify the exact nature of the relationship between tables. The relationship between the Customers and Orders tables, for example, is a one-to-many relationship with referential integrity enforced. This means that the user cannot add orders for customers who don't exist.

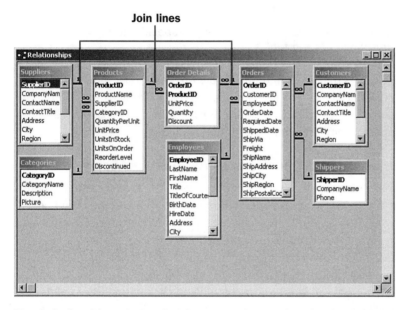

The Relationships window is where you view and maintain the relation-ships in a database. Join lines indicate the relationships between the tables.

Notice in the following figure that the check box **Cascade Update Related Fields** is checked. This means that if the user updates a **CustomerID** field, Access updates all records containing that **CustomerID** value in the Orders table. Because **Cascade Delete Related Records** is not checked in the figure, the user cannot delete from the **Customers** table customers who have corresponding orders in the **Orders** table.

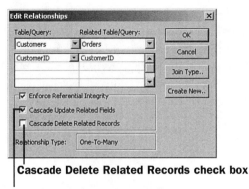

Cascade Delete Related Records check box

Cascade Update Related Fields check box

The Edit Relationships dialog box lets you specify the nature of the relationships between tables.

It also covers the basics of database design. Remember that you should establish relationships both conceptually and literally as early in the design process as possible. Relationships are integral to successfully designing and implementing your application.

Queries: Stored Questions or Actions You Apply to Data

Queries in Access are powerful and multifaceted. A *query* retrieves data from a database based on criteria you specify. An example would be a query that retrieves all employees who live in Florida. Select queries allow you to view, summarize, and perform calculations on the data in tables. Action queries let you add to, update, and delete table data. To run a query, you select **Queries** from the **Objects** list and then double-click the query you want to run, or you can click in the list of queries to select the query you want to run and then click **Open**. When you run a Select query, a datasheet appears (as shown in the following figure), containing all the fields specified in the query and all the records meeting the query's criteria. When you run an *Action query*, which is a query that lets you add to, update, and delete table date, Access runs the specified action, such as making a new table or appending data to an existing table. In general, you can update the data in a query result because the result of a query is actually a dynamic set of records, called a *dynaset*, that is based on the table's data. A dynaset is a subset of data on which you can base a form or report.

Country	Last Name	First Name	Shipped Date	Order ID	Sale Amount
UK	Buchanan	Steven	16-Jul-1996	10248	$440.00
UK	Suyama	Michael	10-Jul-1996	10249	$1,863.40
USA	Peacock	Margaret	12-Jul-1996	10250	$1,552.60
USA	Leverling	Janet	15-Jul-1996	10251	$654.06
USA	Peacock	Margaret	11-Jul-1996	10252	$3,597.90
USA	Leverling	Janet	16-Jul-1996	10253	$1,444.80
UK	Buchanan	Steven	23-Jul-1996	10254	$556.62
UK	Dodsworth	Anne	15-Jul-1996	10255	$2,490.50
USA	Leverling	Janet	17-Jul-1996	10256	$517.80
USA	Peacock	Margaret	22-Jul-1996	10257	$1,119.90
USA	Davolio	Nancy	23-Jul-1996	10258	$1,614.88
USA	Peacock	Margaret	25-Jul-1996	10259	$100.80
USA	Peacock	Margaret	29-Jul-1996	10260	$1,504.65
USA	Peacock	Margaret	30-Jul-1996	10261	$448.00
USA	Callahan	Laura	25-Jul-1996	10262	$584.00
UK	Dodsworth	Anne	31-Jul-1996	10263	$1,873.80
UK	Suyama	Michael	23-Aug-1996	10264	$695.62
USA	Fuller	Andrew	12-Aug-1996	10265	$1,176.00
USA	Leverling	Janet	31-Jul-1996	10266	$346.56
USA	Peacock	Margaret	06-Aug-1996	10267	$3,536.60
USA	Callahan	Laura	02-Aug-1996	10268	$1,101.20
UK	Buchanan	Steven	09-Aug-1996	10269	$642.20

Record: I◄ ◄ [1] ► ►I ►* of 809

When you run a Select query for Employee Sales by Country, you get a datasheet containing all the fields specified in the query and all the records meeting the query's criteria.

When you store a query, Access stores only the query's definition, layout, or formatting properties in the database. It does not store the results of the query. Access offers an intuitive, user-friendly tool that helps you design queries: the *Query Design window*. To open this window, select **Queries** from the **Objects** list in the **Database** window, choose the query you want to modify, and click **Design**. The query pictured in the following figure selects data from Employees, Orders, and Order Subtotals tables. It displays the **Country**, **LastName**, and **FirstName** fields from the **Employees** table, the **ShippedDate** and **OrderID** fields from the **Orders** table, and the **Subtotal** field from the **Order Subtotals** query. The query's output displays only records within a specific **Shipped Date** range. This special type of query is called a *parameter query*. It prompts for criteria at runtime, using the criteria entered by the user to determine which records it includes in the output. Because queries are the foundation for most forms and reports, they are covered throughout this book as they apply to other objects in the database.

KEY TERMS

Query Design window—An intuitive, user-friendly tool that helps you design queries.

Parameter query—A special type of query that prompts for criteria at runtime, using the criteria entered by the user to determine which records it includes in the output.

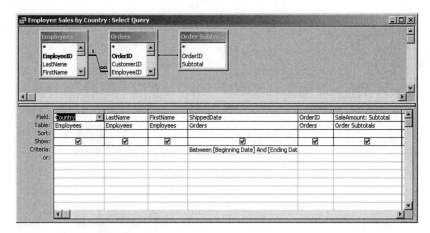

This query design displays data from the Employees and Orders tables and from the Order Subtotals query.

Forms: A Means of Displaying, Modifying, and Adding Data

Although you can enter and modify data in a table's Datasheet view, you can't control the user's actions very well, nor can you do much to facilitate the data-entry process. This is where forms come in. Forms are used to collect and display information, navigate about an application, and more. Access forms can have many traits, and they're very flexible and powerful.

To view a form, you select **Forms** from the **Objects** list. Then you double-click the form you want to view or click in the list of forms to select the form you want to view and then click Open. The Customer Orders form shown in the following figure is actually three forms in one: one main form and two subforms. The main form displays information from the **Customers** table, and the subforms display information from the **Orders** table and the **Order Details** table (tables that are related to the **Customers** table). As the user moves from customer to customer, the form displays the orders associated with that customer. When the user clicks to select an order, the form displays the products included on that order.

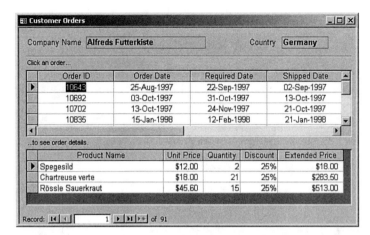

The Customer Orders form, which includes customer, order, and order detail information.

Like tables and queries, you can also view forms in **Design** view. The **Design** view provides tools you can use to edit the layout of a report. To view the design of a form, you select the **Forms** icon from the **Objects** list, choose the form whose design you want to modify, and then click **Design**. The figure that follows shows the Customer Orders form in Design view. Notice the two subforms within the main form.

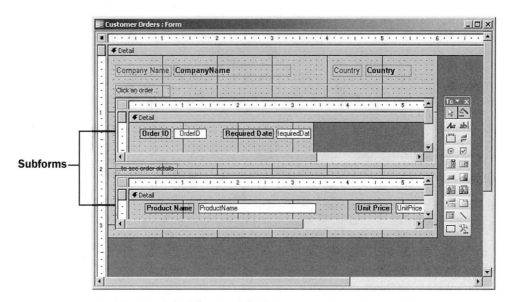

The design of the Customer Orders form shows two subforms.

Reports: Turning Data into Information

Forms allow you to enter and edit information, but with reports, you can display information, usually to a printer. Reports are the primary output device in Microsoft Access. The following figure shows a report in Preview mode. To preview any report, you select **Reports** from the **Objects** list. You double-click the report you want to preview or choose the report you want to preview from the list of reports in the **Database** window, and then you click **Preview**. Notice the graphic in the report, as well as other details, such as the shaded line. Like forms, reports can be elaborate and exciting, and they can contain valuable information.

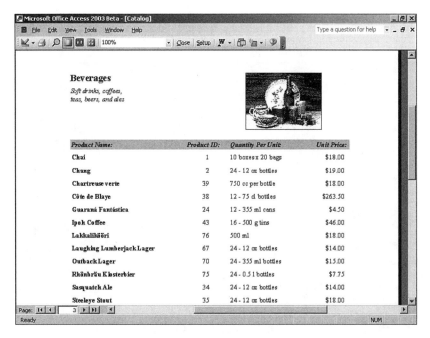

A preview of the Catalog report.

As you may have guessed, you can view reports in Design view, as shown in the following figure. To view the design of a report, you select **Reports** from the **Objects** list, select the report you want to view, and click **Design**. The figure illustrates a report with many sections; in the figure you can see the Page Header, CategoryName Header, Detail section, CategoryName Footer, Page Footer, and Report Footer sections—just a few of the many sections available on a report. Just as a form can contain subforms, a report can contain subreports.

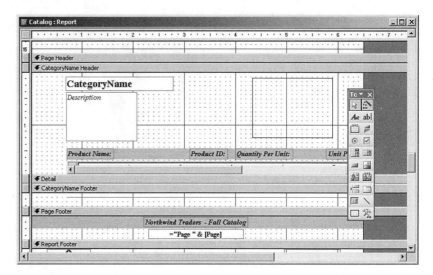

Design view of the Catalog report.

Pages: Forms Viewed in a Browser

Data access pages, discussed earlier in this chapter, first appeared in Access 2000. They allow you to view and update the data in a database from within a browser. Although Access stores them outside the Access database file (that is, the .MDB file), you create and maintain them similarly to the way you create and maintain forms. The following figure shows a data access page viewed within Access. Although Microsoft targets data access pages for use with a browser, you can preview them within the Access application environment.

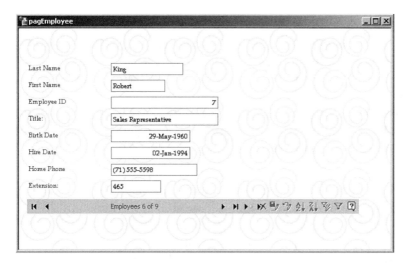

An example of a data access page based on the Employees table.

You can also view and modify data access pages in Design view. The figure that follows shows a data access page in Design view. As you can see, the Design view of a data access page is similar to that of a form in Design view. This makes working with data access pages, and the deployment of an application over an intranet, very easy.

NOTE

Access 2002 introduced the ability to save an Access form as a data access page. This feature makes it easy to develop forms used by Access users and browser-based users simultaneously.

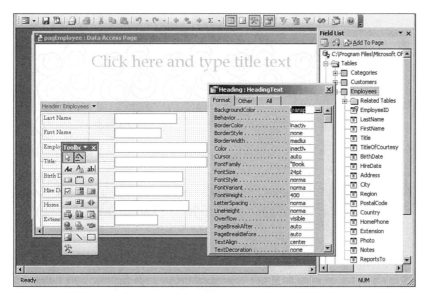

A data access page shown in Design view.

Macros: A Means of Automating a System

Macros provide you with a means of automating application tasks. Macros in Access aren't like the macros in other Office products. You can't record them, as you can in Microsoft Word or Excel, and Access does not save them as Visual Basic for Applications (VBA) code. With Access macros, you can perform most of the tasks that you can manually perform from the keyboard, menus, and toolbars. Macros allow you to build logic into your application flow.

To run a macro, you select **Macros** from the **Objects** list, click the macro you want to run, and then click **Run**. Access then executes the actions in the macro. To view a macro's design, you select **Macros** from the **Objects** list, select the macro you want to modify, and click **Design** to open the **Macro Design** window. The macro pictured in the figure has four columns. The Macro Name column is where you can specify the name of a subroutine within a macro. The Condition column allows you to specify a condition. The Action column is where you specify an action for the macro. (The action in the macro's Action column won't execute unless the condition for that action evaluates to true.) The Comment column lets you document the macro. In the bottom half of the **Macro Design** window, you specify the arguments that apply to the selected action. In the figure, the selected action is MsgBox, which accepts four arguments: Message, Beep, Type, and Title.

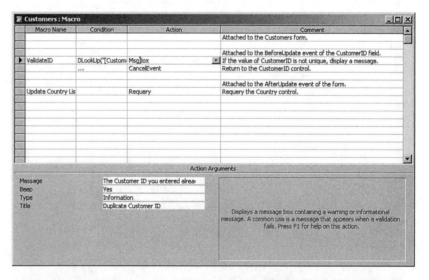

The design of the Customers macro, which contains macro names, conditions, actions, and comments.

Modules: The Foundation of the Application Development Process

Modules, subroutines, and functions allow you to write programming code to automate and provide professional polish for your application. *Modules*, the foundation of any complex Access application, let you create libraries of functions that you can use throughout an application. You usually include subroutines and functions in the modules that you build. A function always returns a value; a subroutine does not. By using code modules, you can do just about anything with an Access application. The figure shows an example of a module. If you want information on modules after reading this book, see *Alison Balter's Mastering Access Office 2003 Desktop Development*, published by Sams, which provides extensive coverage of modules and Access coding techniques.

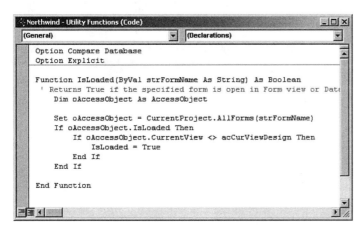

The global code module in Design view, showing the General Declarations section and the IsLoaded function.

Closing an Access Database

Closing an Access database is quite simple: You just select **File**, **Close**. If you have any objects open in **Design** view, Access prompts you to save those objects. You can also close a database by opening another database or by exiting Access.

⊙KEY TERM

Module—Lets you create libraries of functions that you can use throughout an application.

Viewing and Navigating Table Data

Tables are the basis of everything that you do in Access. Most of the data for a database resides in tables, so if you're creating an employee payroll database, the employee data will be stored in a table, your payroll codes might be stored in a table, and your past payroll records could be stored in a table. A table contains data about a specific topic or subject (for example, customers, orders, or employees). Tables are arranged in rows and columns, similarly to a spreadsheet. The columns represent the fields, and the rows represent the records.

A table composed of columns and rows associated with customers.

Opening an Access Table

Before you can view the data in a table and work with its records, you must open the table. To open a table in Datasheet view, follow these steps:

1. Select **Tables** in the list of objects in the **Database** window.

2. Select the table you want to open and click the **Open** button in the database window or double-click the table you want to open.

Navigating Around a Table

You can move around a table by using the keyboard or mouse. When you are editing or adding records, your hands are on the keyboard and you might find it easiest to move around a table by using the keyboard. However, if you are looking for a specific record, you might find it most convenient to use the mouse.

The table that follows shows the keyboard and mouse actions for moving around a table and their resulting effects. As you can see, Microsoft Access provides numerous keyboard and mouse alternatives for moving around a table.

Keyboard and Mouse Actions to Move Around a Table

Keyboard Action	Mouse Action	Effect
Tab or right arrow	Click the right arrow on the bottom scrollbar.	Moves one field to the right of the current field.
Shift+Tab or left arrow	Click the left arrow on the bottom scrollbar.	Moves one field to the left of the current field.
Down arrow	Click the next record button.	Moves down one record.
Up arrow	Click the previous record button.	Moves up one record.
Page Down	(No equivalent mouse action.)	Moves down one screen of records.
Page Up	(No equivalent mouse action.)	Moves up one screen of records.
Home	(No equivalent mouse action.)	Selects the first field of the current record.
End	(No equivalent mouse action.)	Selects the last field of the current record.
Ctrl+Home	Click the first record button.	Moves to the first record of the table.
Ctrl+End	Click the last record button.	Moves to the last record of the table.
F2	Click and drag within a field.	Selects the text in the field.

TIP

The insertion point does not change locations just because you move the mouse; only the mouse pointer moves when you move the mouse. You need to click *within* a field before you begin typing, or the changes occur in the original mouse location.

The Table window includes tools that allow you to scroll through the fields and records, move from record to record, expand and collapse to show and hide related records, and more. The figure that follows illustrates these features. The table that follows provides a list of these features and provides a description of each.

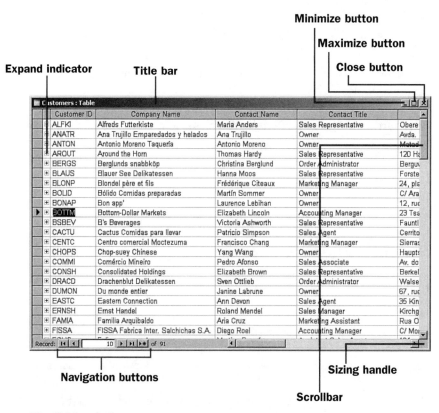

The Table window.

The Components of the Table Window

Table Component	Description
Title bar	You can move a window by putting the mouse pointer on the title bar, holding down the mouse button, and dragging.
Close button	Clicking the close button closes the table.

Table Component	Description
Maximize button	You can click the maximize button, which is a square, to maximize the window. The datasheet then fills the applications window.
Minimize button	You can click the minimize button, which looks like an underscore within a square, to minimize the window. The icon appears on the taskbar. You can restore the window by clicking the icon.
Sizing handle	To change the size of the window, you put the pointer on the lower-right corner, hold down the mouse button, and drag. When the window is the size you want, you release the button.
Scrollbar	You can use the scrollbars to move up and down and right and left in the table.
Navigation buttons	These icons allow you to select the first record, last record, next record, or previous record in the table.
Expand indicator	The expand indicator allows you to view the data hierarchy by showing you any subdata records that are linked to the main record.

Closing a Table

When you are finished working with a table, you need to close it. To close a table, you choose **File, Close** or click the **Close** button in the upper-right corner of the Table window.

Access often prompts you as you close a table, asking if you want to save changes to the layout of the table. It is important that you understand that Access is *not* asking you if you want to save changes to the data. As you'll learn in Chapter 2, Access saves changes to data the moment you move off a record. When you close a table and Access prompts you, it is asking you if you want to save formatting changes, such as changes to column width, to the look of the datasheet, and so on.

PART II

Work with Existing Databases and Objects

2

Working with an Existing Table

IN THIS CHAPTER:

1. Edit Table Data
2. Add Records to a Table
3. Delete Records from a Table
4. Find and Replace Text in a Table
5. Filter Table Data
6. Modify the Appearance of a Datasheet
7. Spell-Check Your Data
8. Using the AutoCorrect Feature

Tables are the foundation of any Access application. In working with tables, the first thing you'll want to be able to do is to open them in **Datasheet** view and navigate around them. Chapter 1 covered navigation techniques. Next, you'll probably want to be able to modify table data. This includes the ability to edit, add, and delete rows.

After you know how to navigate around a table and modify its data, you'll be ready to learn some of the tips and tricks of the trade. This chapter will show you how to find the data that is important to you. You'll learn how to make replacements so that you can make bulk changes to the data in your tables. You'll also learn how to use filters to look at just the data that is important to you at a certain moment in time.

Now we're ready to have some fun. You'll learn how to customize the appearance of a datasheet to your liking. In addition, you'll learn how easy it is to harness the power of the spell-check and autocorrect features right from within Microsoft Access.

1 Edit Table Data

Before You Begin

✔ **2** Add Records to a Table

✔ **42** Build a New Table

See Also

→ **3** Delete Records from a Table

→ **7** Spell-Check Your Data

→ **8** Using the AutoCorrect Feature

🔍 KEY TERM

Record—A new row containing all the same fields as all the existing records in the current table.

You can change the data in your table at any time when you are in the **Datasheet** view of a table, the result of a query, or the **Form** view of a form. Access saves changes you make to a *record* (a new row containing all the same fields as all the existing records in the current table) as soon as you move off the record.

1 Select the Record to Change

Open the table containing the data you want to change by clicking **Tables** in the **Objects** list on the main Access window. On the right side of the window, click the table you want to edit.

When the table opens in a separate window, navigate the table and select the record you want to change by clicking in any field in the table.

2 Select the Field to Change

In the current record, move to the field you want to change by clicking the field or by using the directional keys.

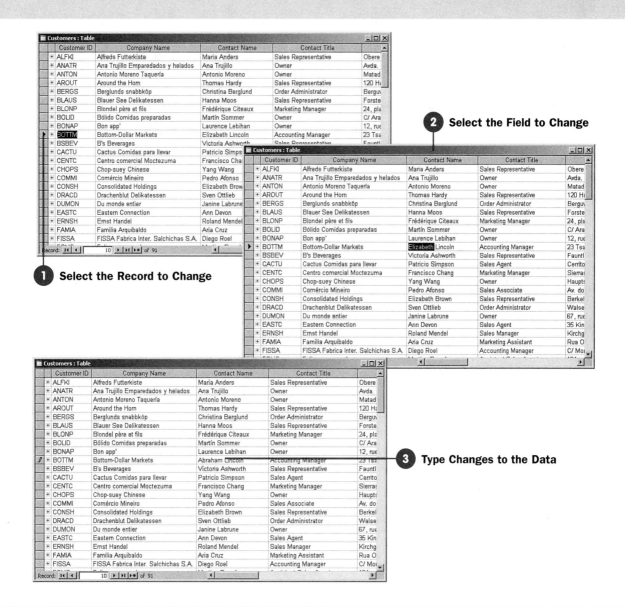

2 Select the Field to Change

1 Select the Record to Change

3 Type Changes to the Data

3 Type Changes to the Data

Type to make the necessary changes to the data in the current field.

TIP

When you begin to type, note that the black arrow at the left of the current record (which marks the current record) changes to a pencil icon to indicate that you are making changes to the current record.

NOTE

If Access cannot undo your correction, the **Undo** tool appears dimmed. After you have made changes to a record and gone on to make changes to another record, you cannot undo the changes made to the first record.

To delete the contents of the current field, select the contents and press the **Delete** key. You can now enter new data in that field or leave that field blank.

 Undo Changes

There are many times when you will want to undo changes that you made to a field or to a record. There are several different options available, depending on whether you are still within a field, have left the field, or have left the record. You can use the **Undo** feature to undo only the last change made to a field or changes made to the most recently modified record.

To undo changes made to the current field, click the **Undo** tool on the toolbar, choose **Edit, Undo Typing** from the menu, or tap the **Esc** key once.

To undo changes after moving to another field (but before you have made changes to that new field), click the **Undo** tool on the toolbar, choose **Edit, Undo Current Field/Record**, or tap the **Esc** key once.

To undo changes after saving the record, click the **Undo** tool on the toolbar, choose **Edit, Undo Saved Record**, or tap the **Esc** key twice. (Remember that when you move to a new record, Access saves all changes to the first record—as long as you do not begin making changes to another record, you can still undo the changes to the most recently modified record.)

---

② **Add Records to a Table**

Before You Begin

✔ **42** Build a New Table

See Also

→ **1** Edit Table Data

→ **3** Delete Records from a Table

→ **7** Spell-Check Your Data

→ **8** Using the AutoCorrect Feature

Access adds records to the end of your table, regardless of how you add those records to the table. You add records to a table when you want to add a new item to the table. For example, if the table keeps track of customers, you add a record to the table each time you add a new customer. If the table keeps track of orders, you add a record to the table each time you add a new order.

2 Click the New Record Navigation Button

Customers : Table

	Customer ID	Company Name	Contact Name	Contact Title	
+	ALFKI	Alfreds Futterkiste	Maria Anders	Sales Representative	Obere
+	ANATR	Ana Trujillo Emparedados y helados	Ana Trujillo	Owner	Avda.
+	ANTON	Antonio Moreno Taquería	Antonio Moreno	Owner	Matad
▶ +	AROUT	Around the Horn	Thomas Hardy	Sales Representative	120 H
+	BERGS	Berglunds snabbköp	Christina Berglund	Order Administrator	Bergu
+	BLAUS	Blauer See Delikatessen	Hanna Moos	Sales Representative	Forste
+	BLONP	Blondel père et fils	Frédérique Citeaux	Marketing Manager	24, pla
+	BOLID	Bólido Comidas preparadas	Martín Sommer	Owner	C/ Ara
+	BONAP	Bon app'	Laurence Lebihan	Owner	12, rue
+	BOTTM	Bottom-Dollar Markets	Elizabeth Lincoln	Accounting Manager	23 Tsa
+	BSBEV	B's Beverages	Victoria Ashworth	Sales Representative	Fauntl
+	CACTU	Cactus Comidas para llevar	Patricio Simpson	Sales Agent	Cerrito
+	CENTC	Centro comercial Moctezuma	Francisco Chang	Marketing Manager	Sierras
+	CHOPS	Chop-suey Chinese	Yang Wang	Owner	Haupt
+	COMMI	Comércio Mineiro	Pedro Afonso	Sales Associate	Av. do
+	CONSH	Consolidated Holdings	Elizabeth Brown	Sales Representative	Berkel
+	DRACD	Drachenblut Delikatessen	Sven Ottlieb	Order Administrator	Walse
+	DUMON	Du monde entier	Janine Labrune	Owner	67, rue
+	EASTC	Eastern Connection	Ann Devon	Sales Agent	35 Kin
+	ERNSH	Ernst Handel	Roland Mendel	Sales Manager	Kirchg
+	FAMIA	Familia Arquibaldo	Aria Cruz	Marketing Assistant	Rua O
+	FISSA	FISSA Fabrica Inter. Salchichas S.A.	Diego Roel	Accounting Manager	C/ Mor

Record: |◄ ◄| 4 |► ►| ►* of 91

4 Add More New Records

Customers : Table

	Customer ID	Company Name	Contact Name	Contact Title	
+	SAVEA	Save-a-lot Markets	Jose Pavarotti	Sales Representative	187 Su
+	SEVES	Seven Seas Imports	Hari Kumar	Sales Manager	90 Wa
+	SIMOB	Simons bistro	Jytte Petersen	Owner	Vinbæ
+	SPECD	Spécialités du monde	Dominique Perrier	Marketing Manager	25, rue
+	SPLIR	Split Rail Beer & Ale	Art Braunschweiger	Sales Manager	P.O. B
+	SUPRD	Suprêmes délices	Pascale Cartrain	Accounting Manager	Boulev
+	THEBI	The Big Cheese	Liz Nixon	Marketing Manager	89 Jeff
+	THECR	The Cracker Box	Liu Wong	Marketing Assistant	55 Gri
+	TOMSP	Toms Spezialitäten	Karin Josephs	Marketing Manager	Luisen
+	TORTU	Tortuga Restaurante	Miguel Angel Paolino	Owner	Avda.
+	TRADH	Tradição Hipermercados	Anabela Domingues	Sales Representative	Av. Inê
+	TRAIH	Trail's Head Gourmet Provisioners	Helvetius Nagy	Sales Associate	722 Da
+	VAFFE	Vaffeljernet	Palle Ibsen	Sales Manager	Smag
+	VICTE	Victuailles en stock	Mary Saveley	Sales Agent	2, rue
+	VINET	Vins et alcools Chevalier	Paul Henriot	Accounting Manager	59 rue
+	WANDK	Die Wandernde Kuh	Rita Müller	Sales Representative	Adena
+	WARTH	Wartian Herkku	Pirkko Koskitalo	Accounting Manager	Torikat
+	WELLI	Wellington Importadora	Paula Parente	Sales Manager	Rua de
+	WHITC	White Clover Markets	Karl Jablonski	Owner	305 - 1
+	WILMK	Wilman Kala	Matti Karttunen	Owner/Marketing Assistant	Kesku
+	WOLZA	Wolski Zajazd	Zbyszek Piestrzeniewicz	Owner	ul. Filt
▌ +	ABCDE	The Alphabet Company	John Letter		

Record: |◄ ◄| 92 |► ►| ►* of 92

1 Open the Table

Open the table that contains data to which you want to add information by clicking **Tables** in the **Objects** list on the main Access window. On the right side of the window, click the table you want to edit. The selected table opens in a separate window.

2 **Click the New Record Navigation Button**

Click the **New Record** navigation button at the bottom of the **Datasheet** window to add a record to the table. Alternatively, choose **Edit**, **Go To**, **New Record** from the menu bar. Access inserts a new *record* at the bottom of the table. You can also press the **Tab** key while entering data into the last row of the table. This process inserts a new row, placing your cursor in the first field of the new row.

3 **Type Information in the Record's Fields**

Type to add the necessary information to the fields within the new record. To move from one field to the next in the new record, press **Tab**; to move back to the preceding field, press **Shift+Tab**. Of course, you can always click in whichever field you want to edit.

Whenever you move off the record—by clicking a new record or using the arrow or **Tab** keys to leave the current record—Access saves the changes you've made to that record.

TIP

You can press **Ctrl+"** to copy the data from the field directly above the current field into the current field.

4 **Add More New Records**

It is important to note that Access always displays one blank record at the end of a table. As you are entering data into the table, you can press the **Tab** key at the end of the current record to insert another new record without moving your hands from the keyboard. You can also click the **New Record** navigation button or choose **Edit**, **Go To**, **New Record** from the menu bar to add additional new records to the bottom of the table.

---

3 **Delete Records from a Table**

Before You Begin

✔ **1** Edit Table Data

✔ **2** Add Records to a Table

See Also

→ **42** Build a New Table

→ **46** Establish Relationships

→ **47** Establish Referential Integrity

There are times when you will want to remove a record from a table. An example is when an order is cancelled. Once the order is cancelled, you may not want to retain its data within the table. This is an example of when you would delete the record from the table.

PART II: Work with Existing Databases and Objects

1 Select Record or Records to Delete

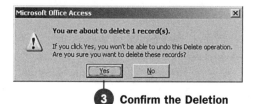

3 Confirm the Deletion

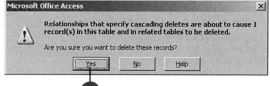

4 Delete a Record with Related Records

1 ## Select Record or Records to Delete

Before you can delete records, you must first select them. To select one record, simply click the gray record selector button at the very left end of the record's row within the datasheet. Alternatively, if the insertion point is already in the record you want to select, choose **Edit**, **Select Record**.

To select multiple records, click and drag within the record selector area. Access selects the contiguous range of records in the area over which you drag. Alternatively, click the gray selector button for the first record you want to select, hold down the **Shift** key, and then click the gray selector button of the last record you want to select. Access selects the entire range of records between the two records you clicked.

2 **Press Delete**

After you have selected the records you want to delete from the table, press the keyboard **Delete** key. A dialog appears prompting you to confirm the deletion.

3 **Confirm the Deletion**

Click the **Yes** button in the dialog box. The selected records are removed from the table.

If the record you want to delete is related to another record in another table in your database, you won't see a confirmation dialog box. Instead, you will see a notification that you cannot delete the selected record. Click **OK** to close that dialog box and continue to step 4.

TIP

When you select records, they appear in reverse type (white text on a black background). You can copy the selected records (press **Ctrl+C**), delete them, or modify them as a group. Remember that deleting records is a permanent process. You cannot undo record deletion.

4 **Delete a Record with Related Records**

Deleting records is not as simple as the preceding steps imply if you have established *referential integrity* between the tables in your database and the row you are attempting to delete. (Refer to **45** About the Types of Relationships, **46** Establish Relationships, and **47** Establish Referential Integrity for information about relationships and referential integrity.)

For example, customers in your **Customers** table probably have orders associated with them; the details of those orders are kept in an **Orders** table. The relationship between the **Customers** table and the **Orders** table prohibits you from deleting customers who have orders. This means that when you attempt to delete a customer who has orders, a dialog appears, notifying you that the process cannot complete.

Access provides a referential integrity option that enables you to "cascade" a deletion down to the child table. For example, if you attempt to delete an order record from the **Orders** table, Access will delete the associated order detail records—including the customer record from the **Customers** table. If you establish referential integrity with the **Cascade Delete** option enabled (see **47** Establish Referential Integrity), when the confirmation dialog box appears, you can click **Yes** to complete the deletion process. Access will delete the parent record, and all associated child records.

4 Find and Replace Text in a Table

When you are working with records in a large data table, you will want a way to locate specific records quickly. Using the **Find** feature, you can easily move to specific records within a table.

The **Find** feature allows you to search in a datasheet for records that meet specific criteria. For example, you can search a **Customers** table to locate the records for those customers who live in Indiana.

1 Define Search Criteria

Select the field containing the criteria for which you are searching. For example, if you want to search a **Customers** table to find those customers for whom your contact is a Sales Representative (and not those customers for whom your contact is the Owner, a Marketing Manager, or an Agent), click any field in the **Contact Title** column. If you want to find all records for a particular city and your table lists the customers' addresses, click the **City** column.

Click the **Find** button on the toolbar. The **Find and Replace** dialog box appears.

Type the criteria in the **Find What** text box. In this example, type **Sales Representative** in the **Find What** box to search the current field (the **Contact Title** field) for this text.

2 Specify Field to Search

Use the **Look In** drop-down list to designate whether you want to search only the current field or all fields in the table for the text you've specified. By default, Access searches through only the field you selected in step 1. From the **Look In** list, you can select the **Entire Table** option to have Access look in every column for the specified text.

Before You Begin

✔ **1** Edit Table Data

✔ **2** Add Records to a Table

See Also

→ **5** Filter Table Data

→ **9** Open a Query in Datasheet View

→ **13** Refine a Query with Criteria

→ **76** Create and Run Action Queries

💡 TIP

When using either the **Find** or **Replace** feature, you can use wildcard characters in the **Find What** text box. Use an asterisk (*) as a placeholder for several characters, use a question mark (?) to replace a single character, or use the pound sign (#) to replace a single number. For example, type **dog*** to find *dog*, *dogs*, and *dogsled*; type **c?t** to find *cat*, *cot*, and *cut*.

2 Specify Field to Search

5 Click Find Next

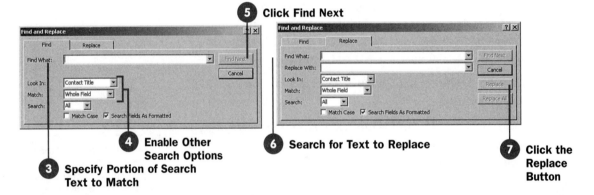

4 Enable Other Search Options

3 Specify Portion of Search Text to Match

6 Search for Text to Replace

7 Click the Replace Button

③ Specify Portion of Search Text to Match

Use the **Match** drop-down list to designate whether you want to match any part of the field you are searching, the whole field you are searching, or the start of the field you are searching. Suppose that you select the **Ship Via** column from the **Look In** drop-down list and type **Federal** in the **Find What** text box. If you select **Whole Field** from the **Match** drop-down list, you will find entries in the **Ship Via** column where *Federal* is the entire entry. If you select **Any Part of Field**, you will find entries where *Federal* is any part of the entry (such as *Federal Shipping*, *Federal Express*, *United Federal Shipping*, and so on). If you select **Start of Field**, you will find *Federal Shipping* and *Federal Express* but not *United Federal Shipping*.

4 Enable Other Search Options

Use the **Search** drop-down list to designate whether you want to search **Up** from the current cursor position, **Down** from the current cursor position, or in **All** directions.

Use the **Match Case** check box to indicate whether you want the search to be case sensitive. For example, select the check box if you want to search for the text exactly as you typed it; deselect the check box to look for the search text regardless of how it is capitalized in the table.

Use the **Search Fields As Formatted** check box to determine whether you want to find data based only on the *display format*. For example, if you are searching a **Date** field that has been formatted to display dates in the date-month-year format, deselect this check box to find *17-Jul-96*; *July 17, 1996*; and *07/17/96*. If you are looking only for those records with the date entered as 17-Jul-96, enable the **Search Fields as Formatted** check box.

5 Click Find Next

Click the **Find Next** button in the **Find** dialog box to find the next record meeting the designated criteria. The **Find** dialog box remains open after the search process completes.

6 Search for Text to Replace

There may be times when you want to update records meeting specific criteria with a new value. The **Replace** feature automatically inserts the new information into the specified field. To replace text in a field with some other text, start by clicking within the field containing the criteria you are searching for. Click the **Find** button on the toolbar. When the Find dialog box opens, select the **Replace** tab.

KEY TERM

Display format—The format in which Access displays data.

TIP

To conduct the same search after you close the **Find** dialog box, press **Shift+F4** to re-open the **Find** dialog box and find the next record meeting the specified criteria.

TIP

Use the **Replace All** option with quite a bit of caution. Remember that the changes you make with the **Find** dialog box are *permanent*. Although **Replace All** can be a useful option, take care that you have a recent backup, and that you are quite certain of what you are doing. In fact, I usually click **Find Next/Replace** a few times to make sure that I know what Access is doing *before* I click **Replace All**.

NOTE

If you are searching a very large table, Access will find a specific value in a field much faster if the field you are searching on is the *primary key* or an *indexed field*. You will learn about primary keys and indexes in **45** About the Types of Relationships and **70** About Working with Field Properties.

Type the criteria you want to search for in the **Find What** text box.

Type the new information (the replacement text) in the **Replace With** text box.

Designate the **Look In, Match, Search, Match Case,** and **Search Fields As Formatted** options as described in steps 2 and 3.

Click the **Find Next** button. Access locates the first record meeting the criteria you designated in the **Find What** text box.

7 Click the Replace Button

Click the **Replace** button; Access deletes this occurrence of the **Find What** text from the table and replaces it with the specified **Replace With** text. Click **Find Next** to search for the next occurrence of the **Find What** text or click **Replace All** to replace all occurrences of the **Find What** text with the **Replace With** text.

8 Finish the Search

Click **Cancel** when done to close the **Find** dialog box. Because Access makes changes to a record when it replaces text and then leaves that record to continue searching, the find-and-replace operations result in changes to individual records that are automatically saved as you progress through the search. In short, the changes you make with the **Replace** tab are permanent.

---

5 Filter Table Data

Before You Begin

✔ **1** Edit Table Data

✔ **2** Add Records to a Table

See Also

→ **4** Find and Replace Text in a Table

→ **9** Open a Query in Datasheet View

→ **13** Refine a Query with Criteria

In a table you can apply *filters* to fields to limit the records you are viewing. These records temporarily disappear. You can view them again any time that you'd like. Filters allow you to hone in on the data that is important to you at a particular moment in time. For example, you might want to view only the customers who are based in the state of Alaska.

1 Open Table in Datasheet View

From the **Database** window, select **Tables** in the object list. The list of tables appears. Double-click to open the table whose data you wish to filter.

1 Open Table in Datasheet View

3 Click Filter by Selection

4 Click Remove Filter

2 Select Record and Field

Click within the record and field that contain the value on which you want to filter. This lets Access know what data you want to use as the example for the filter. For example, if you click within a record where the ContactTitle equals Sales Agent, Access will filter the data to show all of the sales agents.

KEY TERM

Filter—Something you apply to fields in a table to allow you to hone in on the data that is important to you at a particular moment in time.

3 Click Filter by Selection

Click the **Filter by Selection** button that appears on the toolbar. Once you click this button, the data appears filtered to only the specified rows. For example, you can filter the data so that it shows only customers who are Owners.

4 Click Remove Filter

After you have analyzed the filtered data, you may want to remove the filter so that you can once again view all rows, or apply a different filter. The process is very simple. You must simply click the **Remove Filter** button on the toolbar.

6   Modify the Appearance of a Datasheet

Before You Begin

✔ **1** Edit Table Data

✔ **2** Add Records to a Table

You can customize how data in a datasheet appears. For example you can change the column widths, row heights, font, font size, and font color. This makes the data easier to work with. Changes made to the appearance of a Datasheet view affect only the display of the data, not the underlying structure of the table.

1 Format Font Used in Table

One of the things that you can change about a datasheet is the appearance of the text. Choose **Format**, **Font**. The **Font** dialog appears. Select the desired font, color, font size, etc. Click **OK** when finished. Access applies the selection to the entire datasheet.

2 Modify Columns and Rows

You can modify the width of the columns within a datasheet. Move your mouse within the right column separator in the column heading until you get a double-headed arrow. Drag to the right or left to increase or decrease the width of the column. Release the mouse when the column reaches the desired width.

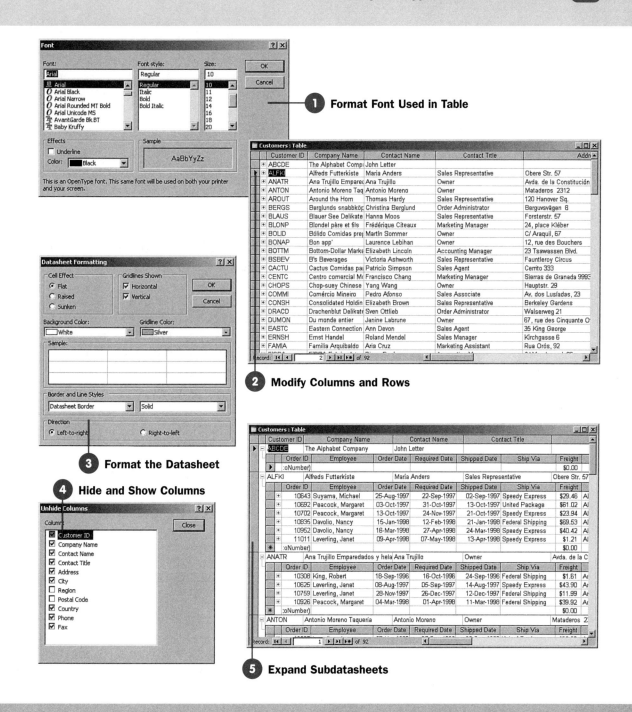

1 Format Font Used in Table

2 Modify Columns and Rows

3 Format the Datasheet

4 Hide and Show Columns

5 Expand Subdatasheets

Whereas the process of changing a column width changes the width of only the selected column(s), the process of changing the row height affects all rows in the table. To change the row height, place the mouse pointer at the lower row border in the record selector area until the mouse pointer turns into a double-headed arrow. The record selector area is the gray button that appears at the very left end of each record's row within the datasheet.

Drag up or down to increase or decrease the height of the row. Release the mouse when the row reaches the desired height.

TIP

In addition to freezing columns, there are other tips and tricks that you should know when working with columns. For instance, to autofit the column size, double-click the column field name border. To select more than one column, click the field selector for the first column and drag to select contiguous columns.

There are times when you will want to ensure that specific columns remain visible, even when you scroll to view other columns in the table. For example, you may want the CustomerID and CompanyName to remain visible, even when you scroll to the right to view other fields. The process of freezing table columns solves this problem. Click the column selectors of the columns that you want to freeze to select the desired columns. The column selectors are the gray buttons containing the field names. Choose **Format, Freeze Columns**. Notice that a slightly darker line appears between those columns and the other columns. Scroll over to the right. Notice that those columns remain on the screen as you view columns to the right. To unfreeze columns, choose **Format, Unfreeze All Columns**.

3 Format the Datasheet

So far, you've learned how to modify the appearance of the text within the datasheet, but you have not learned how to modify the appearance of the actual datasheet. Choose **Format, Datasheet**. The **Datasheet Formatting** dialog appears.

Use the **Cell Effect** option buttons to designate the Cell Effect for the datasheet as **Flat**, **Raised**, or **Sunken**. If you select **Raised** or **Sunken**, the background color defaults to silver.

Use the **Horizontal** and **Vertical** check boxes to designate whether the datasheet will contain no gridlines, just horizontal gridlines, just vertical gridlines, or both horizontal and vertical gridlines (the default). The options that you select here also apply to the printed datasheet.

Use the **Background Color** drop-down to designate a background color for the grid. Use the **Gridline Color** drop-down to specify the color for the gridlines.

Use the **Border** drop-down to select the border you wish to affect. Then use the **Line Styles** drop-down to select the line style you wish to apply to the designated border.

Use the **Direction** option buttons to designate the direction in which you want new objects to display. Left-to-right is standard for most English and European users, meaning that data entry begins in the leftmost column and continues left to right. The navigation buttons appear in the lower left corner of the table. By selecting **Right-to-left**, you switch the direction so that everything is oriented right-to-left, rather than left-to-right.

Once you've formatted the datasheet to your liking, click **OK**. Access applies all the changes that you made and closes the dialog.

4 Hide and Show Columns

Sometimes it will not be necessary to view certain columns in the datasheet. Fortunately, you can hide and unhide columns as necessary. To hide columns, select the column(s) you want to hide. Choose **Format**, **Hide Columns**. The selected columns disappear.

Although you may not need to see the data in a column for awhile, you may need to see it at a later time. To unhide columns, choose **Format**, **Unhide Columns**. The **Unhide Columns** dialog appears. Click to select the columns you want to redisplay. Click **Close** to close the dialog.

5 Expand Subdatasheets

There are times when you will want to show all the subdatasheet data for all of the records in the datasheet. Fortunately, you do not need to click to expand the datasheet for each row individually! Simply choose **Format**, **Subdatasheet**, **Expand All**. All subdatasheets appear. To collapse them again, select **Format**, **Subdatasheet**, **Collapse All**.

7 Spell-Check Your Data

Before You Begin

✔ **1** Edit Table Data

✔ **2** Add Records to a Table

See Also

→ **8** Using the AutoCorrect Feature

Using spell check to correct data entry errors improves the accuracy of the data in your tables. You generally will not want to use spell check for data that contains names and addresses, since this type of data contains many entries that are not in the dictionary.

The spell-check feature within Microsoft Access is shared with the rest of Microsoft Office. So, if you are familiar with spell check in a product such as Microsoft Word, using the spell-check feature should be easy.

1 Select Columns to Check

Click and drag within the gray column headings to select the columns whose data you want to check.

2 Choose Tools, Spelling

Open the **Tools** menu and select **Spelling**. The **Spelling** dialog appears.

3 Determine How to Handle Each Flagged Word

Once the Spelling dialog appears, it immediately shows you the first instance of a word that Access identifies as incorrect. You can choose to correct the error, skip the misspelled word, or select from a variety of other related options. After you determine how to handle the first flagged word, Access identifies the next spelling error. This process repeats until the spell-checker finds no additional errors.

4 Click OK to Return to Datasheet

Once Access has identified all spelling errors in the selected columns, a dialog appears, indicating that the spell check is complete. Click **OK** to return to the datasheet.

Select Columns to Check

Choose Tools, Spelling

Determine How to Handle Each Flagged Word

Click OK to Return to Datasheet

8 Using the AutoCorrect Feature

Before You Begin

✔ **1** Edit Table Data

✔ **2** Add Records to a Table

See Also

→ **7** Spell-Check Your Data

AutoCorrect is another feature shared with the rest of Microsoft Office. It is a feature designed to automatically correct common spelling errors as you type. In addition to catching universally common errors, you can add your own common misspellings or typos to AutoCorrect so that AutoCorrect will immediately correct those mistakes in the future. For example, if you frequently type *reddy* instead of *ready*, you can add that typo and its corrected form to the AutoCorrect list; the next time you type *reddy* and press the spacebar, AutoCorrect will replace your typo with the correct word.

1 Type a Commonly Misspelled Word

Begin typing a sentence in a field in a datasheet and type a commonly misspelled word such as "recieve."

2 Press the Space Bar

Press the **Space** bar. Notice that AutoCorrect changes the spelling of the misspelled word to "receive."

3 Add Term to Correction List

You can add words to AutoCorrect's correction list by choosing **Tools, AutoCorrect Options**. Fill in the **Replace** and **With** text boxes and then click **Add** to add the word to the correction list. Any words you add to AutoCorrect from Access are also available in other Microsoft Office applications.

KEY TERM

AutoCorrect—A feature shared with the rest of Microsoft Office that is designed to automatically correct common spelling errors as you type.

1 **Type a Commonly Misspelled Word**

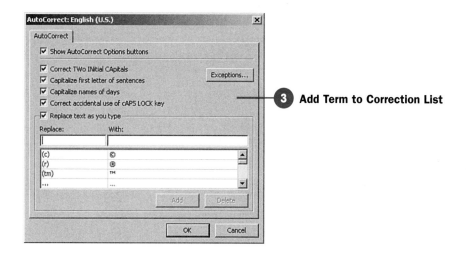

3 **Add Term to Correction List**

3

Working with an Existing Query

IN THIS CHAPTER:

A *Select query* is a stored question about the data stored in a database's tables. Only the question is stored, not the resulting data. Select queries are the foundation of much of what you do in Access. They underlie most forms and reports, and they allow you to view the data you want, when you want.

You use a simple Select query to define the tables and fields whose data you want to view, and also to specify the criteria that limits the data the query's output displays. A Select query is a query of a table or tables that just displays data; the query doesn't modify data in any way. An example is a query that allows you to view customers who have placed orders in the past month.

KEY TERM

Select query—A stored question about the data stored in a database's tables.

You can use more advanced Select queries to summarize data, supply the results of calculations, or cross-tabulate data. You can use *Action queries* to add, edit, or delete data from tables, based on selected criteria, but this chapter covers Select queries.

9 Open a Query in Datasheet View

Before You Begin

✔ **4** Find and Replace Text in a Table

✔ **5** Filter Table Data

See Also

→ **10** Open a Query in Design View

→ **48** Create Queries

→ **52** About Building Queries Based on Multiple Tables

KEY TERM

Datasheet view—Reflects any criteria, sort order, and other parameters defined for the query.

You can easily view the results of a query at any time. This is considered the *Datasheet view* of a query. The Datasheet view of a query reflects any criteria, sort order, and other parameters defined for the query.

1 Select Queries in the List of Objects

Click to select **Queries** in the list of objects in the **Database** window.

2 Click to Select the Query to Run

Locate the query whose results you want to view in Datasheet view. Click to select that query.

3 Select Open on the Database Window Toolbar

Select **Open** on the **Database** window toolbar or double-click the query to run it. The result of the query appears in Datasheet view.

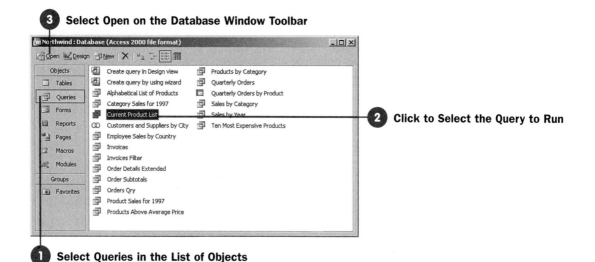

3 Select Open on the Database Window Toolbar

2 Click to Select the Query to Run

1 Select Queries in the List of Objects

There are several different ways that you can cause a query to run. In fact, you have seen two of them already. Here's a list of some of the techniques you can use to run a query:

- Select a query and then select **Open** from the Database window.

- Right-click a query in the Database window and then select **Open**.

- While in the Design view of a query, use the **View** tool to select Datasheet view.

- While in the Design view of a query, right-click the gray area of the query grid and select **Datasheet View**.

- Click the **Run** button (which looks like an exclamation point) on the Query Design toolbar.

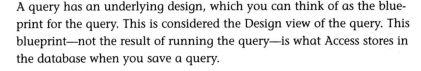

10   **Open a Query in Design View**

Before You Begin

✔ **5**   Filter Table Data

✔ **9**   Open a Query in Datasheet View

See Also

→ **13**   Refine a Query with Criteria

→ **48**   Create Queries

→ **52**   About Building Queries Based on Multiple Tables

A query has an underlying design, which you can think of as the blue-print for the query. This is considered the Design view of the query. This blueprint—not the result of running the query—is what Access stores in the database when you save a query.

① Select the Query to Design

It is not necessary to first run a query to view its design. You can go directly into Design view of a query from the Database window. Simply select the query from the list of queries in the Database window.

② Click the Design Tool on the Database Window Toolbar

Click the **Design** tool on the Database window toolbar. The query appears in Design view.

🔱 TIP

It is easy to toggle back and forth between Datasheet view and Design view. You accomplish it by using the **View** tool on the Query Design and Query Datasheet toolbars. The **View** tool allows you to toggle between the various views available for a query. This makes it very easy for you to switch from Design view to Datasheet view and back as needed.

2 Click the Design Tool on the
Database Window Toolbar

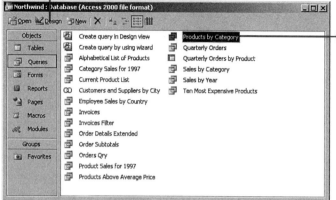

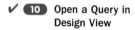

1 Select the Query to Design

11 Add Fields to a Query

When viewing a query in Design view, you might decide to modify the
fields that you want to include in the query's output. In other words, you
might want to add fields to or remove fields from the query grid. You
would do this if you had an existing query and you realized that it was
missing fields, if you had a new query and were adding fields for the
first time, or if you were working with an existing query and realized
that you no longer wanted to include a field in the query.

Sometimes you need to insert a field between two existing fields. For
example, your query might already contain the city and postal code,
and you have decided to add a region field and place it between the city
and the postal code fields. Other times you want to add a field to the
end of the list of existing fields. And sometimes you need to add a contiguous group or a noncontiguous group of fields from the field list to
the query grid. You would add a noncontiguous list of fields when there
are several fields that you want to add to the query, but they do not
appear together in the field list. It would be very tedious if you had to
add each field, one field at a time, in order to accomplish these tasks.
Fortunately, the process for adding fields in all of these scenarios in
Access is simple.

Before You Begin

✔ **10** Open a Query in
Design View

See Also

→ **12** Order a Query
Result

→ **13** Refine a Query
with Criteria

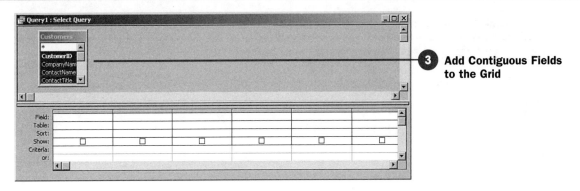

3 Add Contiguous Fields to the Grid

4 Add Non-Contiguous Fields to the Grid

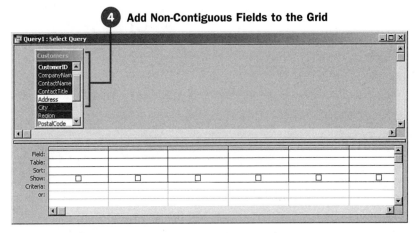

1 Add a Field Between Other Fields

Drag the field from the field list to the grid and drop it where you want it to appear. The fields already included in the query then move over to the right.

2 Add a Field to the End of the Query Grid

Double-click in the field list on the field that you want to add. Access adds the field at the end of the existing field list. This is the technique that I use to add fields to a new query as I build it. I generally double-click each field that I want to add to the query. Access simply adds each field to the query grid in the order in which I select the fields.

PART II: Work with Existing Databases and Objects

3 ## Add Contiguous Fields to the Grid

Click the first field that you want to add to the query.

Scroll through the field list until you can see the last field that you want to add to the query.

Hold down the **Shift** key as you click the last field that you want to add to the query.

Drag the fields as a group to the query grid. The fields are placed on the query grid at the position where you dropped them.

4 ## Add Non-Contiguous Fields to the Grid

Click the first field that you want to add.

Hold down the **Ctrl** key as you click each additional field that you want to add.

Drag the fields to the query grid by clicking any of the selected fields and dragging to the query grid. Access adds the selected fields to the query grid at the position at which you drop them.

12 Order a Query Result

You might want to modify the sort order designated by the designer of a query. As described in the text that follows, you can sort on a single field or on multiple fields, and you can sort in ascending order or in descending order. For example, you might want to sort in ascending order by company name in a company table, but in descending order by sales amount in a sales table so that the highest sales amount appears first. An example where you might want to sort on multiple fields would be employee last name combined with employee first name.

Before You Begin

✔ **10** Open a Query in Design View

✔ **11** Add Fields to a Query

See Also

→ **13** Refine a Query with Criteria

→ **15** Print a Query Result

1 ## Open the Query in Design View

Select **Queries** in the list of objects in the Database window. Click to select the query whose sort order you wish to modify. Click **Design**.

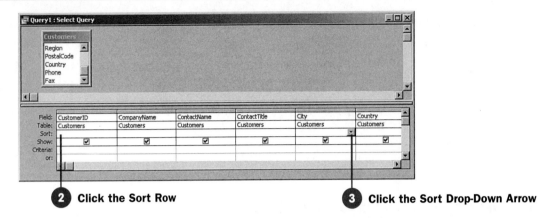

2 Click the Sort Row **3** Click the Sort Drop-Down Arrow

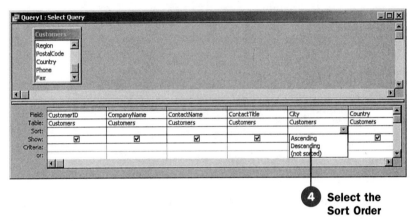

4 Select the Sort Order

2 Click the Sort Row

Click within the query's **Sort** row, which allows you to control sorting options for the query.

3 Click the Sort Drop-Down Arrow

Click the **Sort** drop-down arrow button to display the choices for the sort order.

4 **Select the Sort Order**

Select the sort order:

- Ascending—A to Z or 0 to 9

- Descending—Z to A or 9 to 0

- Not Sorted—No sorting

To sort on more than one field, repeat steps one through four for each additional field that you want to sort by.

Access sorts the data in the query grid from left to right, meaning that if the first name field appears on the query grid before the last name field, the data appears in order by first name and then within first name by last name. Because you probably want the data in order by last name and then by first name, you need to move the last name field so that it appears before the first name field. You must click the gray selector bar that contains the field name. This selects the entire column. You can then drag the field to the new location.

5 **Click the Run Button**

Click the **Run** button. The data appears in the designated sort order.

13 Refine a Query with Criteria

You can limit the records that you see in the result of a query by adding *criteria* to the query. For example, you might want to see just the customers in California, or you might want to view just the orders with sales over $500. You could also view sales that occurred within a specific date range. By using criteria, you can easily accomplish any of these tasks, and many, many more.

1 **Open the Query in Design View**

From the Database window, select **Tables** in the object list. Double-click to open the table whose data you wish to filter.

Before You Begin

✔ **10** Open a Query in Design View

✔ **11** Add Fields to a Query

See Also

→ **15** Print a Query Result

→ **48** Create Queries

→ **50** About Refining a Query with Criteria

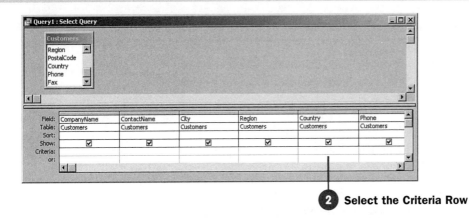

2 Select the Criteria Row

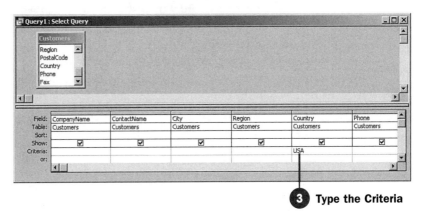

3 Type the Criteria

2 Select the Criteria Row

Select the cell on the **Criteria** row below the field for which you want to add the condition.

3 Type the Criteria

Type the criteria you want to apply for that field. For example, type **USA** in the Country field.

Select the criteria row of any additional fields for which you wish to add criteria. Type the criteria that you want to apply for that field.

There may be times when you want to create a query that contains two or more conditions. You would do this, for example, if you only wanted records in the state of California that had sales within a certain date range to appear in the output. The *And condition* is used to indicate that both of those conditions must be met in order for the row to be included in the resulting recordset. You can use the And condition in the same field or on multiple fields.

By placing criteria for multiple fields on the *same* line of the query grid, you create an And condition. This means that both conditions must be true in order for the records to appear in the result. An example of an And condition on two fields would be State Field = 'TX' And Credit limit >=5000.

There are only a few situations in which you would use an And condition in a single field. This is because in most situations, using the And condition in a single field would yield a recordset with no results. For example, the criteria State = TX And State = CA would yield no results because the state cannot be equal to both values at the same time. On the other hand, HireDate > 7/1/2001 And HireDate < 6/30/2002 would return all employees hired in that date range. To enter this criteria in the criteria cell simply type the first criterion, the keyword And, and then the second criterion.

You can use wildcards to select records that follow a pattern. However, you can use the wildcard characters only in Text or Date/Time fields. You use the * to substitute for multiple characters and the ? to substitute for single characters. Type the criteria, using a wildcard in the desired expression. The expression Like Sales* entered for the Contact Title field returns all rows where the Contact Title begins with Sales.

KEY TERM

And condition—Used to indicate that two or more conditions must be met in order for the row to be included in the resulting recordset.

Examples of Using Wildcards

Expression	Results
Sm?th	Finds **Smith** or **Smyth**.
L*ng	Finds any record that starts with **L** and ends in **ng**.
***th**	Finds any record that ends in **th** (for example, **158th** or **Garth**).
on	Finds any record that has **on** anywhere in the field.
***/2000**	Finds all dates in 2000.
6/*/2000	Finds all dates in June 2000.

Sometimes you want to select records in a table that fall within a range of values. You can use comparison operators (=, <, >, <=, and >=) to create criteria based on the comparison of the value contained in a field to a value that you specify in your criteria. Each record is evaluated, and only records that meet the condition are included in the recordset. Select the cell on the Criteria row below the field for which you want to apply the condition. Type a comparison operator and the criterion you want the query to apply (for example, >**100**).

Many comparison operators are available within Access. The following table gives an example of comparison operators used for a field called Sales. It shows the operators, provides an example of each, and discusses the records that Access would include in the output.

Comparison Operators Used to Compare Against a Field Called Sales

Operator	Indicates	Example	Includes Records Where
>	Greater than	>**7500**	sales are over 7500
>=	Greater than or equal to	>=**7500**	sales are 7500 or more
<	Less than	<**7500**	sales are under 7500
<=	Less than or equal to	<=**7500**	sales are 7500 or less
<>	Does not equal	<>**7500**	sales are not 7500
Between	Range of values	**Between 0 and 7500**	sales are between 0 and 7500

*You can use the word **Not** in place of the <> symbols.*

KEY TERM

Or condition—States that either condition of two conditions should be met in order for the record to appear in the result set.

The *Or condition* states that either condition of two conditions should be met in order for the record to appear in the result set. You can use the Or condition on a single field or on more than one field. To add an Or condition to the query, type the first criterion you want the query to apply. For example, you could type Sales Manager as a criterion for the Contact Title field. Select the cell below the current cell (this is the Or row). Type the second criterion you want the query to apply. For example, you could type Sales Agent as the criterion for the Contact Title field.

An alternative to using the Or condition on a single field is to use the Or condition to create criteria on multiple fields. An example would be City equals London or Contact Title equals Sales Agent. These criteria would return all companies in London, regardless of the contact title, and all sales agents, regardless of the city. Type the first criterion you want the query to apply. Select the cell in the Or row below the second field for which you want to apply the criterion. Type the second criterion you want the query to apply.

Rules for Criteria, Based on Type of Field

Type of Field	Description
Text	After you type the text, Access puts quotes around the text entered.
Number/Currency	You type the digits, without commas or dollar signs but with decimals, if applicable.
Date/Time	You enter any date or time format.
Counter	You type the digits.
Yes/No	For a yes, you type **yes** or **true**. For no, you type **no** or **false**.

NOTE

Although Access is not case sensitive, and you can therefore enter criteria in either upper- or lowercase, the criteria you enter must follow specific rules. These rules vary depending on the type of field the criteria apply to.

4 Click the Run Button

Click the **Run** button. The results of the query appear.

14 Save a Query

If you wish to run your query again at a later time, you are going to want to save it.

1 Click the Save Button

To save a query, click the **Save** button on the toolbar. The Save As dialog box appears.

2 Provide a Name and Click OK

After you provide a name and click **OK**, Access saves the Structured Query Language (SQL) statement underlying the query. It does not save the result of the query.

Before You Begin

✔ **10** Open a Query in Design View

✔ **11** Add Fields to a Query

See Also

→ **15** Print a Query Result

→ **16** Close a Query

1 Click the Save Button

2 Provide a Name and Click Ok

15 Print a Query Result

Before You Begin

✔ **9** Open a Query in Datasheet View

✔ **10** Open a Query in Design View

See Also

→ **25** Open and View a Report

→ **67** Create Groups and Totals Reports

It is easy to print query results. Although not as elegant as a printed report, printed query results are often sufficient to meet people's needs.

1 Run the Query

Run the query whose results you want to print.

2 Click the Print Icon

Click the **Print** icon on the toolbar to send the query directly to the printer; or select **File**, **Print** to invoke the Print dialog box; or click the **Print Preview** icon to preview the query before you send it to a printer.

3 Modify Print Settings

Go to the Print dialog box and click **Setup**, or go to the Print Preview window and click **Setup** to modify the print setup as well as other print settings. Click **OK** when finished.

Click the Print Icon

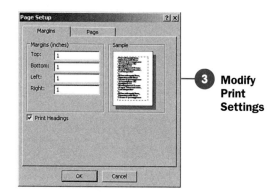

3 Modify Print Settings

---

4 **Click the Print Icon**

From the Print dialog, click **OK** to print, or from the Print Preview window, click the **Print** icon after you have designated all of the desired settings. This will send the document to the printer.

16 **Close a Query**

You close a query by using the close button (the **x**) in the upper-right corner of the Query Design window. How Access responds depends on the following three conditions:

- Whether you previously named and saved the query

- Whether you made design changes to the query

- Whether you made changes to the layout of the query while you were in Datasheet view

Before You Begin

✔ **10** Open a Query in Design View

✔ **14** Save a Query

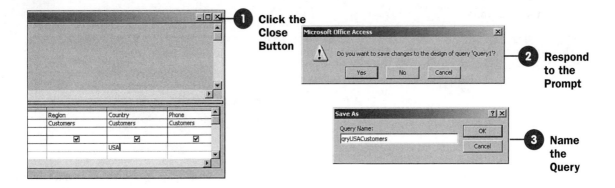

1 Click the Close Button

2 Respond to the Prompt

3 Name the Query

If you did not previously name and save the query, Access prompts you, asking if you want to save the query when you attempt to close it.

If you previously named and saved the query but did not make any design or layout changes to the query, Access provides no prompts. If you made design changes or design and layout changes, Access asks if you want to save those design changes. If you made only layout changes, Access asks if you want to save the layout changes.

1 Click the Close Button

After you have made all of the necessary changes to the query, click the **Close** button.

2 Respond to the Prompt

Designate **Yes**, you want to save the query, **No**, you wish to exit without saving the query, or **Cancel**, you wish to continue working on the query without exiting.

3 Name the Query and Click OK

Provide a name for the query and click **OK**.

4

Working with an Existing Form

IN THIS CHAPTER:

Forms allow you to display data in an esthetically pleasing way. They also provide an excellent mechanism for data entry. Developers often think that forms exist solely for the purpose of data entry. To the contrary, forms serve many different purposes in Access 2003:

- Data entry—They can be used for displaying and editing data.

- Application flow—They can be used for navigating through an application.

- Custom dialog boxes—They can be used to provide messages to users.

- Printing information—They can be used to provide hard copies of data-entry information.

Probably the most common use of an Access form is as a vehicle for displaying and editing existing data or for adding new data. Fortunately, Access offers many features that allow you to build forms that ease data entry for users. Access also makes it easy for you to design forms that let users view and modify data, view data but not modify it, or add new records only. Much of what you can do with forms you can also accomplish from **Datasheet** view. You will find that forms are much easier to look at and work with than **Datasheet** view. They also provide additional protection against data entry errors.

Although not everyone immediately thinks of an Access form as a means of navigating through an application, forms are quite strong in this area. Although the Switchboard Manager makes designing a switchboard form very simple, any type of switchboard is easy to develop. You can be creative with switchboard forms by designing forms that are both utilitarian and exciting.

You can use Access to create custom dialog boxes that display information or retrieve information from users. A custom dialog box can be designed to get the information needed to run a report. The user must fill in the required information before he or she can proceed.

Another strength of Access is its ability to produce professional-looking printed forms. With many other products, it's difficult to print a data-entry form; sometimes the entire form needs to be re-created as a report. In Access, printing a form is simply a matter of clicking a button. You have the option of creating a report that displays the information the user is entering or of printing the form itself.

Access offers many styles of forms. You can display the data in a form one record at a time, or you can let the user view several records at once. You can display forms modally, meaning that the user must respond to and close the form before continuing, or you can display forms so that the user can move through open forms at will. The important thing to remember is that there are many uses for and styles of forms. You will learn about them throughout this chapter, and in Chapter 10, "Create Your Own Forms." As you read the text in this chapter, remember that your forms are limited only by your imagination.

17 Open a Form

A form allows you to display table data or the results of a query. Before you can work with a form, you must first open it.

Before You Begin

→ **18** Work with Data

→ **23** Close a Form

① **Select Forms in the List of Objects**

Click to select forms in the list of objects in the **Database** window.

② **Click to Select the Form to Open**

Locate the form that you want to view. Click to select that form.

③ **Select Open on the Database Window Toolbar**

Select **Open** on the **Database** window toolbar or double-click the form to run it. The form appears.

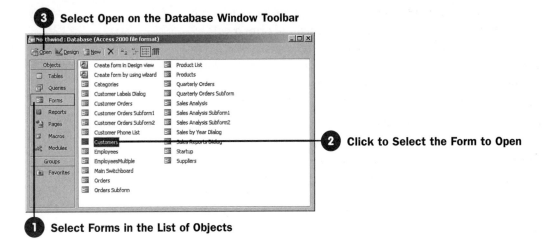

③ Select Open on the Database Window Toolbar

② Click to Select the Form to Open

① Select Forms in the List of Objects

18 Work with Data

Before You Begin

✔ **17** Open a Form

See Also

→ **19** Find Data

→ **20** Replace Data

→ **21** Sort Data

→ **22** Filter Data

🔍 KEY TERM

Navigation bar—Appears at the bottom of the Form window; allows you to move from record to record.

After you have opened a form, you probably want to work with the data you have bound it to. You most likely want to move from record to record, edit data, add new records, delete records, and copy records. The process of editing data includes learning important techniques such as how to select records, delete field contents, undo changes, and search and replace. The steps that follow cover all these techniques.

① Click the Record Navigation Tools

The *Navigation bar* appears at the bottom of the **Form** window. It allows you to move from record to record. The **First Record** navigation button moves you to the first record, the **Previous Record** navigation button moves you to the previous record, and the **Record Number** navigation button allows you to quickly move to a desired record. To the right of the **Record Number** tool are the **Next Record** button, the **Last Record** button, and the **New Record** button.

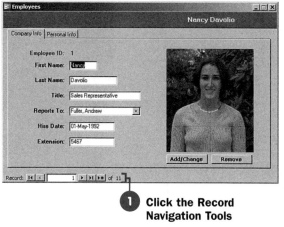

2 Change a Field in a Record

1 Click the Record Navigation Tools

6 Delete a Record

You can also use keystrokes to move from record to record. Pressing **Page Down** moves you forward through the records, one record at a time. Pressing **Page Up** moves you backward through the records, one record at a time. Pressing **Ctrl+End** moves you to the last record, and pressing **Ctrl+Home** moves you to the first record.

2 Change a Field in a Record

Select the record you want to change by using any of the techniques covered in step 1.

Select the field you want to change by clicking the field or using the directional keys.

Type to make the necessary changes to the data.

3 Delete Field Contents

Now that you know how to modify the contents of a field, let's talk about how to delete the contents of a field. In this step, make sure that you understand that you are not deleting records; you are simply deleting the contents of an individual field *within* a record. You would do this, for example, if you entered a region for a company and then realized that the company was located in a country that did not have regions. Simply select the field contents you wish to delete.

Press the **Delete** key. The contents of the field are deleted.

NOTES

A couple of items are important to note. First, if you press the **Esc** key twice, Access cancels all changes you made to that record. Second, it is important to recognize that Access saves the record you are working with as soon as you move off of it and onto another record.

You can add records to a table by choosing **Edit**, **Go To**, **New Record**. Access always displays at the end of a table one blank record that is ready to act as the new record. You can press the **Tab** key to add a record when you are on the last field of the last record in the table.

4 Undo Changes to a Control

When you are in the process of making changes to a *control*, you might realize that you really didn't want to make changes to that control or to that record. To undo changes to the current control, you can either click the **Undo** tool on the toolbar, select **Edit**, **Undo Typing**, or press the **Esc** key once.

The process of undoing changes after you move to another control is slightly different from the process of undoing changes you've made to the current control. You can either click the **Undo** tool on the toolbar, select **Edit**, **Undo Current Field/Record**, or press the **Esc** key once.

When you make changes to a control and then move to another record, Access saves all changes to the modified record. As long as you do not begin making changes to another record, you can still undo the changes you made to the most recently modified record. To do this, you can either click the **Undo** tool on the toolbar, select **Edit**, **Undo Saved Record**, or press the **Esc** key twice. If Access is unable to undo a change, the **Undo** tool appears dimmed.

If you have made changes to a record and then have gone on to make changes to another record, you cannot undo the changes that you made to the first record.

5 Create a New Record

Click the **New Record** tool on the **Navigation** bar at the bottom of the form.

Type the data for the new record. Press **Tab** to go to the next control. Repeat this step to enter all the data for the record. Press **Tab** to move to another new record. Access saves the record.

6 Delete a Record

To select a record, you simply click the gray record selector button to the left of a record within a form. Access selects the record. As an alternative, select **Edit, Select Record**.

To select multiple records (when the form is in **Continuous Forms** view or **Datasheet** view), you click and drag within the record selector area. *Continuous Forms view* allows you to view multiple rows of data in a form at a time. Access selects the contiguous range of records in the area over which you click and drag. As an alternative, you can click the selector button for the first record you want to select, hold down the **Shift** key, and then click the selector button of the last record you want to select. Access selects the entire range of records between the two selector buttons.

If you want to select a single record when the cursor is within the record, you can simply select **Edit, Select Record**.

After you have selected records, they appear in black and you can copy them, delete them, or modify them as a group.

Press the **Delete** key. A dialog box appears, asking if you're sure you want to delete the record(s).

Click **OK** to confirm the deletion and to close the dialog box.

KEY TERM

Continuous Forms view— **Allows you to view multiple rows of data in a form at a time.**

TIP

Deleting records is a permanent process. You cannot undo a deletion.

7 Copy a Record

Select the record you want to copy. You can select the record by clicking the gray record selector or by selecting **Edit, Select Record**.

Select **Edit, Copy**.

Select **Edit, Paste Append**. Access copies the original record and places you in the new record (the copy).

Copying a record often results in what is called a referential integrity error. This occurs, for example, when copying a record would cause a duplicate primary key (that is, unique record identifier). In such a situation, you see an error message. You can either change the data in the field or fields that constitute the duplicate key, or you can press the **Esc** key to cancel the process of appending the new row.

19 Find Data

If you are editing records in a form, you need to find specific records quickly. The same procedure used in **Datasheet** view helps you to quickly locate data in a form.

1 Select the Criteria Field

Select the field that contains the criteria for which you are searching.

2 Click Find

Click the **Find** button on the toolbar. The **Find and Replace** dialog box appears.

3 Designate Search Criteria

Type the criteria in the **Find What** text box.

Use the **Look In** drop-down list box to designate whether to search only the current field or all fields in the table.

Use the **Match** drop-down list box to designate whether to match any part of the field you are searching, the whole field you are searching, or the start of the field you are searching. For example, if you type the word **Federal** in the **Find What** text box and you select **Whole Field** in the **Match** drop-down list box, you find only entries where Ship Via is set to Federal. If you select **Any Part of Field**, you find Federal Shipping, Federal Express, United Federal Shipping, and so on. If you select **Start of Field**, you find Federal Shipping and Federal Express, but you do not find United Federal Shipping.

Use the **Search** drop-down list box to designate whether to search only up from the current cursor position, only down, or in all directions.

Use the **Match Case** check box to indicate whether you want the search to be case sensitive.

2 **Click Find**

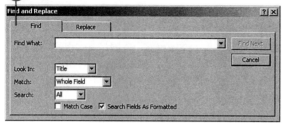

3 **Designate Search Criteria**

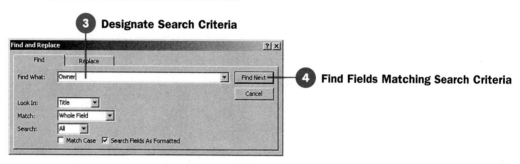

4 **Find Fields Matching Search Criteria**

Use the **Search Fields As Formatted** check box to indicate whether you want to find data only based on the display format (for example, 17-Jul-96 for a date).

4 **Find Fields Matching Search Criteria**

Click the **Find Next** button to find the next record that meets the designated criteria.

To continue searching after you close the dialog box, use the **Shift+F4** keystroke combination or the **Find Again** menu option.

20 Replace Data

There may be times when you want to update records that meet specific criteria. You might want to do this, for example, if a company changes its name or if you realize that you have improperly entered an employee's Social Security number. The **Replace** feature automatically inserts new information into the specified fields.

1 Select the Criteria Field

Select the field that contains the criteria for which you are searching.

2 Click Find

Click the **Find** button on the toolbar. The **Find and Replace** dialog box appears.

3 Click the Replace Tab

Click the **Replace** tab to select it.

4 Designate Criteria to Replace

Type the criteria in the **Find What** text box.

Type the new information (the replacement value) in the **Replace With** text box.

Use the **Look In** drop-down list box to designate whether to search only the current field or all fields in the table.

Use the **Match** drop-down list box to designate whether to match any part of the field you are searching, the whole field you are searching, or the start of the field you are searching. For example, if you type the word **Federal** in the **Find What** text box and you select **Whole Field** in the **Match** drop-down list box, you find only entries where Ship Via is set to Federal. If you select **Any Part of Field**, you find Federal Shipping, Federal Express, United Federal Shipping, and so on. If you select **Start of Field**, you find Federal Shipping and Federal Express, but you do not find United Federal Shipping.

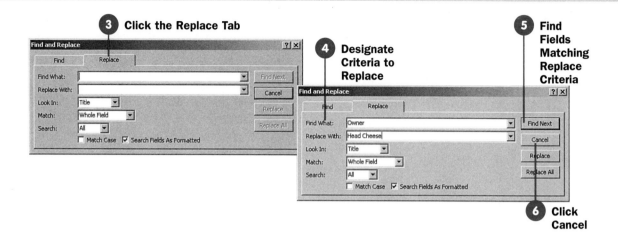

3 Click the Replace Tab

4 Designate Criteria to Replace

5 Find Fields Matching Replace Criteria

6 Click Cancel

Use the **Search** drop-down list box to designate whether to search only up from the current cursor position, only down, or in all directions.

Use the **Match Case** check box to indicate whether you want the search to be case sensitive.

Use the **Search Fields As Formatted** check box to indicate whether you want to find data only based on the display format (for example, 17-Jul-96 for a date).

5 **Find Fields Matching Replace Criteria**

Click the **Find Next** button to find the next record that meets the designated criteria.

When you click the **Replace** button, text in the first occurrence is replaced.

Repeat this step to find all occurrences of the value in the **Find What** text box and replace them. As an alternative, you can click the **Replace All** button to replace all occurrences at once.

6 **Click Cancel**

Click **Cancel** when you are finished replacing all occurrences.

TIP

You should use **Replace All** with quite a bit of caution. Remember that the changes you make are *permanent*. Although **Replace All** is a viable option, when you use it, you need to make sure you have a recent backup and that you are quite certain of what you are doing. In fact, I usually do a few replaces to make sure that I see what Access is doing *before* I click **Replace All**.

21 **Sort Data**

KEY TERM

Wildcard character—A character you use in place of an unknown character.

When using either **Find** or **Replace**, you can use several wildcard characters. A *wildcard character* is a character you use in place of an unknown character. The table that follows describes the wildcard characters.

Wildcard Characters You Can Use When Searching

Wildcard Character	Description
*	Acts as a placeholder for multiple characters.
?	Acts as a placeholder for a single character.
#	Acts as a placeholder for a single number.

21 Sort Data

Before You Begin

✔ **17** Open a Form

✔ **18** Work with Data

See Also

→ **12** Order a Query Result

→ **22** Filter Data

You can change the order of records by using sort buttons. You use this feature when you want to view your records in a particular order. For example, you might want to first view the records in order by company name, and later view them in order by most recent order date. The wonderful thing is that with this easy-to-use feature, changing the sort order involves a simple mouse click.

1 Click Within the Field

Click anywhere within the field.

2 Sort the Information

Click the **Sort Ascending** button or click the **Sort Descending** button. Access reorders the form data based on the designated column.

Another way to sort is to right-click a field and then choose Sort Ascending or Sort Descending.

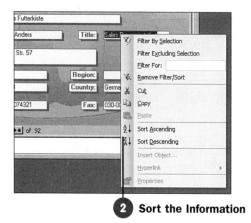

2 Sort the Information

From the **Form** view, you can apply a filter to view a select group of records. You do this when you want to focus on a select group of records. For example, you might just want to work with the records in the Customers table for which the contact title is Owner. You can use the **Filter by Form** feature to accomplish this task. When you learn how to use the **Filter by Form** feature, you need to know how to remove filters and how to work with multiple filter criteria.

1 Open the Form

Open the form whose data you wish to filter.

2 Choose Records, Filter, Filter by Form

Choose **Records, Filter, Filter by Form**. The **Filter by Form** feature appears.

3 Click in the Criteria Field

Click in the field whose data you want to use as the filter criteria.

4 Select Data to Filter On

Select the field data to filter on from the drop-down list.

Before You Begin

✔ **13** Refine a Query with Criteria

See Also

→ **21** Sort Data

→ **24** Highlight Important Data with Conditional Formatting

◣ NOTE

To remove a filter, you simply choose **Records, Remove Filter/Sort** or click the **Remove Filter** toolbar button. Access then displays all the records in the record source underlying the form.

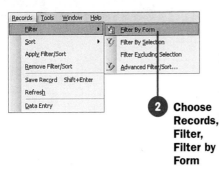

2 Choose Records, Filter, Filter by Form

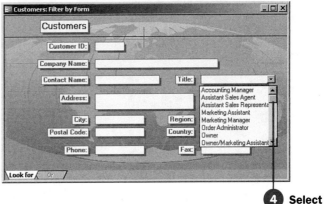

4 Select Data to Filter On

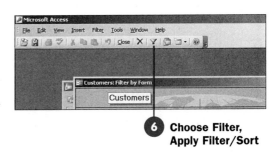

6 Choose Filter, Apply Filter/Sort

5 Select the Or Tab

---

5 Select the Or Tab

Select the **Or** tab and repeat steps 3 and 4 to apply as many additional filter options as desired.

6 Choose Filter, Apply Filter/Sort

Choose **Filter**, **Apply Filter/Sort** or click the **Apply Filter** tool on the toolbar. Access filters the data to just the designated rows.

---

23 Close a Form

If you try to close a form without having made any design changes—
that is, changes that you make to the design of the form—Access does
not prompt you to save. This is because Access saves all data changes as
you move from row to row. If you close a form and save design changes,
those changes are permanent for all users of the form.

1 Click the Close Button

To close a form, you click the **Close** button (**x**) in the upper-right
corner of the form.

2 Respond Whether You Want to Save

If you have made design changes to the form, a dialog appears
asking if you want to save. If you click **Yes**, Access saves the design
changes. If you click **No**, Access abandons the design changes.
Finally, if you click **Cancel**, Access returns you to the form, without
closing it.

Before You Begin

✔ **17** Open a Form

1 Click the Close Button

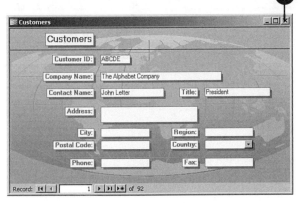

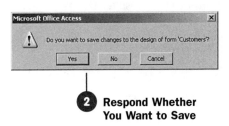

2 Respond Whether You Want to Save

---

24 Highlight Important Data with Conditional Formatting

Before You Begin

✔ **17** Find Data

✔ **22** Filter Data

See Also

→ **74** Apply Advanced Filters

At some point you might need to have a control stand out if it meets certain criteria. You can add formatting to the control to set what condition should be met in order for a particular type of formatting to appear in the record. An example would be for the inventory amount to appear in red if the inventory amount is less than the reorder amount.

1 Open Form in Design View

Open the form that you want to format in **Design** view.

2 Click Control to Format

Click in the control that will contain the conditional formatting.

3 Open the Conditional Formatting Dialog Box

Choose **Format, Conditional Formatting**. The **Conditional Formatting** dialog appears.

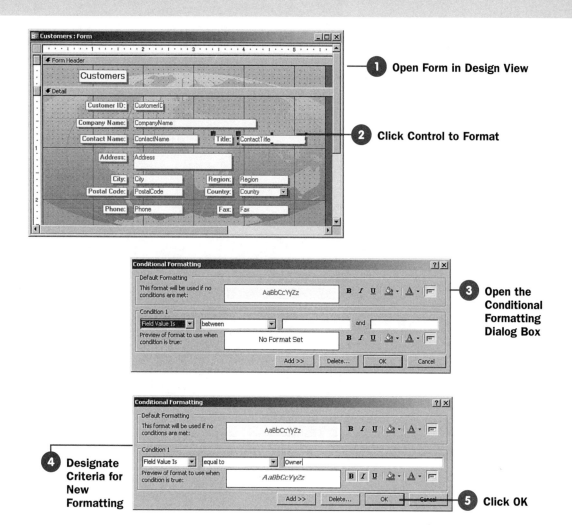

1. Open Form in Design View

2. Click Control to Format

3. Open the Conditional Formatting Dialog Box

4. Designate Criteria for New Formatting

5. Click OK

4 Designate Criteria for New Formatting

Select the condition (equal to, greater than, and so on).

Type the appropriate criteria.

Select the desired formatting.

5 Click OK.

Click **OK**. Access applies the conditional formatting expression.

5

Working with an
Existing Report

IN THIS CHAPTER:

KEY TERM

Report—Provides printed output of the data in a database.

Reports provide printed output of the data in a *database*. They are generally a major objective of any database application that you develop.

25 Open and View a Report

See Also

→ **26** Move from Page to Page

→ **27** Zoom In and Out

→ **28** View Multiple Pages

Microsoft Access provides an excellent means of working with existing reports. You can either send a report directly to the printer, or you can first preview a report that you want to work with.

1 Select Reports in the List of Objects

Click the **Reports** list of objects in the **Database** window.

2 Click to Select the Report to Open

Locate the report that you want to view. Click to select that report.

3 Select Preview on the Database Window Toolbar

Select **Preview** on the **Database** window toolbar or double-click the report to run it. The report appears in preview mode.

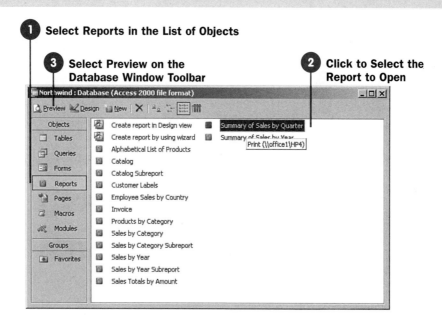

1 Select Reports in the List of Objects

3 Select Preview on the Database Window Toolbar

2 Click to Select the Report to Open

26 Move from Page to Page

A report is a way to present the data from a table or query in a format-ted document. Although you can print datasheets, reports control how you present and summarize the data. When you open a report, you can use the navigation buttons to easily move from page to page. You accomplish this by using the page navigation buttons at the bottom of the report window. By using these buttons, you can easily navigate to the first page of the report, the previous page, the next page, or the last page of the report. By typing a number into the text box on the *Navigation bar*, you can easily navigate to any page in the report.

Before You Begin

✔ **25** Open and View a Report

See Also

→ **27** Zoom In and Out

→ **28** View Multiple Pages

→ **29** Print a Report

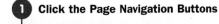

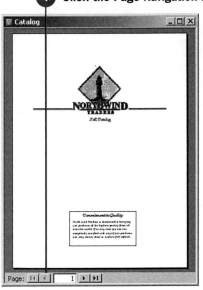

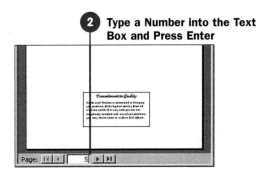

❶ Click the Page Navigation Buttons

The *Navigation bar* appears at the bottom of the Report window. It allows you to move from page to page of the report. The **First Page** navigation button moves you to the first page, the **Previous Page** navigation button moves you to the previous page, and the **Page Number** navigation button allows you to quickly move to a desired page. To the right of the **Page Number** button are the **Next Page** button and the **Last Page** button.

You can also use keystrokes to move from page to page. Pressing **Page Down** moves you forward through the pages, one page at a time. Pressing **Page Up** moves you backward through the pages, one page at a time.

❷ Type a Number into the Text Box and Press Enter

Type a number into the text box on the *Navigation bar*. Press **Enter**. Access will take you to the specified page of the report.

27 Zoom In and Out

When previewing reports, you can change the amount of text (and the size of the text) that you see onscreen in a report. You do this by zooming in and out of the report page. There are two different techniques that you can use to set the zoom level.

1 Zoom In and Out

Place the mouse pointer over the report so that it appears as a magnifying glass. Click the mouse. The page zooms in. Click the mouse again. The page zooms out.

2 Use the Zoom Drop-down List Box

Click the **Zoom** drop-down list box. Select a size. The report zooms to the designated level.

Before You Begin

✔ **25** Open and View a Report

✔ **26** Move from Page to Page

See Also

→ **28** View Multiple Pages

→ **29** Print a Report

 TIP

The **Fit** option within the **Zoom** drop-down list box fits the report within the available screen real estate of the report window.

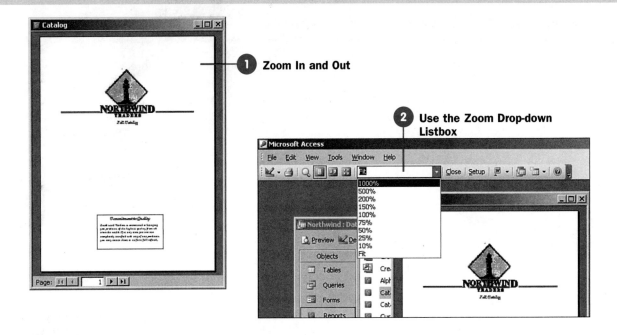

1 Zoom In and Out

2 Use the Zoom Drop-down Listbox

---

28 View Multiple Pages

Before You Begin

✔ **25** Open and View a Report

✔ **26** Move from Page to Page

✔ **27** Zoom In and Out

See Also

→ **29** Print a Report

While you're previewing an Access report, you can preview more than one page at a time.

1 Click the Two Pages Button

To view two pages, you click the **Two Pages** button on the **Print Preview** toolbar.

2 Click the Multiple Pages Button

To view multiple pages, you click the **Multiple Pages** button. Select how many pages you want to view.

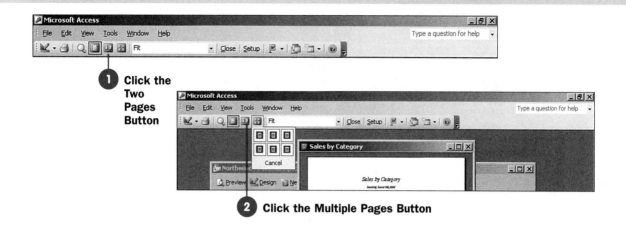

1 Click the
Two
Pages
Button

2 Click the Multiple Pages Button

---

29 Print a Report

Before you print a report, you can change the report margins, orientation, paper size, and several other important options. You accomplish this by using the **Page Setup** feature.

1 Open the Page Setup Dialog Box

While previewing the report, click the **Setup** button on the **Preview** toolbar. The **Page Setup** dialog box appears.

2 Modify the Margins

Click the **Margins** tab and modify the top, bottom, left, and right margins.

3 Customize Page Settings

Click the **Page** tab and customize important settings such as the orientation, paper size and source, and printer you wish to use.

4 Designate Column Settings

Click the **Columns** tab and designate column size and other information applicable for multicolumn reports. Click **OK** to accept the designated settings.

Before You Begin

✔ **25** Open and View a
Report

See Also

→ **30** Close a Report

→ **31** Print Database
Objects

CHAPTER 5: Working with an Existing Report

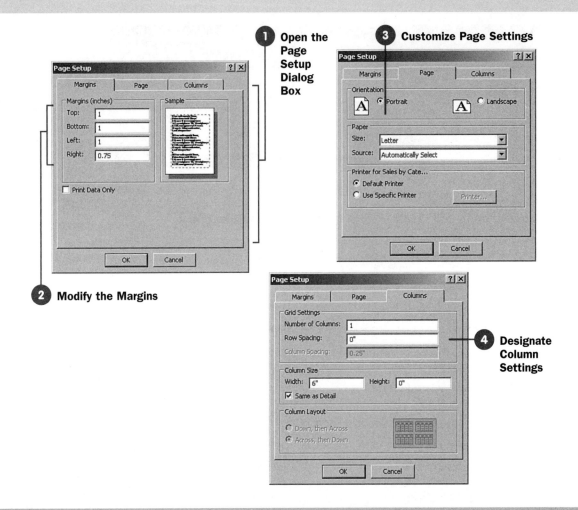

1 Open the Page Setup Dialog Box

3 Customize Page Settings

2 Modify the Margins

4 Designate Column Settings

5 Print the Report

Click **Print** on the toolbar to send your report to the printer.

You can print the reports you create by using the Print dialog box that you access by selecting **File**, **Print** or using the **Print** button from the **Standard** toolbar. You can also print a report while you are in Print Preview mode by clicking the **Print** button on the **Print Preview** toolbar. To print a report by using the File menu, click **Reports** in the list of objects in the **Database** window, select the report you want to print, and select **File**, **Print**. Complete the dialog, entering information such as the number of copies you want to print, and the printer you want to print to, and click **OK** to complete the process.

You can print a report using the **Print** button from the Standard toolbar. Click **Reports** in the list of objects in the **Database** window. Click to select the report you want to print. Click the **Print** tool on the **Standard** toolbar. Access immediately sends the report to the printer without invoking the Print dialog box or asking for further confirmation.

You can print a report by right-clicking it in the **Database** window and then selecting **Print**. Access sends the report directly to the printer.

30 Close a Report

When you are finished working with a report, you need to close it.

1 Click the Close Button

To close a report, you click the **Close** button (**x**) in the upper-right corner of the report.

2 Respond Whether You Want to Save

If you have made design changes to the report, a dialog appears asking if you want to save. If you click **Yes**, Access saves the design changes. If you click **No**, Access abandons the design changes. Finally, if you click **Cancel**, Access returns you to the report, without closing it.

Before You Begin

✔ **25** Open and View a Report

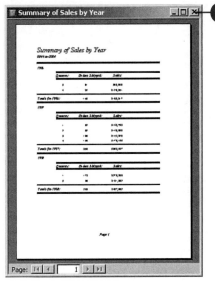

1 Click the Close Button

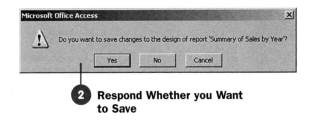

2 Respond Whether you Want to Save

---

31 Print Database Objects

Before You Begin

✔ **25** Open and View a Report

✔ **29** Print a Report

Sometimes it is unnecessary to go through the process of building a report. It might be sufficient, for example, to simply print the datasheet that shows the result of running a query. Access allows you to print table datasheets, query results, and forms.

1 Select Tables in the Object List

Select **Tables** in the list of database objects.

2 Double-click the Table You Want to Print

Double-click the table whose data you want to print.

3 Preview the Table

Click the **Print Preview** button to preview the data before you print it, or click **Print** to send the data directly to a printer.

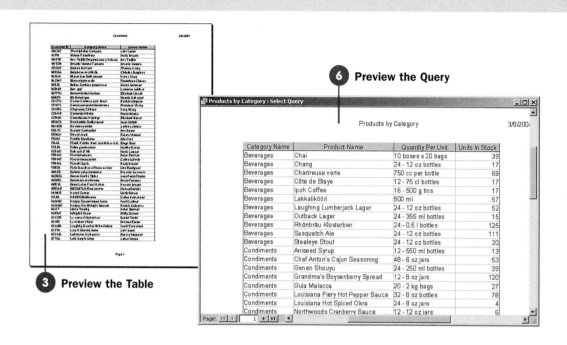

3 Preview the Table

6 Preview the Query

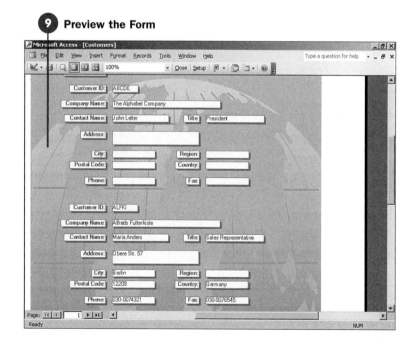

9 Preview the Form

As an alternative, if you want to modify print settings, you can select **File**, **Print**. The **Print** dialog box appears. Modify any print settings and click **OK** to proceed.

4 Select Queries in the Object List

Click **Queries** in the list of objects in the **Database** window.

5 Double-click the Query You Want to Print

Double-click the query whose result set you want to print.

6 Preview the Query

Click the **Print Preview** button to preview the data before you print it, or click **Print** to send the data directly to a printer.

As an alternative, if you want to modify print settings, you can select **File**, **Print**. The **Print** dialog box appears. Modify any print settings and click **OK** to proceed.

7 Select Forms in the Object List

Select **Forms** in the list of database objects.

8 Double-click the Form You Want to Print

Double-click the form you want to print.

9 Preview the Form

Click the **Print Preview** button to preview the data before you print it, or click **Print** to send the form directly to a printer.

As an alternative, if you want to modify print settings, you can select **File**, **Print**. The **Print** dialog box appears. Modify any print settings and click **OK** to proceed.

PART III

Create Your Own Database and Objects

6

Use Wizards to Create a Database

IN THIS CHAPTER:

NOTE

Before you begin the tasks in this chapter, be sure to read Chapter 1 for information on relational databases and the database window, as well as on how to open an existing database.

Access provides many wizards that facilitate the process of creating a database and the objects within it. These wizards can provide everything you need. Sometimes, however, you might run the wizards and then have to modify the design of the objects that the wizards create, or you might find it easier to build the objects from scratch. This chapter focuses on the wizards, and in later chapters, you'll learn how to modify the objects that the wizards create and to build the objects from scratch.

32 Use a Database Template to Create a Database

See Also

✔ **33** Create a New Empty Database

✔ **34** Create a Table Using the Table Wizard

You can use the Database Wizard to create a new database based on a template (a Customer database, for example). You can select options provided by the wizard to make the database suit your specific needs. After you have completed the process of running the wizard, you can then modify the design of any of the objects that the wizard creates.

1 Select File, New

With the **Database** window active, select **File, New**. The **New File panel** appears on the right side of the screen.

2 Select On My Computer

Select **On my computer** from the list of options that appears below **Templates** on the right side of the screen. The **Templates** dialog box appears.

3 Select the Databases Tab

Select the **Databases** tab in the **Templates** dialog box. Double-click the desired template (for example, Contact Management).

4 Type Filename and Location

Type the filename and location for the new database. Click the **OK** button. The **Database Wizard** appears. Click **Next**. The wizard prompts you with a list of selected tables and fields.

5 Include Optional Fields

Scroll down to view the list of optional fields for each table. Click to include the desired optional fields. Click **Next** to continue.

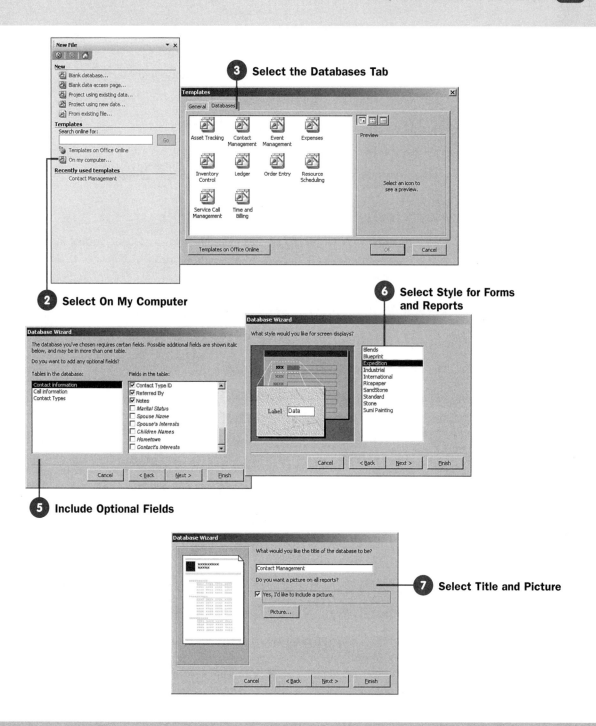

3 Select the Databases Tab

2 Select On My Computer

6 Select Style for Forms and Reports

5 Include Optional Fields

7 Select Title and Picture

6 **Select Style for Forms and Reports**

Select a style for the forms and click **Next**. Select a style for the reports and click **Next**.

7 **Select Title and Picture**

Select a title for the database and, if you want to, select a picture that Access should include on reports. Click **Next**. Click **Finish** to complete the process.

8 **Press F11 and Click Tables**

Press **F11**, and the **Database** window appears. Click **Tables** in the list of objects. Notice what tables the wizard has added to the database.

9 **View Other Object Categories**

Click the various object categories (tables, queries, and so on) to view the other types of objects that the **Database Wizard** created.

33 Create a New Empty Database

Before You Begin

✔ **32** Use a Database Template to Create a Database

See Also

→ **34** Create a Table Using the Table Wizard

→ **35** Create a Query Using the Query Wizard

→ **36** Create a Form Using the Form Wizard

→ **37** Create a Report Using the Report Wizard

When none of the available databases that the wizard creates gives you what you need, you need to create a database on your own. An example would be if you needed to create a database for a fundraising organization. Since none of the wizard-generated databases relates to fundraising, you would probably want to create a blank database and build the database and its objects on your own.

1 **Choose File, New**

Choose **File, New**.

2 **Select Blank Database**

Select **Blank Database** from the list of options on the right-hand side of the screen.

3 **Select a Drive and Folder**

Select a drive and/or folder where you will place the database.

2 **Select Blank Database**

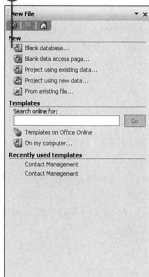

3 **Select a Drive and Folder**

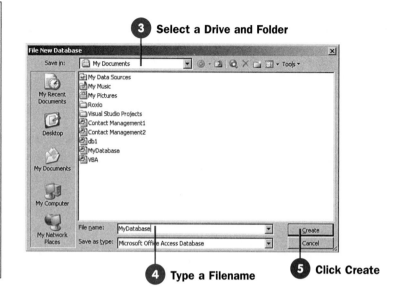

4 **Type a Filename**

5 **Click Create**

4 Type a Filename

Type a filename for the database.

5 Click Create

Click the **Create** button. Access creates an empty database file.
You can add the necessary tables, queries, forms, reports, data
access pages, macros, and modules that comprise a functional
application.

NOTE

Database filenames must
follow these rules. They can
contain up to 255 charac-
ters. Database names can
contain spaces, but you
should avoid special characters such as asterisks.
Access assigns the exten-
sion .MDB to a database
that you create.

34 Create a Table Using the Table Wizard

Before You Begin

✔ **32** Use a Database Template to Create a Database

✔ **33** Create a New Empty Database

See Also

➜ **42** Build a New Table

➜ **43** About Selecting the Appropriate Field Type for Your Data

The **Table Wizard** can assist you with the process of building basic tables. It provides you with the table structures necessary to collect data for many common personal and business systems. Using the Table wizard can save you a lot of time and energy in building the tables that comprise your database.

The first step in the Table Wizard lets you choose specific fields from one of many predefined tables. The tables are categorized as business and personal. After you have selected a type of table, you can specify which fields you want to include in the table. In the next step of the **Table Wizard**, you name the table and indicate whether you want Access to set the primary key for you. (Primary keys are covered in more detail in **45** About the Types of Relationships and **47** Establish Referential Integrity)

In the next step of the **Table Wizard**, Access tries to identify relationships between the new table and existing tables (if there are any existing tables). The process of establishing relationships is an important part of Access development. Relationships allow you to normalize a database and to "flatten out" the data structure at runtime. To *normalize* means to test tables against a series of rules to ensure that the application runs as efficiently as possible. Relationships also help you ensure the integrity of an application's data. For example, you can define a relationship so that it's impossible to enter orders for customers who don't exist.

The final dialog box of the **Table Wizard** allows you to indicate whether you want to modify the design of the table, enter data into the table, or let Access automatically build both the table and a data-entry form for you.

❶ Select Tables in the Database Window

Select the **Tables** icon from the list of objects in the **Database** window.

❷ Double-click Create Table by Using Wizard

Double-click the **Create Table by Using Wizard** icon. The Table Wizard appears.

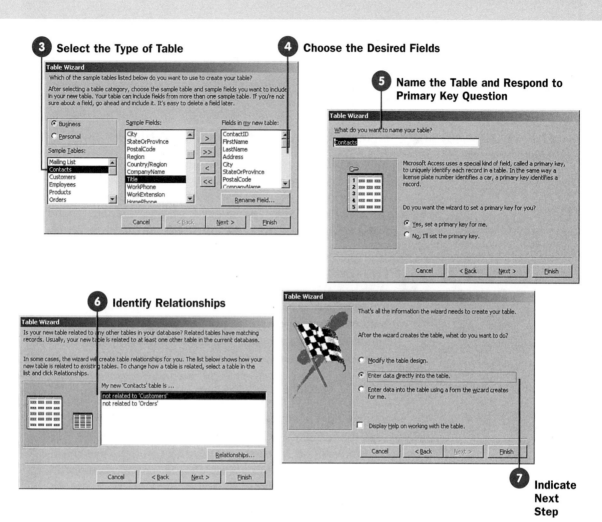

3 Select the Type of Table

If you select the **Business** option, you see a set of business-related tables; if you select **Personal**, you see a set of tables for personal topics.

4 Choose the Desired Fields

To do this, double-click the field you want or click the **right-arrow button**. After you have selected the table and fields you want, click **Next**. A dialog box appears.

5 Name the Table and Respond to Primary Key Question

Provide a name for the table. If you haven't entered a *unique identifier* (that is, some field that differentiates each record from the next) for the table, select **Yes**. Access then adds an **AutoNumber** field to the table and designates it as the primary key.

6 Identify Relationships

Although Access automatically identifies relationships if it can, you can modify or add relationships by clicking the **Relationships** button. When you're satisfied with the relationships that you have established, click **Next**.

7 Indicate Next Step

Indicate what you want Access to do when the wizard is finished running. Click **Finish** to complete the process. Access creates the table with the options that you specified.

35 Create a Query Using the Query Wizard

Just as the Table Wizard facilitates the process of creating tables, the **Simple Query Wizard** helps you to build basic queries. These basic queries limit the fields that Access displays from a table, but in no way modify the sort order or the records that Access displays. An example would be a query that displays the Customer ID, Company Name, Contact Name, and Contact Title from the Customers table.

1 Select Queries

Select the **Queries** icon from the list of objects in the **Database** window.

3 Select a Table or Query
and Fields to Include

4 Rename
Query and
Run or
Modify
Design

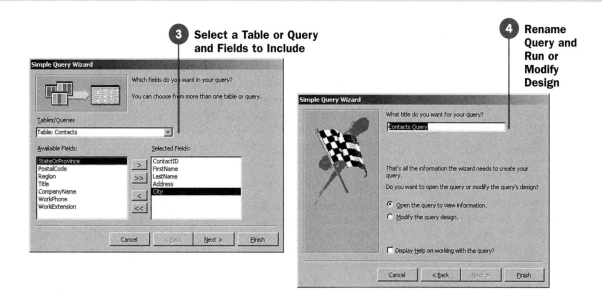

2 **Double-click Create Query by Using a Wizard**

Double-click the **Create Query by Using a Wizard** icon. The
Simple Query Wizard appears.

3 **Select a Table or Query and Fields to Include**

From the **Tables/Queries** drop-down list box, select the table or
query on which you want to base the query. Then select the fields
that you want to include in the query. Click **Next** to continue with
the wizard.

4 **Rename Query and Run or Modify Design**

The second and final step of the **Simple Query Wizard** prompts
you to name the query and allows you to either immediately run
the query or modify the design of the query. Click **Finish** to complete the process.

36 Create a Form Using the Form Wizard

36 Create a Form Using the Form Wizard

Before You Begin

✔ **17** Open a Form

✔ **33** Create a New Empty Database

✔ **34** Create a Table Using the Table Wizard

See Also

→ **56** Add Controls

→ **57** About Selecting Controls

→ **58** Move, Size, and Delete Controls

Just as the wizards we've looked at so far in this chapter can give you a jump start when creating tables and queries, the **Form Wizard** can give you the help you need to get started with building forms. It does this by walking you step-by-step through the process of building a form. After the wizard is complete, you have a form that displays all of the data you want, the way that you want to display it.

1 Select Create Form by Using a Wizard

Select the **Create Form by Using a Wizard** icon with the **Forms** icon selected from the Objects list. You can also select **Form Wizard** from the **New Form** dialog box and click **OK**.

Another way to start the **Form Wizard** is to click the **Tables** or **Queries** icon in the **Objects** list and then select the table or query you want the form to be based on. From the **New Object** drop-down list box on the toolbar, you select **Form**; this opens the **New Form** dialog box. Then you select **Form Wizard**. You don't have to use the **Tables/Queries** drop-down list box to select a table or query because Access automatically selects the table or query you selected before invoking the wizard.

2 Designate Table or Query to Use as the Foundation

Select a particular table or query. Access displays its fields in the **Available Fields** list box.

3 Select Fields to Include

To select the fields to include on the form, double-click the name of the field or click on the field, and then click the **right-arrow button**. Select the fields you want and then click **Next**.

4 Specify the Layout

In the second step of the **Form Wizard** you specify the layout for the form you're designing. You can select from Columnar, Tabular, Datasheet, Justified, PivotTable, and PivotChart layouts; the most common choice is Columnar. Select a **form layout** and then click **Next**.

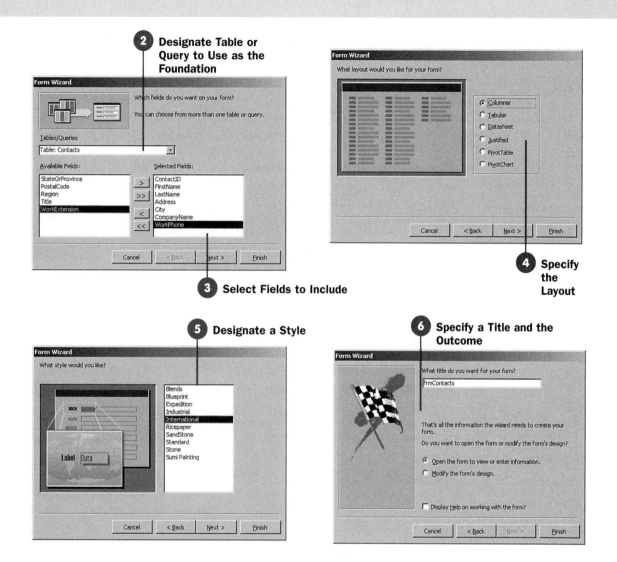

2 Designate Table or Query to Use as the Foundation

3 Select Fields to Include

4 Specify the Layout

5 Designate a Style

6 Specify a Title and the Outcome

5 Designate a Style

In the third step of the **Form Wizard**, you select a style for a form from several predefined styles. Although you can use **Design view** to modify all the properties set by the wizard after the wizard creates the form, to save time it's best to select the appropriate style while you're running the wizard. Select a style for your form and then click **Next**.

6 **Specify a Title and the Outcome**

In the final step of the **Form Wizard**, supply a title for the form. (If you just accept the default, the form will have the same name as the underlying table or query, which could be confusing.) Unfortunately, the form's title becomes the name of the form as well. For this reason, you should type the text you want to use as the name of the form. Later, if you want to change the title of the form, you can do so in **Design view**.

This last step of the **Form Wizard** also lets you specify whether you want to view the results of your work or open the form in **Design view**. It's usually best to view the results and then modify the form's design after you have taken a peek at what the **Form Wizard** has done. Click **Finish**.

37 Create a Report Using the Report Wizard

Before You Begin

✔ **25** Open and View a Report

✔ **33** Create a New Empty Database

✔ **34** Create a Table Using the Table Wizard

See Also

➜ **66** About Working with Controls

➜ **67** Create Groups and Totals Reports

The final wizard that we're going to take a look at in this chapter is the **Report Wizard**. No matter how experienced you are as an Access user or developer, the **Report Wizard** can save you much time and effort. For instance, in the **Report Wizard** you can lay out controls and create summary calculations much more quickly than you can in **Design view**.

1 **Double-click Create Report by Using a Wizard**

Click **Reports** in the **Objects** list and then double-click the **Create Report by Using a Wizard** icon. This launches the **Report Wizard**.

Another way to start the **Report Wizard** is to select **Tables** or **Queries** from the **Objects** list in the **Database** container and then click the table or query that you want the report to be based on. From the **New Object** drop-down list box on the toolbar, you select **Report**. In the New Report dialog box, you select **Report Wizard**. You don't have to use the Tables/Queries drop-down list box to select a table or query because the one you selected before invoking the wizard is automatically selected for you.

4 **Designate How to View Data**

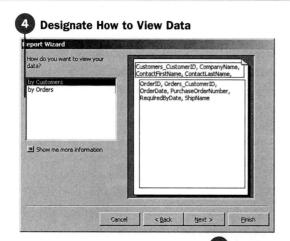

5 **Add Group Levels**

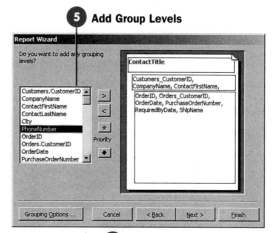

6 **Choose Sorting Levels**

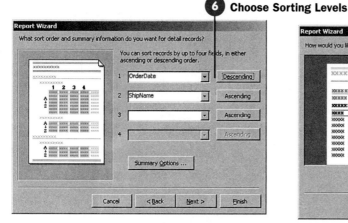

7 **Select Layout and Orientation**

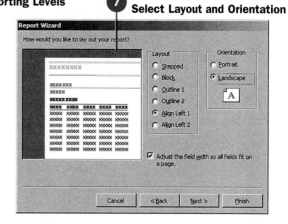

8 **Designate a Style**

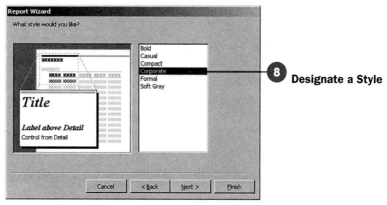

2 **Select Table or Query That Supplies the Data**

Select the table or query that will supply data to the report.

I prefer to base reports on queries or on embedded SQL statements. This generally improves performance because it returns the smallest dataset possible. Basing reports on queries also enhances your ability to produce reports based on varying criteria.

3 **Select Fields to Include on Report**

To add fields to the report, use the Available Fields list box to double-click the name of the field you want to add or click the field name and then click the **right-arrow button**. When you are done selecting a table or query and the fields you want to include on the report, click **Next**.

4 **Designate How to View Data**

If you based your report on data from more than one table or on a query that retrieves data from multiple tables, the **Report Wizard** shows a dialog box that lets you determine how to view the data. For example, the **Report Wizard** may prompt you to select whether to view the data by category or by product. If this dialog box appears, make a selection and click **Next**.

5 **Add Group Levels**

Add group levels if you need to visually separate groups of data or include summary calculations (subtotals) in a report. After adding the required groupings, click **Next**.

6 **Choose Sorting Levels**

Because the order of a query underlying a report is overridden by any sort order designated in the report, it's a good idea to designate a sort order for the report.

You can add up to four sorting levels by using the **Report Wizard**. If you click the **Ascending** buttons to the right of the drop-down list boxes, they toggle to read **Descending**, causing the data to sort in descending order. After you select the fields you want to sort on, click **Next**.

7 **Select Layout and Orientation**

In the next step of the **Report Wizard**, you decide on the report's layout and orientation. The layout options vary depending on what selections you have made in the wizard's previous steps. The orientation can be Portrait or Landscape.

This step of the **Report Wizard** also allows you to specify whether you want Access to adjust the width of each field so that all the fields fit on each page. Supply Access with this information and then click **Next**.

8 **Designate a Style**

Choose a style for the report. The choices are Bold, Casual, Compact, Corporate, Formal, and Soft Gray. You can preview each look before you make a decision by simply clicking the style. Later on, you can modify any of the style attributes that the **Report Wizard** applies, as well as other report attributes that the wizard defines. You accomplish this in **Design view** any time after the wizard produces the report. After you select a style, click **Next**.

9 **Enter a Title and Designate an Outcome**

The final step of the **Report Wizard** prompts you for the report's title. Access uses this title as both the name and the caption for the report. (You can supply a standard Access report name and modify the caption after the **Report Wizard** has finished its process.)

You're then given the opportunity to preview the report or modify the report's design. If you opt to modify the report's design, Access places you in **Design view** rather than in **Print Preview view**. You can then preview the report at any time.

You can optionally mark the check box **Display Help on Working with the Report** to have Access display the **Help** window and list the associated report topics.

7

Design and Create Your Own Tables

IN THIS CHAPTER:

It is useful to think of the process of table design as being similar to the process of building a foundation for a house. Just as a house with a faulty foundation will fall over, an application with a poor table design will be difficult to build, maintain, and use. This chapter covers all the ins and outs of table design in Access 2003. After this chapter, you will be ready to build the other components of an application, knowing that the tables you design provide the application with a strong foundation.

38 About Task Analysis

Before You Begin

✔ **32** Use a Database Template to Create a Database

✔ **33** Create a New Empty Database

See Also

→ **39** About Database Analysis and Design

→ **40** About Relational Database Design

The first step in the development process is task analysis, which involves considering each and every process that occurs during the user's work-day—a cumbersome but necessary task. When I first started working for a large corporation as a mainframe programmer, I was required to carefully follow a task-analysis checklist. I had to find out what each user of the system did to complete his or her daily tasks, document each procedure, determine the flow of each task to the next, relate each task of each user to his or her other tasks as well as to the tasks of every other user of the system, and tie each task to corporate objectives. In this day and age of rapid application development and changing technology, task analysis in the development process seems to have gone out the window. I maintain that if you don't take the required care to complete this process, you will have to rewrite large parts of the application.

39 About Database Analysis and Design

Before You Begin

✔ **32** Use a Database Template to Create a Database

✔ **33** Create a New Empty Database

See Also

→ **40** About Relational Database Design

→ **41** About the Application Development Process

After you have analyzed and documented all the tasks involved in a system, you're ready to work on the data analysis and design phase of an application. The process involves the following steps:

- Identify information needed. Identify each piece of information needed to complete each task. For example, you may want your system to store the customer names, customer addresses, order numbers, customer numbers, order dates, freight amounts, ship-to information, and other important information associated with customers and orders.

- Assign data elements to subjects. You must assign data elements to subjects, and each subject will become a separate table in the database. For example, a subject might be a customer; every data element relating to that customer—the name, address, phone number, credit limit, and any other pertinent information—would become fields within the customer table.

- Determine the data type for each element. Select the appropriate data types for each field in each table. For example, whereas your **CustomerID** field will probably be **Numeric**, the **CreditLimit** field will be **Currency**, and the **EntryDate** field will be **Date/Time**.

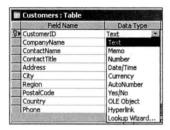

Select the appropriate data types for each field in each table.

- Determine how subjects are related. Determine conceptually how the subjects are related, and then use the **Relationships** window to establish the relationship between each subject (table).

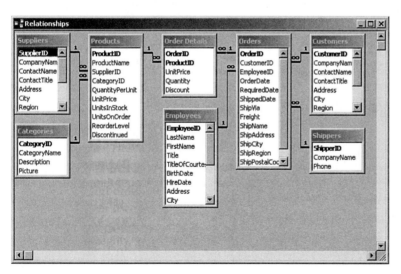

Determine conceptually how the subjects are related.

- Determine the required size for each element. You always want to select the smallest data type possible. This acts both to reduce storage requirements and to improve performance. When selecting a size, make sure that you leave room for growth (for example, select **Long Integer** instead of **Integer**).

- Determine validation rules for each element. Determine how the system should validate each entry. You can enter the validation rules directly into the **Design view** of the table.

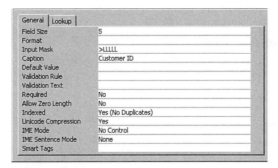

Determine the required size for each element, and how the system should validate each entry.

- Determine which elements are updateable. Determine whether you will allow the user to update each data element.

- Determine which elements are calculated. Determine whether the user will enter each update or the system will calculate it.

In the preceding chapters we have briefly mentioned some terms that are integrally important now that you will be designing your own objects. The following are the most important of these terms and what they mean:

- *Column or field*—A single piece of information about an object (for example, a company name).

- *Row or record*—A collection of information about a single entity (for example, all the information about a customer).

- *Table*—A collection of all the data for a specific type of entity (for example, all the information for all the customers stored in a database). It is important that each table contain information about only a single entity. In other words, you would not store information about an order in the **Customers** table.

- *Primary key field*—A field or a combination of fields in a table that uniquely identifies each row in the table (for example, the **CustomerID**).

- *Natural key field*—A primary key field that is naturally part of the data contained within the table (for example, a Social Security number). Generally it is better to use a contrived key field, such as an **AutoNumber** field, than a natural key field as the primary key field.

- *Composite key field*—A primary key field comprising more than one field in a table (for example, **LastName** and **FirstName** fields). It is preferable to create a primary key based on an **AutoNumber** field than to use a composite key field.

- *Relationship*—Two tables in a database sharing a common key value. An example is a relationship between the Customers table and the Orders table: The **CustomerID** field in the Customers table is related to the **CustomerID** field in the Orders table.

- *Foreign key field*—A field on the many side of the relationship in a one-to-many relationship. Whereas the table on the one side of the relationship is related by the primary key field, the table on the many side of the relationship is related by the foreign key field. For example, one customer has multiple orders, so whereas the **CustomerID** field is the primary key field in the **Customers** table, it is the foreign key field in the **Orders** table.

KEY TERMS

Natural key field—A primary key field that is naturally part of the data contained within the table (for example, a Social Security number).

Composite key field—A primary key field comprising more than one field in a table (for example, **LastName** and **FirstName** fields).

Foreign key field—A field on the many side of the relationship in a one-to-many relationship. Whereas the table on the one side of the relationship is related by the primary key field, the table on the many side of the relationship is related by the foreign key field.

40 About Relational Database Design

Normalization is a fancy term for the process of testing a table design against a series of rules to ensure that the application will operate as efficiently as possible. These rules are based on set theory and were originally proposed by Dr. E. F. Codd. Although you could spend years studying normalization, its main objective is to create an application that runs efficiently with as little data manipulation and coding as possible. With that in mind, you should do a number of things to ensure that you properly normalize your database:

- Ensure that fields are atomic. Fields should be atomic—that is, each piece of data should be broken down as much as possible. For

Before You Begin

✔ **32** Use a Database Template to Create a Database

✔ **33** Create a New Empty Database

See Also

→ **42** Build a New Table

→ **43** About Selecting the Appropriate Field Type for Your Data

example, rather than create a field called **Name**, you should create two fields: one for the first name and another for the last name. This method makes the data much easier to work with. If you need to sort or search by first name separately from the last name, for example, you can do so without any extra effort. The Northwind **Customers** table is an example of a table where the **ContactName** is *not* atomic. It would be very difficult to sort the data in this field by last name.

The Contact Name field is not atomic—that is, it is not broken down into first and last name.

- Verify that there are no repeating values. There should be no repeating values—that is, fields should not appear such as Phone1Type, Phone1Number, Phone2Type, Phone2Number, Phone3Type, Phone3Number. That works great until someone has a fourth phone number. If storing a large number of phone numbers for each company is important to you, you should create a **Phone** table and relate it to the **Customers** table with a one-to-many relationship from **Customers** to **Phones**.

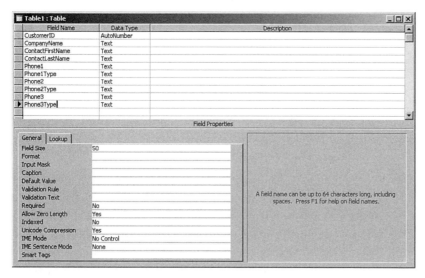

The Phone and Phone Type demonstrate repeating values—that is, multiple fields that contain similar information.

- Assign a unique identifier to each record. Each record should contain a unique identifier so that you have a way of safely identifying the record. For example, if you're changing customer information, you can make sure you're changing the information associated with the correct customer. This unique identifier is called the *primary key*.

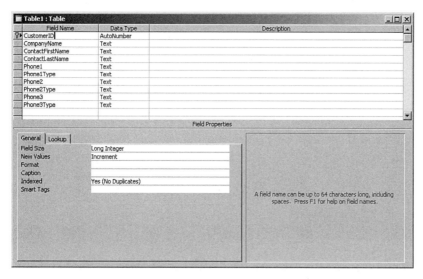

The CustomerID field demonstrates an example of a primary key field—that is, a field that will not allow duplicate values.

KEY TERM

Primary Key—A field (or fields) that uniquely identifies a record.

The primary key is a field (or fields) that uniquely identifies the record. Sometimes you can assign a natural primary key. For example, a Social Security number in an Employees table should serve to uniquely identify each employee to the system. At other times, you might need to create a primary key. Because two customers could have the same name, for example, a customer name might not uniquely identify the customer to the system. It might be necessary to create a field that would contain a unique identifier for each customer, such as a customer ID.

- Evaluate the unique identifier. A primary key should be short, stable, and simple. Short means it should be small in size (not a 50-character field). Stable means the primary key should be a field whose value rarely, if ever, changes. For example, whereas a customer ID would rarely change, a company name is rather likely to change. Simple means it should be easy for a user to work with.

- Ensure that you are not duplicating information. Make sure that you are not storing the same information in more than one place. For example, you should place the company name in the **Customers** table. It should not appear in the **Orders** table. Besides saving disk space, by storing the company name in only one place, you can modify it in one place if it changes.

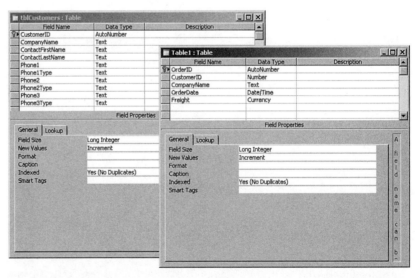

Tables that show an example of duplicated information—that is, the CompanyName appears in two tables.

- Ensure that all columns depend on the primary key. Every field in a table should supply additional information about the record that the primary key serves to identify. For example, every field in a Customers table should describe the customer who has a particular customer ID.

41 About the Application Development Process

The application development process is divided into seven basic stages: task analysis, data analysis and design, development, prototyping, testing, implementation, and maintenance. The development of the application is the subject of this book. The previous sections covered task analysis and data analysis and design. The text that follows discusses the other four stages.

Prototyping

Although the task analysis and data analysis phases of application development haven't changed much since the days of mainframes, the prototyping phase has changed. In working with mainframes or DOS-based languages, it was important to develop detailed specifications for each screen and report. I remember requiring users to sign off on every screen and report. Even a change such as moving a field on a screen required a change order and approval for additional hours. After the user signed off on the screen and report specifications, the programmers would spend days working arduously to develop each screen and report. They would return to the user after many months, only to hear that everything was wrong. This meant back to the drawing board for the developer and many additional hours before the user could once again review the application.

The process is quite different now. As soon as you have outlined the tasks and the data analysis is complete, you can design the tables and establish relationships among them. The form and report prototype process can then begin. Rather than the developer going off for weeks or months before having further interaction with the user, the developer needs only a few days, using the Access wizards to quickly develop form and report prototypes. They can then present these to the users, get users' feedback, and continue to refine the application. Application development today is an iterative process.

Before You Begin

✔ **39** About Database Analysis and Design

✔ **40** About Relational Database Design

See Also

→ **45** About the Types of Relationships

→ **46** Establish Relationships

→ **47** Establish Referential Integrity

Testing

As far as testing goes, you just can't do enough. I recommend that if an application is going to be run in Windows 2003 and Windows XP, you test in both of these environments. I also suggest that you test an application extensively on the lowest-common-denominator piece of hardware so that you can ensure that it will work on all the machines in the environment; an application might run great on your machine but show unacceptable performance on a user's slower machine.

It usually helps to test your application both in pieces and as an integrated application. Recruit several people to test your application and make sure they range from the most savvy of users to the least computer-adept person you can find. These different types of users will probably find completely different sets of problems. Most importantly, make sure you're not the only tester of your application because you're the person least likely to find errors in your own programs.

Implementation

After you have tested an application, it is finally ready to go out into the world—at least you hope it is! At this point, you need to distribute the application to a subset of users and make sure they know they're performing the test implementation. You should make them feel honored to participate as the first users of the system but warn them that problems might occur, and it's their responsibility to make you aware of them. If you distribute your application on a wide-scale basis and it doesn't operate exactly as it should, it will be difficult to regain the confidence of your users. That's why it is so important to roll out your application slowly.

Maintenance

Because Access is a rapid application development environment, the maintenance period tends to be much more extended than that for a mainframe or DOS-based application. Users are much more demanding; the more you give them, the more they want. For a consultant, this is great. You just don't want to get into a fixed-bid situation: Because the scope of the application changes, you could very well end up on the losing end of that deal.

There are three categories of maintenance activities: bug fixes, specification changes, and frills. You need to handle bug fixes as quickly as possible. The implications of specification changes need to be clearly explained to the user, including the time and cost involved in making the requested changes. As far as frills go, you should try to involve the users as much as possible in adding frills by teaching them how to enhance forms and reports and by making the application as flexible and user defined as possible. Of course, the final objective of any application is a happy group of productive users.

42 Build a New Table

One of the steps in the data analysis and design phase of application development is to design the table structures needed by the application. Designing tables from scratch offers flexibility and encourages good design principles. It is almost always the best choice when you're creating a custom business solution. Although it requires some knowledge of database and table design, it gives you much more control and precision than designing a table with a wizard or from **Datasheet** view. It allows you to select each field name and field type and to define field properties.

1 Open the Table Design Window

To design a table from scratch, you select **Tables** from the list of objects and double-click the **Create Table in Design View** icon.

2 Type the Field Name

Define each field in the table by typing its name in the **Field Name** column.

Field names can be up to 64 characters long. For practical reasons, you should try to limit them to 10–15 characters, which is enough to describe the field without making the name difficult to type.

Field names can include any combination of letters, numbers, spaces, and other characters, excluding periods, exclamation points, accents, and brackets. I recommend that you stick to letters. Spaces in field names can be inconvenient when you're building queries, modules, and other database objects. You shouldn't be concerned that users will see the field names without the spaces.

Before You Begin

✔ **32** Use a Database Template to Create a Database

✔ **33** Create a New Empty Database

✔ **34** Create a Table Using the Table Wizard

See Also

→ **43** About Selecting the Appropriate Field Type for Your Data

→ **44** Set a Primary Key

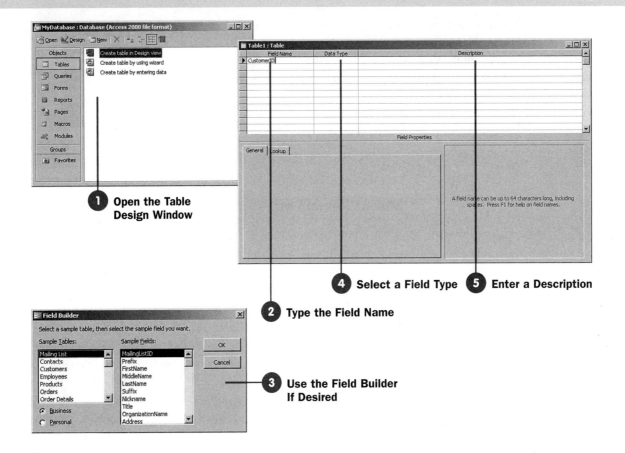

① Open the Table
Design Window

④ Select a Field Type ⑤ Enter a Description

② Type the Field Name

③ Use the Field Builder
If Desired

A field name can't begin with leading spaces. As mentioned previously, field names shouldn't contain any spaces, so the rule to not begin a field name with spaces shouldn't be a problem. Field names also cannot include ASCII control characters (ASCII values 0–31).

You should try not to duplicate property names, keywords, function names, or the names of other Access objects when naming fields (for example, naming a field **Date**). Although the code might work in some circumstances, you might get unpredictable results in others.

3 Use the Field Builder If Desired

If you prefer, you can click the **Build** button on the toolbar (the button with the ellipsis [...]) to open the **Field Builder** dialog box. The **Field Builder** lets you select from predefined fields that have predefined properties. Of course, you can modify the properties at any time.

4 Select a Field Type

Tab to the **Data Type** column. Select the default field type, which is Text, or use the drop-down combo box to select another field type. You can find details on which field type is appropriate for data in **43** **About Selecting the Appropriate Field Type for Your Data**. Note that if you use the **Field Builder**, it sets a data type value for you that you can modify.

NOTE

If you use the **Field Builder**, it sets a data type value for you that you can modify.

5 Enter a Description

Tab to the **Description** column and enter a description for the data. What you type in this column appears on the status bar when the user is entering data into the field. This column is also great for documenting what data is actually stored in the field.

6 Continue Entering Fields

Continue entering fields. If you need to insert a field between two existing fields, click the **Insert Rows** button on the toolbar. Access inserts the new field above the field you were on. To delete a field, select it and click the **Delete Rows** button.

7 Click Save When Done

To save your work, click the **Save** tool on the toolbar. The **Save As** dialog box appears. Enter a table name and click **OK**. Another dialog box appears, recommending that you establish a primary key. Every table should have a primary key. Primary keys are discussed in the "Set a Primary Key" Task later in this chapter.

TIP

Access supplies default names for the tables that you create (for example, Table1, Table2). I suggest that you supply more descriptive names. I generally follow the industrywide naming convention of prefixing all my table names with tbl.

43 **About Selecting the Appropriate Field Type for Your Data**

Before You Begin

✔ **34** Create a Table Using the Table Wizard

✔ **42** Build a New Table

See Also

→ **44** Set a Primary Key

→ **46** Establish Relationships

⚑ NOTE

If it is unimportant that leading zeros be stored in a field and you simply need them to appear on forms and reports, you can accomplish this by using the **Format** property of the field.

Another step in the data analysis and design phase is to select the data type for each field in each table. The data type you select for each field can greatly affect the performance and functionality of an application. Several factors can influence your choice of data type for each field in a table:

- The type of data that's stored in the field

- Whether the field's contents need to be included in calculations

- Whether you need to sort the data in the field

- The way you want to sort the data in the field

- How important storage space is to you

The type of data you need to store in a field has the biggest influence on which data type you select. For example, if you need to store numbers that begin with leading zeros, you can't select a **Number** field because leading zeros entered into a **Number** field are ignored. This rule affects data such as ZIP codes (some of which begin with leading zeros) and department codes.

If the contents of a field need to be included in calculations, you must select a **Number** or **Currency** data type. You can't perform calculations on the contents of fields defined with the other data types. The only exception to this rule is **Date** data type fields, which you can include in date/time calculations.

You must also consider whether you will sort or index the data in a field. You can't sort the data in **OLE Object** and **Hyperlink** fields, so you shouldn't select these field types if you must sort or index the data in the field. Furthermore, you must think about the way you want to sort the data. For example, in a **Text** field, a set of numbers would be sorted in the order of the numbers' leftmost character, then the second character from the left, and so on (that is, 1, 10, 100, 2, 20, 200), because data in the **Text** field is sorted as characters rather than numbers. On the other hand, in a **Number** or **Currency** field, the numbers would be sorted in ascending value order (that is, 1, 2, 10, 20, 100, 200). You might think you would never want data sorted in a character sequence, but sometimes it makes sense to sort certain information, such as department codes, in this fashion. Access 2003 gives you the ability to sort or group based on a **Memo** field, but it performs the sorting or grouping only based on the first 255 characters. Finally, you should consider how important disk space is to you. Each field type takes up a different amount of storage space on a hard disk, and this could be a factor when you're selecting a data type for a field.

Nine field types are available in Access: **Text**, **Memo**, **Number**, **Date/Time**, **Currency**, **AutoNumber** (known as Counter in Access 2.0), **Yes/No**, **OLE Object**, and **Hyperlink**. The table that follows briefly describes the appropriate uses for each field type and the amount of storage space each type needs.

Appropriate Uses and Storage Space for Access Field Types

Field Type	Appropriate Uses	Storage Space
Text	Data containing text, a combination of text and numbers, or numbers that don't need to be included in calculations. Examples are names, addresses, department codes, and phone numbers.	Based on what's actually stored in the field; ranges from 0 to 255 bytes.
Memo	Long text and numeric strings. Examples are notes and descriptions.	Ranges from 0 to 65,536 bytes.
Number	Data that's included in calculations (excluding money). Examples are ages, codes (such as employee IDs), and payment methods.	1, 2, 4, or 8 bytes, depending on the field size selected (or 16 bytes for replication ID).
Date/Time	Dates and times. Examples are date ordered and birth date.	8 bytes.
Currency	Currency values. Examples are amount due and price.	8 bytes.
AutoNumber	Unique sequential or random numbers. Examples are invoice numbers and project numbers.	4 bytes (16 bytes for replication ID).
Yes/No	Fields that contain one of two values (for example, yes/no, true/false). Sample uses are indicating bills paid and tenure status.	1 bit.

Field Type	Appropriate Uses	Storage Space
OLE Object	Objects such as Word documents or Excel spreadsheets. Examples are employee reviews and budgets.	0 bytes to 1GB, depending on what's stored within the field.
Hyperlink	Text or a combination of text and numbers, stored as text and used as a hyperlink for a Web address (uniform resource locator [URL]) or a universal naming convention (UNC) path. Examples are Web pages and network files.	0 to 2,048 bytes for each of the three parts that compose the address (up to 64,000 characters total).

Although Microsoft loosely considers the **Lookup Wizard** a field type, it is really not its own field type. You use it to create a field that allows the user to select a value from another table or from a list of values via a combo box that the wizard helps define for you. The **Lookup Wizard** requires the same storage size as the primary key for the lookup field.

The most difficult part of selecting a field type is knowing which type is best in each situation. The following detailed descriptions of each field type and when you should use them should help you with this process.

Text Fields: The Most Common Field Type

Most fields are **Text** fields. Many developers don't realize that it's best to use **Text** fields for any numbers that are not used in calculations. Examples of such numbers are phone numbers, part numbers, and ZIP codes. Although the default size for a **Text** field is 50 characters, you can store up to 255 characters in a **Text** field. Because Access allocates disk space dynamically, a large field size doesn't use hard disk space, but you can improve performance if you allocate the smallest field size possible. You can control the maximum number of characters allowed in a **Text** field by using the **FieldSize** property.

Memo Fields: For Long Notes and Comments

A **Memo** field can store up to 65,536 characters of text, meaning that it can hold up to 16 pages of text for each record. **Memo** fields are excellent for any type of notes you want to store with table data. Remember that in Access 2003 you can sort by a **Memo** field.

Number Fields: For When You Need to Calculate

You use **Number** fields to store data that you must include in calculations. If currency amounts are included in calculations or if calculations require the highest degree of accuracy, you should use a **Currency** field rather than a **Number** field.

The **Number** field is actually several types of fields in one because Access 2003 offers seven sizes of numeric fields. **Byte** can store integers from 0 to 255, **Integer** can hold whole numbers from −32,768 to 32,767, and **Long Integer** can hold whole numbers ranging from less than negative two billion to just over two billion. Although all three of these sizes offer excellent performance, each type requires an increasingly large amount of storage space. Two of the other numeric field sizes, **Single** and **Double**, offer floating decimal points and, therefore, much slower performance than **Integer** and **Long Integer**. **Single** can hold fractional numbers to 7 significant digits; **Double** extends the precision to 14 significant digits. **Decimal**, a numeric data type, allows storage of very large numbers and provides decimal precision up to 28 digits! The final size, **Replication ID**, supplies a unique identifier required by the data synchronization process.

Date/Time Fields: For Tracking When Things Happened

You use the **Date/Time** field type to store valid dates and times. **Date/Time** fields allow you to perform date calculations and make sure dates and times are always sorted properly. Access actually stores the date or time internally as an 8-byte floating-point number. Access represents time as a fraction of a day.

Currency Fields: For Storing Money

The **Currency** field is a number field that is used when currency values are being stored in a table. A **Currency** field prevents the computer from rounding off data during calculations. It holds 15 digits of whole dollars, plus accuracy to one one-hundredth of a cent. Although very accurate, this type of field is quite slow to process.

AutoNumber Fields: For Unique Record Identifiers

The **AutoNumber** field in Access 2003 is equivalent to the **Counter** field in Access 2.0. Access automatically generates **AutoNumber** field values when the user adds a record. In Access 2.0, counter values have to be

NOTES

Any date and time settings you establish in the **Windows Control Panel** are reflected in your data. For example, if you modify **Short Date Style** in **Regional Settings** within the **Control Panel**, your forms, reports, and datasheets will immediately reflect those changes.

Any changes to the currency format made in the **Windows Control Panel** are reflected in your data. Of course, Access doesn't automatically perform any actual conversion of currency amounts. As with dates, if you modify the currency symbol in **Regional Settings** within the **Control Panel**, your forms, reports, and datasheets will immediately reflect those changes.

sequential. The **AutoNumber** field type in Access 2003 can be either sequential or random. The random assignment is useful when several users are adding records offline because it's unlikely that Access will assign the same random value to two records. A special type of **AutoNumber** field is a **Replication ID**. This randomly produced, unique number helps with the replication process by generating unique identifiers used to synchronize database replicas.

You should note a few important points about sequential **AutoNumber** fields. If a user deletes a record from a table, its unique number is lost forever. Likewise, if a user is adding a record but cancels the action, the unique counter value for that record is lost forever. If this behavior is unacceptable, you can generate your own counter values.

Yes/No Fields: For When One of Two Answers Is Correct

You should use **Yes/No** fields to store a logical **true** or **false**. What Access actually stores in the field is –1 for yes, 0 for no, or Null for no specific choice. The display format for the field determines what the user actually sees (normally Yes/No, True/False, On/Off, or a fourth option—Null— if you set the **TripleState** property of the associated control on a form to **True**). **Yes/No** fields work efficiently for any data that can have only a true or false value. Not only do they limit the user to valid choices, but they also take up only 1 bit of storage space.

OLE Object Fields: For Storing Just About Anything

OLE Object fields are designed to hold data from any OLE server application that is registered in Windows, including spreadsheets, word processing documents, sound, and video. There are many business uses for **OLE Object** fields, such as storing resumes, employee reviews, budgets, or videos. However, in many cases, it is more efficient to use a **Hyperlink** field to store a link to the document rather than store the document itself in an **OLE Object** field.

Hyperlink Fields: For Linking to the Internet

Hyperlink fields are used to store uniform resource locator addresses, which are links to Web pages on the Internet, on an intranet, or UNC paths, which are links to a file location path. The **Hyperlink** field type is broken into three parts:

- What the user sees

- The URL or UNC

- A subaddress, such as a range name or bookmark

After the user places an entry in a **Hyperlink** field, the entry serves as a direct link to the file or page it refers to.

44 Set a Primary Key

Another step in the data analysis and design phase of the application development process is to assign a primary key to each table in the database. A primary key is a field or a combination of fields in a table that uniquely identifies each row in the table (for example, **CustomerID**). The most important index in a table is called the primary key index. It ensures uniqueness of the fields that make up the index and also gives the table a default order. You must set a primary key for the fields on the one side of a one-to-many relationship.

❶ Select the Field(s) Included in the Primary Key

Click and drag to select the fields that you wish to include in the primary key index.

❷ Click the Primary Key Button

Click the **Primary Key** toolbar button to set the primary key.

❸ Click the Indexes Tool

Click the **Indexes** tool to open the **Indexes** window.

❹ Review the Primary Key Index Information

Notice that the index name of the field designated as the primary key of the table is called **PrimaryKey**. Note that the **Primary** and **Unique** properties for this index are both set to Yes (true).

Before You Begin

✔ **42** Build a New Table

✔ **43** About Selecting the Appropriate Field Type for Your Data

See Also

➜ **46** Establish Relationships

➜ **47** Establish Referential Integrity

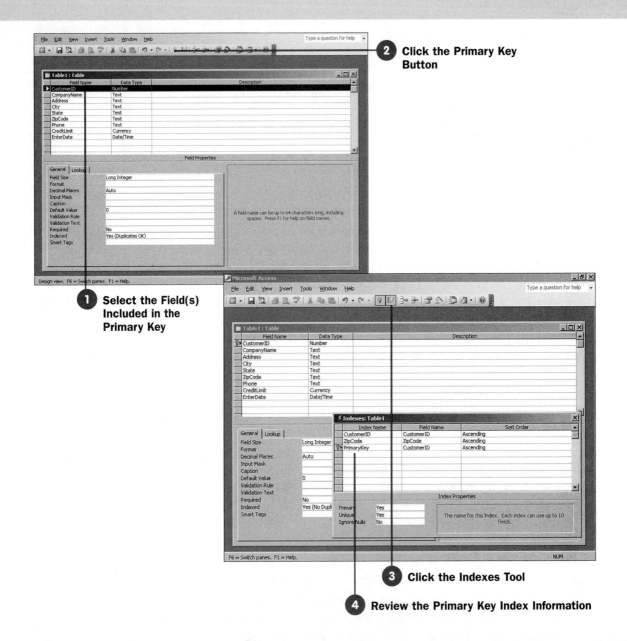

2 Click the Primary Key Button

1 Select the Field(s) Included in the Primary Key

3 Click the Indexes Tool

4 Review the Primary Key Index Information

8

Create Your Own Relationships

IN THIS CHAPTER:

KEY TERMS

Relationship—Exists between two tables when one or more key fields from one table are matched to one or more key fields in another table.

Data normalization—The process of eliminating duplicate information from a system by splitting information into several tables, each containing a unique value (that is, a primary key).

Referential integrity—A series of rules that the database engine applies to ensure that it properly maintains relationships between tables.

A *relationship* exists between two tables when one or more key fields from one table are matched to one or more key fields in another table. The fields in both tables usually have the same name, data type, and size. Relationships are a necessary by-product of the data normalization process. *Data normalization*, introduced in Chapter 7, "Design and Create Your Own Tables," is the process of eliminating duplicate information from a system by splitting information into several tables, each containing a unique value (that is, a primary key). Although data normalization brings many benefits, it means you need to relate an application's tables to each other so that users can view the data in the system as a single entity. After you define relationships between tables, you can build queries, forms, reports, and data access pages that combine information from multiple tables. In this way, you can reap all the benefits of data normalization while ensuring that a system provides users with all the information they need.

Referential integrity is another very important topic covered in this chapter. Referential integrity consists of a series of rules that the database engine applies to ensure that it properly maintains relationships between tables.

45 About the Types of Relationships

Before You Begin

✔ **39** About Database Analysis and Design

✔ **40** About Relational Database Design

✔ **42** Build a New Table

See Also

→ **46** Establish Relationships

→ **47** Establish Referential Integrity

Three types of relationships can exist between tables in a database: one-to-many, one-to-one, and many-to-many. Setting up the proper type of relationship between two tables in a database is imperative. The right type of relationship between two tables ensures

- Data integrity

- Optimal performance

- Ease of use in designing system objects

The reasons behind these benefits are covered throughout this chapter. Before you can understand the benefits of relationships, though, you must understand the types of relationships available.

One-to-Many Relationships

A *one-to-many relationship* is by far the most common type of relationship. In a one-to-many relationship, a record in one table can have many related records in another table. A common example is a relationship set up between a Customers table and an Orders table. For each customer in the Customers table, you want to have more than one order in the Orders table. On the other hand, each order in the Orders table can belong to only one customer. The Customers table is on the "one" side of the relationship, and the Orders table is on the "many" side. In order for you to implement this relationship, the field joining the two tables on the "one" side of the relationship must be unique.

In the Customers and Orders tables example, the CustomerID field that joins the two tables must be unique within the Customers table. If more than one customer in the Customers table has the same customer ID, it is not clear which customer belongs to an order in the Orders table. For this reason, the field that joins the two tables on the "one" side of the one-to-many relationship must be a primary key or have a unique index. In almost all cases, the field relating the two tables is the primary key of the table on the "one" side of the relationship. The field relating the two tables on the "many" side of the relationship is the foreign key.

> **KEY TERM**
>
> *One-to-many relationship—* A record in one table can have many related records in another table.

One-to-One Relationships

In a *one-to-one relationship*, each record in the table on the "one" side of the relationship can have only one matching record in the table on the other side of the relationship. This relationship is not common and is used only in special circumstances. Usually, if you have set up a one-to-one relationship, you should have combined the fields from both tables into one table. The following are the most common reasons to create a one-to-one relationship:

- The number of fields required for a table exceeds the number of fields allowed in an Access table.

- Certain fields that are included in a table need to be much more secure than other fields in the same table.

- Several fields in a table are required for only a subset of records in the table.

> **KEY TERM**
>
> *One-to-one relationship—* Each record in the table on the "one" side of the relationship can have only one matching record in the table on the other side of the relationship.

The maximum number of fields allowed in an Access table is 255. There are very few reasons a table should ever have more than 255 fields. In fact, before you even get close to 255 fields, you should take a close look at the design of the system. On the rare occasion when having more than 255 fields is appropriate, you can simulate a single table by moving some of the fields to a second table and creating a one-to-one relationship between the two tables. For example, I once developed an application that monitored various blood gases every 15 minutes. The users needed to track more than 255 factors relating to blood gases. We made a decision to place the additional data in a second table and relate the tables with a one-to-one relationship.

The second reason to separate data that logically would belong in the same table into two tables involves security. An example is a table that contains employee information. Certain information, such as employee name, address, city, state, ZIP code, home phone, and office extension, might need to be accessed by many users of the system. Other fields, including the hire date, salary, birth date, and salary level, might be highly confidential. Field-level security is not available in Access. You can simulate field-level security by using a special attribute of queries called Run with Owner's Permissions. The alternative to this method is to place the fields that all users can access in one table and the highly confidential fields in another. You give only a special Admin user (that is, a user with special security privileges—not one actually named Admin) access to the table that contains the confidential fields.

The last situation in which you would want to define one-to-one relationships is when you will use certain fields in a table for only a relatively small subset of records. An example is an Employees table and a Vesting table. Certain fields are required only for employees who are vested. If only a small percentage of a company's employees are vested, it is not efficient, in terms of performance or disk space, to place all the fields containing information about vesting in the Employees table. This is especially true if the vesting information requires a large number of fields. By breaking the information into two tables and creating a one-to-one relationship between the tables, you can reduce disk-space requirements and improve performance. This improvement is particularly pronounced if the Employees table is large.

Many-to-Many Relationships

In a *many-to-many relationship*, records in two tables have matching records. You cannot directly define a many-to-many relationship in Access; you must develop this type of relationship by adding a table called a junction table. You relate the junction table to each of the two tables in one-to-many relationships. For example, with an Orders table and a Products table, each order will probably contain multiple products, and each product is likely to be found on many different orders. The solution is to create a third table, called OrderDetails. You relate the OrderDetails table to the Orders table in a one-to-many relationship based on the OrderID field. You relate it to the Products table in a one-to-many relationship based on the ProductID field.

KEY TERM

Many-to-many relationship—Records in two tables have matching records.

46 Establish Relationships

You use the Relationships window to establish relationships between Access tables. The Relationships window enables you to view, add, modify, and remove relationships between tables. By looking at the Relationships window, you can see the types of relationships for each table. All the one-to-many and one-to-one relationships defined in a database are represented with join lines. If you enforce referential integrity between the tables involved in a one-to-many relationship, the join line between the tables appears with the number 1 on the "one" side of the relationship and with a link symbol on the "many" side of the relationship. A one-to-one relationship appears with a 1 on each end of the join line.

Before You Begin

✔ **39** About Database Analysis and Design

✔ **40** About Relational Database Design

✔ **42** Build a New Table

See Also

→ **47** Establish Referential Integrity

1 Open the Relationships Window

To open the **Relationships** window, click **Relationships** on the toolbar with the **Database** window active, or choose **Tools, Relationships**. If you have not established any relationships, you will need to use the **Show Table** dialog box to add tables to the **Relationships** window.

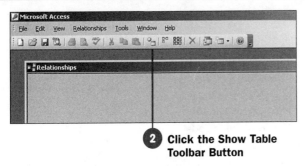

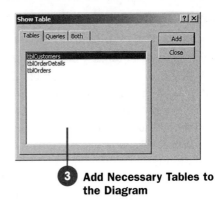

2 Click the Show Table
Toolbar Button

3 Add Necessary Tables to
the Diagram

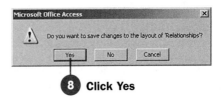

5 Modify Referential Integrity
Settings

8 Click Yes

7 Close the
Relationships
Window

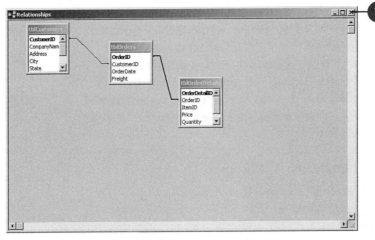

2 Click the Show Table Toolbar Button

If this is the first time that you've opened the **Relationships** window of a particular database, the **Relationships** window appears

empty. If the **Relationships** window is empty, or the tables you want to include in the relationship do not appear, click the **Show Table** button on the toolbar or choose **Relationships, Show Table**.

③ Add Necessary Tables to the Diagram

To add the desired tables to the **Relationships** window, select a table and then click **Add**. Repeat this process for each table you want to add. To select multiple tables at once, press **Shift** while clicking to select contiguous tables or press **Ctrl** while clicking to select noncontiguous tables; then click **Add**. Click **Close** when you are finished.

When you're adding tables to the **Relationships** window by using the **Show Tables** dialog box, it is easy to accidentally add a table to the window many times. This is because the tables you are adding can hide behind the **Show Tables** dialog box, or they can appear below the portion of the **Relationships** window that you are viewing. If this occurs, you see multiple occurrences of the same table when you close the **Show Tables** dialog box. Access gives each occurrence of the table a different alias, and you must remove the extra occurrences.

In addition to adding tables to the **Relationships** window, you also can add queries to the **Relationships** window by using the **Show Tables** dialog box. Although this method is rarely used, it might be useful if you regularly include the same queries within other queries and want to permanently establish relationships between them.

④ Click and Drag a Field from One Table to the Other

Click and drag the field from one table to the matching field in the other table. The **Edit Relationships** dialog box appears.

⑤ Modify Referential Integrity Settings

Determine whether you want to establish referential integrity and whether you want to cascade update related fields or cascade delete related records by enabling the appropriate check boxes. These topics are covered later in this chapter, in **47** **Establish Referential Integrity**.

6 Click Create New

Click **Create New** to close the **Edit Relationships** dialog and establish the relationship.

7 Close the Relationships Window

Close the **Relationships** window. If you have made changes to the layout of the **Relationships** window, Access prompts you to save.

It is important to understand the correlation between the **Relationships** window and the actual relationships established within a database. The **Relationships** window lets you view and modify the existing relationships. When you establish relationships, Access creates the relationship the moment you click **Create**. You can delete the tables from the **Relationships** window (by selecting them and pressing **Delete**), but the relationships still exist. The **Relationships** window provides a visual blueprint of the relationships that are established. If you modify the layout of the window by moving around tables, adding tables to the window, or removing tables from the window, Access prompts you to save the layout after you close the **Relationships** window. Access is not asking whether you want to save the relationships you have established; it is simply asking whether you want to save the visual layout of the window.

8 Click Yes

Access immediately saves changes to relationships when you close the **Edit Relationships** dialog. When you close the **Relationships** window, you are only saving layout changes. Click **Yes** to save any *layout* changes that you made.

NOTE

If you remove tables from the **Relationships** window (remember that this does not delete the relationships) and you want to once again show all relationships that exist in the database, you can click **Show All Relationships** on the toolbar or choose **Relationships**, **Show All**. All existing relationships are then shown.

TIPS

To modify an existing relationship, double-click the line joining the two tables whose relationship you want to modify. Make the required changes, and click **OK**.

To delete a relationship, click the join line and press **Delete**.

47 Establish Referential Integrity

Referential integrity consists of a series of rules that the Jet Engine applies to ensure that Jet properly maintains the relationships between tables. At the most basic level, referential integrity rules prevent the creation of orphan records in the table on the "many" side of the one-to-many relationship. After you establish a relationship between a Customers table and an Orders table, for example, all orders in the Orders table must be related to a particular customer in the Customers table. Before you can establish referential integrity between two tables, the following conditions must be met:

Before You Begin

✔ **39** About Database Analysis and Design

✔ **40** About Relational Database Design

✔ **42** Build a New Table

✔ **46** Establish Relationships

See Also

→ **70** About Working with Field Properties

→ **71** Look Up Values in a Table or Query

- The matching field on the "one" side of the relationship must be a primary key field or must have a unique index.

- The matching fields must have the same data types. (For linking purposes, AutoNumber fields match Long Integer fields.) With the exception of Text fields, the matching fields also must have the same size. Number fields on both sides of the relationship must have the same size (for example, Long Integer).

- Both tables must be part of the same Access database.

- Both tables must be stored in the proprietary Access file (.MDB) format. (They cannot be external tables from other sources.)

- The database that contains the two tables must be open.

- Existing data within the two tables cannot violate any referential integrity rules. All orders in the Orders table must relate to existing customers in the Customers table, for example.

When the **Cascade Update Related Fields** option is selected, the user can change the primary key value of the record on the "one" side of the relationship. When the user attempts to modify the field joining the two tables on the "one" side of the relationship, the Jet Engine cascades the change down to the foreign key field on the "many" side of the relationship. This is useful if the primary key field is modifiable. For example, a purchase number on a purchase order master record might be updateable. If the user modifies the purchase order number of the parent record, you would want to cascade the change to the associated detail records in the purchase order detail table.

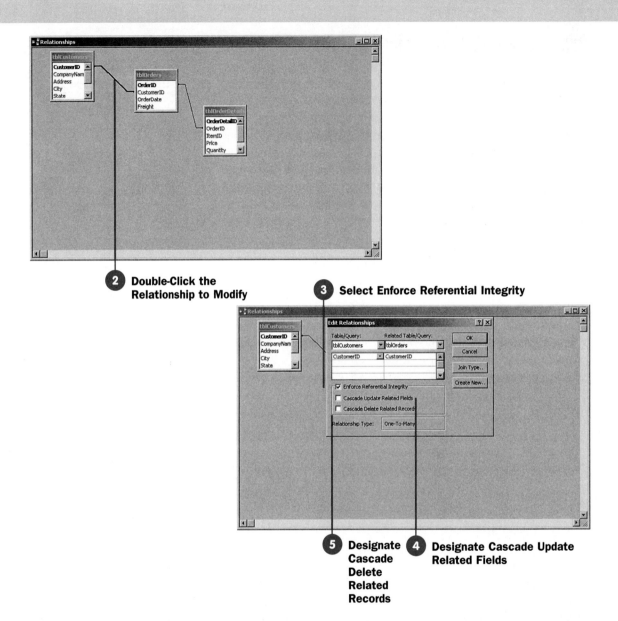

2 Double-Click the Relationship to Modify

3 Select Enforce Referential Integrity

5 Designate Cascade Delete Related Records

4 Designate Cascade Update Related Fields

When the **Cascade Delete Related Records** option is selected, the user can delete a record on the "one" side of a one-to-many relationship, even if related records exist in the table on the "many" side of the relationship. A user can delete a customer even if the customer has existing orders, for example. The Jet Engine maintains referential integrity between the tables because it automatically deletes all related records in the child table.

The **Cascade Delete Related Records** option is not always appropriate. It is an excellent feature, but you should use it prudently. Although it is usually appropriate to cascade delete from an Orders table to an Order Details table, for example, it generally is not appropriate to cascade delete from a Customers table to an Orders table. This is because you generally do not want to delete all your order history from the Orders table if for some reason you want to delete a customer. Deleting the order history causes important information, such as the profit and loss history, to change. It is therefore appropriate to prohibit this type of deletion and handle the customer in some other way, such as marking him or her as inactive or archiving his or her data. On the other hand, if you delete an order because the customer cancelled it, you probably want to remove the corresponding order detail information as well. In this case, the **Cascade Delete Related Records** option is appropriate. You need to make the most prudent decision in each situation, based on business needs. You need to carefully consider the implications of each option before you make a decision.

After you establish referential integrity between two tables, the Jet Engine applies the following rules:

- You cannot enter a value that does not exist in the primary key of the primary table into the foreign key of the related table. For example, you cannot enter a value that does not exist in the CustomerID field of the Customers table into the CustomerID field of the Orders table.

- You cannot delete a record from the primary table if corresponding records exist in the related table. For example, you cannot delete a customer from the Customers table if related records (for example, records with the same value in the CustomerID field) exist in the Orders table.

- You cannot change the value of a primary key on the "one" side of a relationship if corresponding records exist in the related table. For example, you cannot change the value in the CustomerID field of the Customers table if corresponding orders exist in the Orders table.

NOTE

Although Text fields involved in a relationship do not have to be the same size, it is prudent to make them the same size. Otherwise, you degrade performance as well as risk the chance of unpredictable results when you create queries based on the two tables.

If you attempt to violate any of these three rules and you have enforced referential integrity between the tables, Access displays an appropriate error message. The Jet Engine's default behavior is to prohibit the deletion of parent records that have associated child records and to prohibit the change of a parent record's primary key value when that parent has associated child records. You can override these restrictions by using the **Cascade Update Related Fields** and **Cascade Delete Related Records** check boxes that are available in the **Relationships** dialog box when you establish or modify a relationship.

As you can see, establishing a relationship is quite easy. Establishing the right kind of relationship is a little more difficult. When you attempt to establish a relationship between two tables, Access makes some decisions based on a few predefined factors:

- Access establishes a one-to-many relationship if one of the related fields is a primary key or has a unique index.

- Access establishes a one-to-one relationship if both of the related fields are primary keys or have unique indexes.

- Access creates an indeterminate relationship if neither of the related fields is a primary key and neither has a unique index. You cannot establish referential integrity in this case.

1 Open the Relationships Window

Click **Relationships** on the toolbar with the **Database** window active. This will open the **Relationships** window.

2 Double-click the Relationship to Modify

Double-click the line joining the two tables whose relationship you wish to modify.

3 Select Enforce Referential Integrity

Click the **Enforce Referential Integrity** check box to establish referential integrity between the two tables.

4 Designate Cascade Update Related Fields

If desired, click to select the **Cascade Update Related Fields** option. The **Cascade Update Related Fields** option is available only if you have established referential integrity between tables.

5 **Designate Cascade Delete Related Records**

If desired, click to select the **Cascade Delete Related Records** option. The **Cascade Delete Related Records** option is available only if you have established referential integrity between tables.

If you attempt to delete a record from the table on the "one" side of a one-to-many relationship and no related records exist in the table on the "many" side of the relationship, you get the usual warning message. On the other hand, if you attempt to delete a record from the table on the "one" side of a one-to-many relationship and related records exist in the child table, Access warns you that you are about to delete the record from the parent table as well as any related records in the child table.

 NOTE

There is no need to select the **Cascade Update Related Fields** option when the related field on the "one" side of the relationship is an **AutoNumber** field. You can never modify an **AutoNumber** field. The **Cascade Update Related Fields** option has no effect on **AutoNumber** fields.

9

Create Your Own Queries

IN THIS CHAPTER:

Although tables act as the ultimate foundation for any application you build, queries are very important as well. Most of the forms and reports that act as the user interface for an application are based on queries. Having an understanding of queries—what they are and when and how to use them—is imperative for your success as an Access application developer or end user. The time and effort that you take to learn how to effectively build queries will pay for itself many times over.

48 Create Queries

Before You Begin

✔ **10** Open a Query in Design View

✔ **11** Add Fields to a Query

✔ **13** Refine a Query with Criteria

See Also

→ **49** Order a Query Result

→ **50** About Refining a Query with Advanced Criteria

→ **52** About Building Queries Based on Multiple Tables

Creating a basic query is easy because Microsoft has provided a user-friendly, drag-and-drop interface.

1 Build a New Query

There are two ways to start a new query in Access 2003. The first way is to select the **Queries** icon from the Objects list in the Database window; then double-click the **Create query in Design view** icon or the **Create query by using wizard** icon.

The second method is to select the **Queries** icon from the **Objects** list in the **Database** window and then click the **New** command button on the **Database** window toolbar. The **New Query** dialog box appears. Select whether to build the query from scratch or to use one of the wizards to help you. The Simple Query Wizard walks you through the steps of creating a basic query. The other wizards help you create three specific types of queries: Crosstab, Find Duplicates, and Find Unmatched queries. You can learn about these types of queries in an advanced text such as *Alison Balter's Mastering Microsoft Office Access 2003*, published by Sams.

2 Add Tables to the Query

If you choose to use **Design** view rather than one of the wizards, the **Show Table** dialog box appears. In this dialog box, select the tables or queries that supply data to a query. Access doesn't care whether you select tables or queries as the foundation for queries.

1 **Build a New Query**

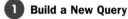
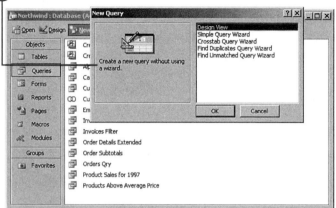
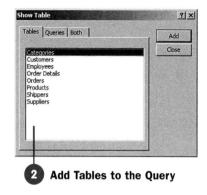

2 **Add Tables to the Query**

3 **Add Fields to the Query**

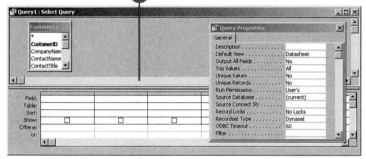

4 **Remove Fields from the Query**

7 **Save and Name the Query**

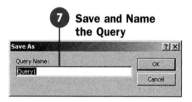

Select a table or query by double-clicking the name of the table or query you want to add or by right-clicking the table and then selecting **Add** from the context menu. Select multiple tables or queries by holding down the **Shift** key while you select a contiguous range of tables or the **Ctrl** key while you select noncontiguous tables. After selecting the tables or queries you want, click **Add** and then click **Close**. This brings you to the **Query Design** window.

An alternate way to add a table is to first select **Tables** from the **Objects** list in the **Database** window and then select the table on which you want to base the query. With the table selected, select **New Query** from the **New Object** drop-down list box on the toolbar or choose **Insert|Query**. The **New Query** dialog box appears. This is an efficient method of starting a new query based on only one table because the **Show Table** dialog box never appears.

3 Add Fields to the Query

The query window is divided into two sections: The top half of the window shows the tables or queries that underlie the query you're designing, and the bottom half shows any fields that you will include in the query output. Add a field to the query design grid on the bottom half of the query window in one of the following ways:

- Double-click the name of the field you want to add.

- Click and drag a single field from the table in the top half of the query window to the query design grid below.

- Select multiple fields at the same time by using the **Shift** key (for a contiguous range of fields) or the **Ctrl** key (for a noncontiguous range). Double-click the title bar of the field list to select all fields and then click and drag any one of the selected fields to the query design grid.

- Double-click the **asterisk** in the field list to include all fields within the table in the query result.

4 Remove Fields from the Query

Find the field you want to remove, and click the **column selector** (that is, the small horizontal gray button) immediately above the name of the field. The entire column of the query design grid

TIP

Although double-clicking the asterisk in the field list to add a field to the query design grid is handy in that changes to the table structure affect the query's output, this "trick" is dangerous. It includes all table fields in the query result, whether you need them or not. This can cause major performance problems in a LAN, WAN, or client/server application.

should become black. Press the **Delete** key or select **Delete** from the **Edit** menu. Access removes the field from the query.

5 Add Additional Fields to the Query

To insert a new field after the existing fields, it's easiest to **double-click** the name of the field you want to add. To insert the new field between two existing fields, it's best to **click and drag** the field you want to add and drop it onto the field you want to appear to the right of the inserted field.

6 Move a Field to a Different Location on the Query Grid

To move a single column, select a column while in the query's **Design** view by clicking its **column selector**. Then click the selected column a second time, and drag it to a new location on the query design grid. To move more than one column at a time, drag across the column selectors of the columns you want to move. Click any of the selected columns a second time, and then drag them to a new location on the query design grid.

Moving a column in **Datasheet** view doesn't modify the query's underlying design because subsequent reordering in **Design** view isn't reflected in **Datasheet** view. In other words, **Design** view and **Datasheet** view are no longer synchronized, and you must reorder both manually. This actually serves as an advantage in most cases. As you will learn in **52** **About Building Queries Based on Multiple Tables**, if you want to sort by the **StateProvince** field and then by the **CompanyName** field, the **StateProvince** field must appear to the left of the **CompanyName** field in the design of the query. If you want the **CompanyName** field to appear to the left of the **StateProvince** field in the query's result, you must make that change in **Datasheet** view. The fact that Access maintains the order of the columns separately in both views allows you to easily accomplish both objectives.

7 Save and Name the Query

Click the **Save** button on the toolbar. If the query is a new one, Access prompts you to name the query.

 **NOTES**

You might want to permanently alter a field's position in the query output as a convenience to users or to use the query as a foundation for forms and reports. The fields' order in the query becomes the default order on forms and reports you build using the wizards. You can save yourself a lot of time by ordering the field in queries effectively.

Access supplies default names for the queries that you create (for example, Query1, Query2). I suggest that you supply a more descriptive name. A query name should begin with *qry* so that you can easily recognize and identify it as a query.

It's important to understand that when you save a query, you're saving only the query's definition, not the actual query result.

Access 2003 provides shortcut keys that allow you to easily toggle between the various query views: **Ctrl+>**, **Ctrl+period**, **Ctrl+<**, and **Ctrl+comma**. **Ctrl+>** and **Ctrl+period** take you to the next view; **Ctrl+<** and **Ctrl+comma** take you to the previous view.

8 **Run the Query**

The easiest way to run a query is to click the **Run** button on the toolbar. (It looks like an exclamation point.)

You can click the **Query View** button to run a query, but this method works only for Select queries, not for Action queries. The **Query View** button has a special meaning for Action queries. Clicking **Run** is preferable because when you do that, you don't have to worry about what type of query you're running.

After running the query, you should see what looks like a datasheet that contains only the fields you selected. To return to the query's design, click the **Query View** button.

49 Order a Query Result

Before You Begin

✔ **10** Open a Query in Design View

✔ **11** Add Fields to a Query

✔ **13** Refine a Query with Criteria

See Also

→ **50** About Refining a Query with Advanced Criteria

→ **52** About Building Queries Based on Multiple Tables

When you run a new query, the query output appears in no particular order. Generally, however, you want to order query output. This is so the records appear in an order that is meaningful to you. For example, you may want to view the records in order by the CompanyName field. You can do this by using the Sort row of the query design grid.

1 **Click the Sort Cell**

In **Design** view, click within the query design grid in the **Sort** cell of the column you want to sort.

2 **Select Ascending or Descending from the Drop-down**

Use the drop-down combo box to select an ascending or descending sort. **Ascending** or **Descending** appears in the sort cell for the field, as appropriate.

1 **Click the Sort Cell**

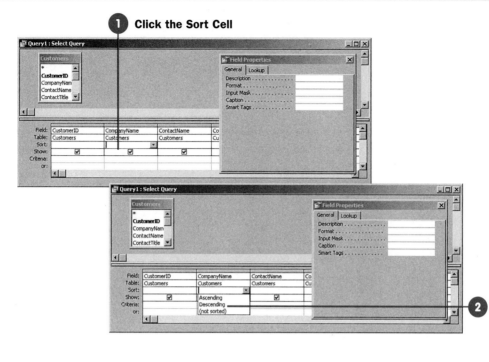

2 **Select Ascending or Descending from the Drop-down**

3 **Repeat Steps 1 and 2 as Necessary**

Repeat steps 1 and 2 to sort by additional columns. The columns you want to sort must be placed in order, from left to right, on the query design grid, with the column you want to act as the primary sort on the far left and the secondary, tertiary, and any additional sorts following to the right. If you want the columns to appear in a different order in the query output, move them manually in **Datasheet** view after you run the query.

50 About Refining a Query with Advanced Criteria

Before You Begin

✔ **10** Open a Query in Design View

✔ **11** Add Fields to a Query

✔ **13** Refine a Query with Criteria

See Also

→ **51** Update Query Results

→ **52** About Building Queries Based on Multiple Tables

So far in this chapter, you have learned how to select the fields you want and how to indicate the sort order for query output. One of the important features of queries is the ability to limit output by using selection criteria. Access allows you to combine criteria by using several operators to limit the criteria for multiple fields. The following table covers the operators and their meanings.

Access Operators

Operator	Meaning	Example	Result of Example
=	Equal to	="Sales"	Finds only records with "Sales" as the field value.
<	Less than	<100	Finds all records with values less than 100 in that field.
<=	Less than or equal to	<=100	Finds all records with values less than or equal to 100 in that field.
>	Greater than	>100	Finds all records with values greater than 100 in that field.
>=	Greater than or equal to	>=100	Finds all records with values greater than or equal to 100 in that field.
<>	Not equal to	<>"Sales"	Finds all records with values other than Sales in the field.

Operator	Meaning	Example	Result of Example
And	Both conditions must be true	Created by adding criteria on the same line of the query design grid to more than one field	Finds all records where the conditions in both fields are true.
Or	Either condition can be true	"CA" or "NY" or "UT"	Finds all records with the value "CA", "NY", or "UT" in the field.
Like	Compares a string expression to a pattern	Like "Sales*"	Finds all records with the value "Sales" at the beginning of the field (the asterisk is a wildcard character).
Between	Finds a range of values	Between 5 and 10	Finds all records with the values 5–10 (inclusive) in the field.
In	Same as Or	In("CA", "NY","UT")	Finds all records with the value "CA", "NY", or "UT" in the field.
Not	Same as <>	Not "Sales"	Finds all records with values other than Sales in the field.
Is Null	Finds nulls	Is Null	Finds all records where no data has been entered in the field.
Is Not	Finds all records that are not null	Is Not Null	Finds all records where data has been Null entered into the field.

Criteria entered for two fields on a single line of the query design grid are considered an **And** condition, which means that both conditions need to be true for the record to appear in the query output. Entries made on separate lines of the query design grid are considered an **Or** condition, which means that either condition can be true for Access to include the record in the query output.

Take a look at the example in the following figure; this query would output all records in the United States. It also outputs all records in which the **ContactTitle** field begins with either **Sales** or **Marketing** and the **Country** equals **Canada**. Finally, it outputs all of the customers in **London** or **Paris**, regardless of their contact title or country. Notice that the word **Sales** and the word **Marketing** are immediately followed by an asterisk. This means that salesmen and marketing managers would be included in the output.

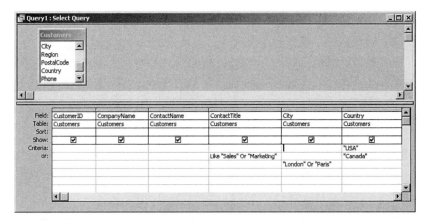

Example based on multiple criteria.

Working with Dates in Criteria

Access gives you significant power for adding date functions and expressions to query criteria. Using these criteria, you can find all records in a certain month, on a specific weekday, or between two dates. The table that follows lists the Date criteria expressions and examples.

Date Criteria Expressions

Expression	Meaning	Example	Result
Date()	Current date	Date()	Records the current date within a field.
Day(Date)	The day of a date	Day([OrderDate])=1	Records the order date on the first day of the month.
Month(Date)	The month of a date	Month([OrderDate])=1	Records the order date in January.
Year(Date)	The year of a date	Year([OrderDate])=1991	Records the order date in 1991.
Weekday(Date)	The weekday of a date	Weekday([OrderDate])=2	Records the order date on a Monday.
Between Date And Date	A range of dates	Between #1/1/95# and #12/31/95#	Finds all records in 1995.
DatePart	A specific part of a date	DatePart(Interval, ("q",[OrderDate])=2 Date)	Finds all records in the second quarter.

The **Weekday (Date, [FirstDayOfWeek])** function works based on your locale and how your system defines the first day of the week. **Weekday()** used without the optional **FirstDayOfWeek** argument defaults to **vbSunday** as the first day. A value of **0** defaults **FirstDayOfWeek** to the system definition. Other values can be set also.

The following figure illustrates the use of a date function. Notice that **DatePart("m",[OrderDate])** is entered as the expression, and the value 7 is entered for the criterion. **Year([OrderDate])]** is entered as another expression, with the number **1996** as the criterion. Therefore, this query outputs all records in which the order date is in July of 1996.

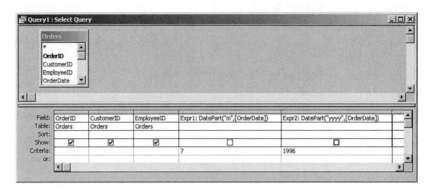

*Query showing the use of the **DatePart** function.*

51 Update Query Results

Before You Begin

✔ **10** Open a Query in Design View

✔ **11** Add Fields to a Query

✔ **13** Refine a Query with Criteria

→ **50** About Refining a Query with Advanced Criteria

See Also

→ **52** About Building Queries Based on Multiple Tables

If you haven't realized it yet, you can usually update the results of a query (sometimes the type of query you create does not allow modifications to the output). This means that if you modify the data in the query output, Access permanently modifies the data in the tables underlying the query. It's essential that you understand how Access updates query results; otherwise, you might mistakenly update table data without realizing you've done so.

❶ Build a New Query

Build a query based on a table of your choice.

❷ Select the Table Underlying the Query

Use the **Show Table** dialog to select the table underlying the query.

❸ Add the Fields

Add fields to the query design.

❹ Run the Query

Run the query.

1 Build a New Query

2 Select the Table Underlying the Query

5 Change Data in the Query

Customer ID	Company Name	Contact Name	Contact Title
ABCDE	The Alphabet Company	John Letter	President
ALFKI	Alfreds Futterkiste	Maria Anderson	Sales Representative
ANATR	Ana Trujillo Emparedados y helados	Ana Trujillo	Owner
ANTON	Antonio Moreno Taquería	Antonio Moreno	Owner
AROUT	Around the Horn	Thomas Hardy	Sales Representative
BERGS	Berglunds snabbköp	Christina Berglund	Order Administrator
BLAUS	Blauer See Delikatessen	Hanna Moos	Sales Representative
BLONP	Blondel père et fils	Frédérique Citeaux	Marketing Manager
BOLID	Bólido Comidas preparadas	Martín Sommer	Owner
BONAP	Bon app'	Laurence Lebihan	Owner
BOTTM	Bottom-Dollar Markets	Elizabeth Lincoln	Accounting Manager
BSBEV	B's Beverages	Victoria Ashworth	Sales Representative
CACTU	Cactus Comidas para llevar	Patricio Simpson	Sales Agent
CENTC	Centro comercial Moctezuma	Francisco Chang	Marketing Manager

Record: 2 of 92

5 Change Data in the Query

Change data in one or more fields in a row of the query output.
Make note of which record you changed.

6 Close the Query

Close the query, saving changes if you desire.

7 Note the Changes in the Base Table

Open the table underlying the query and notice that the changes
you made while viewing the query result are permanent.

CHAPTER 9: Create Your Own Queries

52 About Building Queries Based on Multiple Tables

Before You Begin

✔ **10** Open a Query in Design View

✔ **11** Add Fields to a Query

✔ **13** Refine a Query with Criteria

→ **50** About Refining a Query with Advanced Criteria

See Also

→ **53** Create Calculated Fields

→ **75** Create and Run Parameter Queries

If you have properly normalized your table data, you probably want to bring the data from your tables back together by using queries. Fortunately, you can do this quite easily by using Access queries.

The query in the following figure joins the **Customers**, **Orders**, **Products**, and **Order Details** tables, pulling fields from each. Notice in the figure that I have selected the **CustomerID** and **CompanyName** fields from the **Customers** table, the **OrderID** and **OrderDate** fields from the **Orders** table, the **ProductName** fields from the **Products** table, and the **UnitPrice** and **Quantity** fields from the **Order Details** table.

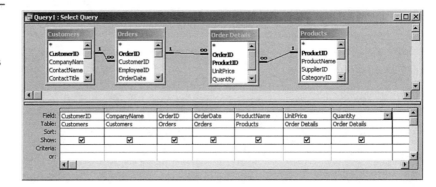

A query joining the Customers, Orders, Products, and Order Details tables.

After you run this query, you should see the results shown in the following figure. Notice that you get a record in the query's result for every record in the **Order Details** table. In other words, there are 2,155 records in the **Order Details** table, and that's how many records appear in the query output. By creating a multitable query, you can look at data from related tables, along with the data from the **Order Details** table.

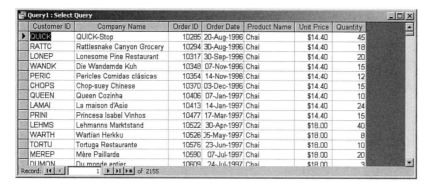

The results of querying multiple tables.

Pitfalls of Multitable Queries

You should be aware of some pitfalls of multitable queries: They involve what happens when you update data in the output of the query, as well as which records you see in the query output.

It's important to remember that you cannot update certain fields in a multitable query. For instance, you cannot update the join fields on the "one" side of a one-to-many relationship (unless you've activated the **Cascade Update Referential Integrity** feature). You also can't update the join field on the "many" side of a relationship after you've updated data on the "one" side. More importantly, which fields you can update, and the consequences of updating them, might surprise you. If you update the fields on the "one" side of a one-to-many relationship, you must be aware of that change's impact. You're actually updating that record in the original table on the "one" side of the relationship, and several records on the "many" side of the relationship may be affected.

For example, the following figure shows the result of a query based on the **Customers**, **Orders**, **Products**, and **Order Details** tables. I have changed **Chai** to **Latte** on a specific record of the query output. You might expect this change to affect only that specific order detail item.

NOTES

Chapter 8 discusses how setting up the right type of relationship ensures ease of use in designing system objects. By setting up relationships between tables in a database, Access knows how to properly join them in the queries that you build.

To remove a table from a query, click anywhere on the table in the top half of the query design grid and press the **Delete** key. Add tables to the query at any time by clicking the **Show Table** button on the toolbar. If you prefer, select the **Database** window and click and drag tables directly from the **Database** window to the top half of the query design grid.

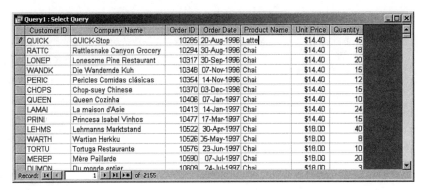

Changing a record on the "one" side of a one-to-many relationship.

However, pressing the **down-arrow** key to move off the record shows
that all records associated with **Chai** are changed, as depicted in the figure that follows. This happens because all the orders for **Chai** were actually getting their information from one record in the **Products** table—
the record for product ID 1—and that is the record I modified while
viewing the query result.

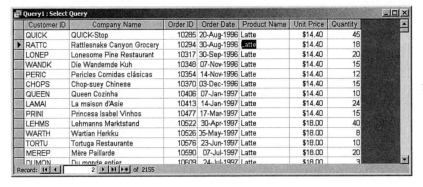

*The result of changing a record on the "one" side of a one-to-many
relationship.*

The second pitfall of multitable queries has to do with figuring out
which records result from a multitable query. So far, you have learned
how to build only inner joins. You need to understand that the query
output contains only customers who have orders and orders that have
order details. This means that not all the customers or orders might be
listed. You can also build queries in which you can list all customers,
regardless of whether they have orders, or you can list only the customers that do not have orders.

AutoLookup in Multitable Queries

The **AutoLookup** feature is automatically available in Access. As you fill in key values on the "many" side of a one-to-many relationship in a multitable query, Access automatically looks up the non-key values in the parent table. Most database developers refer to this as *enforced referential integrity*. A foreign key must first exist on the "one" side of the query to be entered successfully on the "many" side. As you can imagine, you don't want to be able to add to a database an order for a non-existent customer.

For example, I have based the query in the following figure on the **Order Details** and **Products** tables. The fields included in the query are **ProductID**, **UnitPrice**, and **Quantity** from the **Order Details** table and **ProductName**, **SupplierID**, and **CategoryID** from the **Products** table. If you change the **ProductID** field associated with an order detail row, Access looks up the **ProductName**, **SupplierID**, and **CategoryID** fields from the **Products** table and immediately displays them in the query result.

KEY TERM

Enforced referential integrity—A rule by which Access looks up key values on the "many" side of a one-to-many relationship in a multitable query as you fill in those key values. The value entered on the "many" side must exist on the "one" side of the relationship.

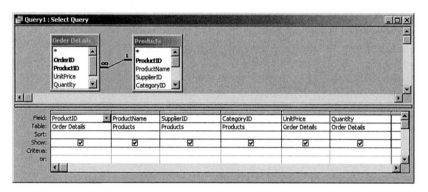

Using AutoLookup in a query with multiple tables.

Notice in the following figure how the information for **Chai** is displayed in the query result.

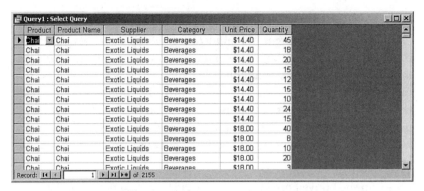

*The result of the **AutoLookup** query after the query is run.*

As you can see in the figure that follows, the **ProductName** and **Supplier** fields change automatically when the **ProductID** field is changed to **Escargots de Bourgogne**. Don't be confused by the combo box used to select the product ID. The presence of the combo box within the query is a result of Access's Lookup feature, covered in Chapter 12, "Power Table Techniques." The product ID associated with a particular order is actually being modified in the query. If you add a new record to the query, Access fills in the product information as soon as you select the product ID associated with the order.

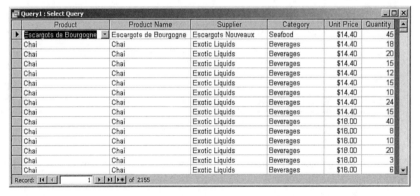

*The result of the **AutoLookup** feature changing data in a query with multiple tables.*

53 Create Calculated Fields

One of the rules of data normalization is that you shouldn't include the results of calculations in a database. You can, however, output the results of calculations by building those calculations into queries, and you can display the results of the calculations on forms and reports by making the query the foundation for a form or report. You can also add to forms and reports controls that contain the calculations you want. In certain cases, this can improve performance.

The columns of a query result can hold the result of any valid expression. This makes queries extremely powerful. For example, you could enter the following expression:

Left([FirstName],1) & "." & Left([LastName],1) & "."

This expression would give you the first character of the first name, followed by a period, the first character of the last name, and another period. An even simpler expression would be this one:

[UnitPrice]*[Quantity]

This calculation would simply multiply the **UnitPrice** field by the **Quantity** field. In both cases, Access would automatically name the resulting expression. For example, in the calculation that results from concatenating the first and last initials, Access gives the expression a name (often referred to as an alias). To give the expression a name that you desire, such as Initials, you must enter it as follows:

Initials:Left([FirstName],1) & "." & Left([LastName],1) & "."

The text preceding the colon is the name of the expression—in this case, **Initials**. If you don't explicitly give an expression a name, the name defaults to **Expr1**.

1 Insert a New Column

Either insert a new column at the end of the existing columns, or select a column with the column selector and then use the **Insert** key to insert a new column between existing columns.

2 Click the Field Row for the New Column

Click the **Field Row** for the new column.

Before You Begin

✔ **10** Open a Query in Design View

✔ **11** Add Fields to a Query

→ **50** About Refining a Query with Advanced Criteria

→ **52** About Building Queries Based on Multiple Tables

See Also

→ **54** Get Help from the Expression Builder

NOTE

Access automatically surrounds field names included in an expression with square brackets, unless the field name has spaces, in which case you must enclose the field name in brackets; otherwise, the query won't run properly.

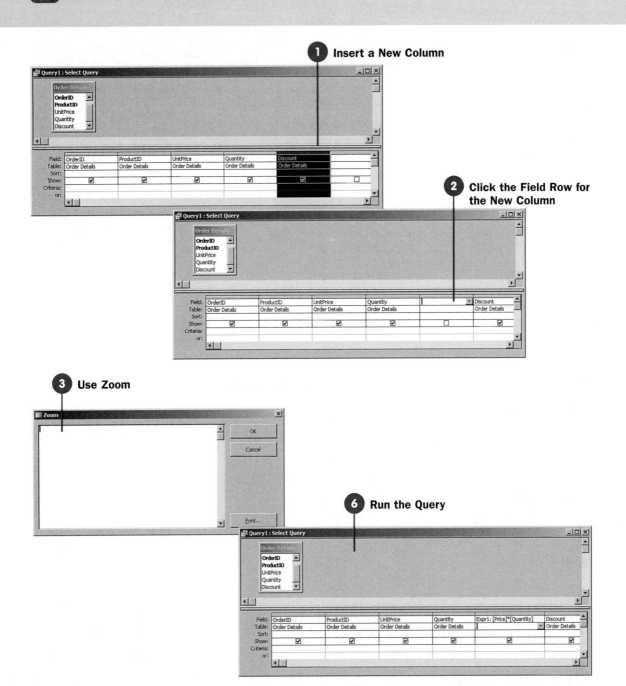

1 Insert a New Column

2 Click the Field Row for the New Column

3 Use Zoom

6 Run the Query

PART III: Create Your Own Database and Objects

3 **Use Zoom**

To more easily see what you are typing, press **Shift+F2** (Zoom) to open the **Zoom** dialog.

4 **Type the Expression**

Type the desired expression.

5 **Click OK**

Click **OK** to close the **Zoom** window.

6 **Run the Query**

Run the query to view the results of the expression that you created.

54 Get Help from the Expression Builder

The **Expression Builder** is a helpful tool for building expressions in queries as well as in many other situations in Access. You build expressions to include combinations of fields or results of calculations in your queries. Examples are combining the first and last name, or multiplying the price times the quantity.

1 **Insert a New Column**

Either insert a new column at the end of the existing columns, or select a column with the column selector and then use the **Insert** key to insert a new column between existing columns.

2 **Click the Field Row for the New Column**

Click the field row for the new column.

3 **Click Build**

Click the **Build** button on the toolbar. The **Expression Builder** appears. Notice that the **Expression Builder** is divided into three columns.

Before You Begin

✔ **10** Open a Query in Design View

✔ **11** Add Fields to a Query

→ **50** About Refining a Query with Advanced Criteria

→ **53** Create Calculated Fields

See Also

→ **75** Create and Run Parameter Queries

3 **Click Build**

4 **Select an Element in the Left Column**

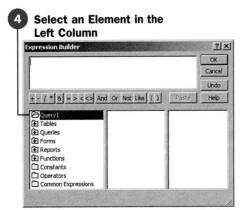
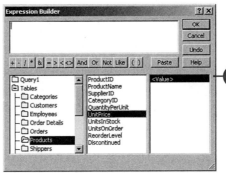

6 **Double-click an Element from the Right Column**

④ Select an Element in the Left Column

The left column shows the objects in the database. Select an element from the left column. You may have to double-click to expand the list of elements before you can single-click to select the element that you want.

⑤ Select an Element from the Middle Column

Click to select an element from the middle column.

⑥ Double-click an Element from the Right Column

Double-click an element from the right column. Access inserts the expression into the **Expression Builder**.

⑦ Click OK

Click **OK**. Access closes the dialog and inserts the expression into the field row of the query.

10

Create Your Own Forms

IN THIS CHAPTER:

Most Access applications are centered on forms. Forms are used to collect and display information, navigate about an application, and more. This chapter covers all the basics of creating and working with forms. It begins by looking at the various uses of forms. Then it delves into many important form and control properties.

55 Create a Form in Design View

Before You Begin

✔ **17** Open a Form

✔ **23** Close a Form

See Also

➜ **56** Add Controls

➜ **60** About Selecting the Correct Control

➜ **63** Work with Combo Boxes and List Boxes

Although the form wizards are both powerful and useful, in many cases it's best to build a form from scratch, especially if you're building a form that's not bound to data.

1 Click Forms in the Objects List

Click **Forms** in the **Objects List**.

2 Double-click Create Form in Design View

Double-click the **Create form in Design view** icon, or click **New** on the **Database** window toolbar to open the **New Form** dialog box and select **Design view** (the default choice).

3 Select Table or Query for Form's Foundation

If you clicked **New** to open the **New Form** dialog box and your form will be bound to data, use the drop-down list in the **New Form** dialog box to select the table or query that will serve as the form's foundation. Click **OK**. The **Form Design** window appears. You can now modify the form's design.

② Double-Click Create Form in Design View

③ Select Table or Query for Form's Foundation

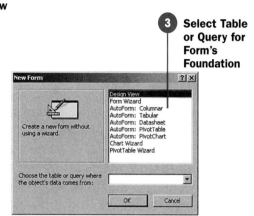

56 Add Controls

You can use the **Field List** window to easily add fields to a form. The **Field List** window contains all the fields that are part of the form's record source. The *record source* for a form is the table, query, or embedded Structured Query Language (SQL) statement that produces the data for the form. For example, the form's record source could be the **Customers** table. The fields listed in the **Field List** window are the fields that make up the **Customers** table.

① Make Sure the Field List Is Visible

Make sure the **Field List** window is visible. If it isn't, click the **Field List** button on the toolbar (the ninth tool from the right).

② Locate the Field(s) to Add

Locate the field(s) within the field list that you want to add.

Before You Begin

✔ **17** Open a Form

✔ **23** Close a Form

✔ **55** Create a Form in Design View

See Also

→ **58** Move, Size, and Delete Controls

→ **59** Align Controls

→ **60** About Selecting the Correct Control

KEY TERM

Record source—The table, query, or embedded Structured Query Language (SQL) statement that produces the data for a form.

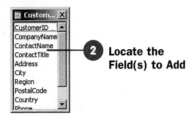

② **Locate the Field(s) to Add**

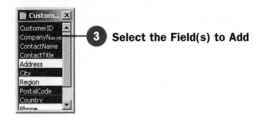

③ **Select the Field(s) to Add**

③ **Select the Field(s) to Add**

Click and drag the field from the field list to the place on the form where you want it to appear. The location you select becomes the upper-left corner of the text box, and the attached label appears to the left of where you dropped the control.

A *control* is an object that you add to a form or report. Types of controls include text boxes, combo boxes, list boxes, and check boxes.

To add multiple fields to a form at the same time, select several fields from the field list. Hold down the **Ctrl** key to select noncontiguous (not together) fields or the **Shift** key to select contiguous (together) fields. For example, if you hold down the **Ctrl** key and click three noncontiguous fields, each of these three fields is selected. If you click a field, hold down the **Shift** key, and click another field, all fields between the two selected fields are selected. If you want to select all the fields in a list, double-click the **Field List** title bar.

④ **Click and Drag the Field(s) to the Form**

Click and drag the selected field(s) to the form.

KEY TERM

Control—An object that you add to a form or report.

57 About Selecting Controls

You must select controls before you move them, size them, align them, or change their properties. It is therefore very important that you know the various ways to select controls.

The easiest way to select a single object on a form is to click it. After you have selected the object, you can move it, size it, or change any of its properties. Selecting multiple objects is a bit trickier, but you can accomplish it in several ways. Different methods are more efficient in different situations.

It's important to understand which objects you've actually selected. The following figure shows a form with four selected objects. The **CustomerID** text box, the **Company Name** label, and the **Contact Title** label and **Contact Title** text box are all selected; however, the **Customer ID** label and **CompanyName** text box aren't selected. If you look closely at the figure, you can see that the selected objects are completely surrounded by selection handles. The **Customer ID** label and **CompanyName** text box each have just a single selection handle because each is attached to an object that is selected. If you changed any properties of the selected objects, the **Customer ID** label and **CompanyName** text box would be unaffected.

Before You Begin

✔ **17** Open a Form

✔ **23** Close a Form

✔ **55** Create a Form in Design View

✔ **56** Add Controls

See Also

→ **58** Move, Size, and Delete Controls

→ **59** Align Controls

→ **60** About Selecting the Correct Control

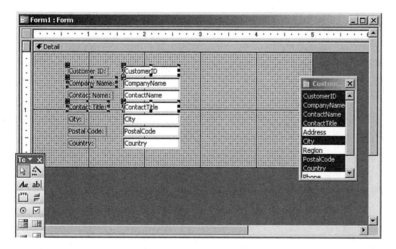

Selecting objects on a form.

One way to select multiple objects is to hold down the **Shift** key and click each object you want to select. Access surrounds each selected object with selection handles, indicating that you have selected it.

You can also select objects by lassoing them. Objects to be lassoed must be adjacent to one another on the form. To lasso objects, you place the mouse pointer on a blank area of the form (that is, not over any objects) and then click and drag the mouse pointer around the objects you want to select. You can see a thin line around the objects the mouse pointer is encircling. When you let go of the mouse button, any objects that were within the lasso, including those only partially surrounded, are selected. If you want to deselect any of the selected objects to exclude them, you hold down the **Shift** key and click the object(s) you want to deselect.

One of my favorite ways to select multiple objects is to use the horizontal and vertical rulers that appear at the edges of the **Form Design** window. You click and drag within the ruler, and as you do this, two horizontal lines appear, indicating which objects are selected. As you click and drag across the horizontal ruler, two vertical lines appear, indicating the selection area. When you let go of the mouse button, any objects within the lines are selected. As with the process of lassoing, to remove any objects from the selection, you hold down the **Shift** key and click the object(s) you want to deselect.

58 Move, Size, and Delete Controls

Before You Begin

✔ **17** Open a Form

✔ **55** Create a Form in Design View

✔ **56** Add Controls

✔ **57** About Selecting Controls

See Also

➜ **59** Align Controls

➜ **60** About Selecting the Correct Control

You must know several important tricks of the trade for selecting, moving, aligning, and sizing form objects. These tips will save you hours of frustration and wasted time.

1 Place Your Mouse Over a Control

Place you mouse over the control you want to move.

2 Click and Drag

Click and drag. An outline appears, indicating the object's new location. When the object reaches the position you want, you release the mouse. The attached label automatically moves with its corresponding control.

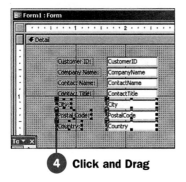

4 **Click and Drag**

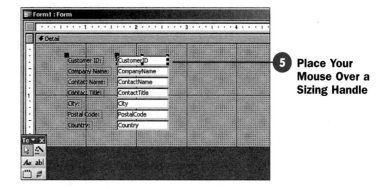

5 **Place Your Mouse Over a Sizing Handle**

7 **Select Other Sizing Options**

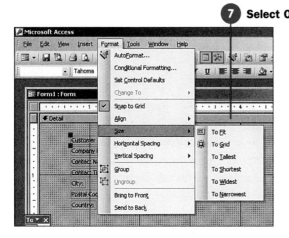

8 **Select Spacing Options**

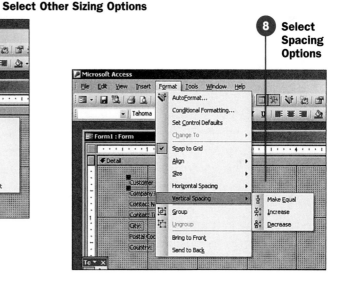

3 **Select Multiple Controls**

Select the controls that you want to move.

4 **Click and Drag**

Place the mouse over any of the selected objects and click and drag. An outline appears, indicating the proposed new position for the objects. You release the mouse when you have reached the position you want for the objects.

Sometimes you want to move a control independently of its attached label, and this requires a special technique. If you click a control, such as a text box, as you move the mouse over the border of the control, a hand icon with five fingers pointing upward appears. If you click and drag, both the control and the attached label move as a unit, and the relationship between them is maintained. If you place the mouse pointer over the larger handle in the upper-left corner of the object, the mouse pointer appears as a hand with only the index finger pointing upward. If you click and drag here, the control moves independently of its attached label and the relationship between the objects changes.

5 Place Your Mouse Over a Sizing Handle

Place your mouse over a sizing handle, except for the handle in the upper-left corner of the object.

6 Click and Drag

Click and drag. The handles at the top and bottom of the object allow you to change the object's height, and the handles at the left and right of the object let you change the object's width. You can use the handles in the upper-right, lower-right, and lower-left corners of the object to change the width and height of the object simultaneously.

You can select several objects and size them all at once. Each of the selected objects increases or decreases in size by the same percentage; their relative sizes stay intact.

You use the upper-left handle to move an object independently of its attached label. This means, for example, that you can place the label associated with a text box above the text box rather than to its left.

7 Select Other Sizing Options

Access offers several powerful methods of sizing multiple objects, which you access by selecting **Format**, **Size**. They include

- **To Fit**—Sizes the selected objects to fit the text within them.

- **To Grid**—Sizes the selected objects to the nearest gridlines.

- **To Tallest**—Sizes the selected objects to the height of the tallest object in the selection.

- **To Shortest**—Sizes the selected objects to the height of the shortest object in the selection.

- **To Widest**—Sizes the selected objects to the width of the widest object in the selection.

- **To Narrowest**—Sizes the selected objects to the width of the narrowest object in the selection.

Probably the most confusing of the options is **Format, Size, To Fit**. This option is somewhat deceiving because it doesn't perfectly size text boxes to the text within them. In today's world of proportional fonts, it isn't possible to perfectly size a text box to the largest possible entry it contains. Generally, however, you can visually size text boxes to a sensible height and width. You use a field's **Size** property to limit what's typed in the text box. If the entry is too large to fit in the allocated space, the user can scroll to view the additional text. The **Format, Size, To Fit** option is much more appropriate for labels than it is for text boxes.

 TIP

To quickly size a label to fit the text within it, select the label and **double-click** any of its sizing handles, except the sizing handle in the upper-left corner of the label.

8 Select Spacing Options

To make the vertical distance between selected objects equal, choose **Format, Vertical Spacing, Make Equal**.

You can make the horizontal distance between objects equal by choosing **Format, Horizontal Spacing, Make Equal**. Other related commands that are useful are **Format, Vertical Spacing, Increase** (or **Decrease**) and **Format, Horizontal Spacing, Increase** (or **Decrease**). These commands maintain the relationships between objects while proportionally increasing or decreasing the distances between them.

9 Select One or More Controls

Select the controls that you wish to delete.

10 Tap Your Delete Key

Tap your **Delete** key to delete the objects.

59 Align Controls

Before You Begin

✔ **17** Open a Form

✔ **55** Create a Form in
Design View

✔ **56** Add Controls

✔ **57** About Selecting
Controls

✔ **58** Move, Size, and
Delete Controls

See Also

→ **60** About Selecting
the Correct Control

→ **61** Change the Tab
Order of Controls

NOTE

Don't confuse the **Format,
Align** feature with the **Align**
tools (**Align Left**, **Center**,
and **Align Right**) on the
Formatting toolbar.
Whereas **Format, Align**
aligns objects one to the
other, the **Align** tools justify
the text inside an object.

TIP

To add the **Format, Align**
options to the toolbar,
select **Tools, Customize**,
and click to display the
appropriate toolbar on the
Toolbars tab. The alignment tools appear in the
Form/Report Design category. Drag and drop the
desired tools from the
Commands list onto the
appropriate toolbar.

Access makes it easy to align objects. If you align attached labels, the
controls (such as text boxes) remain in their original positions. If you
select the text boxes as well, the text boxes try to align with the
attached labels. Because the Align feature doesn't allow the objects to
overlap, the text boxes end up immediately next to their attached
labels.

❶ Select the Objects to Align

Use one of the techniques covered earlier in the chapter to select
the objects you wish to align.

❷ Select Format, Align

Select **Format, Align**.

❸ Select the Type of Alignment

Select the type of alignment. You can align the left, right, top, or
bottom edges of any objects on a form.

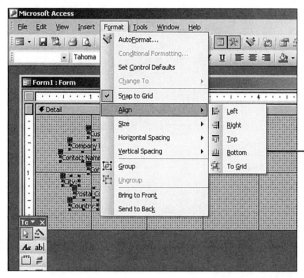

3 Select the Type of Alignment

---

60 About Selecting the Correct Control

Windows programming in general, and Access programming in particular, isn't limited to just writing code. Your ability to design a user-friendly interface can make or break the success of an application. Access and the Windows programming environment offer a variety of controls, and each one is appropriate in different situations. The following sections discuss each type of control and describe when and how it should be used. The following figure shows each control. As you go through each section, you can refer to this figure to get an idea of how each control looks and behaves.

Before You Begin

✔ **17** Open a Form

✔ **55** Create a Form in Design View

✔ **56** Add Controls

✔ **57** About Selecting Controls

See Also

→ **61** Change the Tab Order of Controls

→ **62** About Form Properties

NOTE

The **Display Control** property determines the default control type for an object; this default is set in the design of the underlying table.

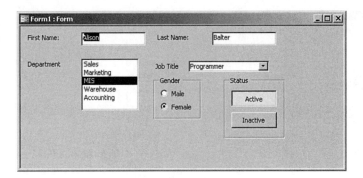

An introduction to the available controls.

Labels

You use labels to display information to users. Access automatically adds attached labels to a form when you add other controls, such as text boxes and combo boxes, to the form. You can delete or modify these attached labels as necessary. The default caption of a label is based on the **Caption** property of the field that underlies the control it's attached to. If you enter nothing into a field's **Caption** property, Access uses the field name for the label's caption.

You can use the **Label** tool, found in the toolbox, to add any text to a form. To do so, you click the **Label** tool and then click and drag the label to place it on the form. Labels are often used to provide descriptions of forms or to supply instructions to users. You can customize labels by modifying their font, size, color, and so on. Although developers can use Visual Basic for Applications (VBA) code to modify label properties at runtime, users don't have this ability.

TIP

To disassociate a label from its attached control, cut the label and paste it back on the form *without* selecting the control it was attached to. This allows you to perform tasks such as hiding the control without hiding the label.

Sometimes an attached label gets detached from its associated text box. In this case, the label will no longer move, size, or become selected with the text box that it applies to. To reassociate the label with the text box, you cut the label (by using **Ctrl+X**), click to select the text box, and then press **Ctrl+V** to paste.

Text Boxes

You use text boxes to get information from users. ***Bound text boxes*** display and retrieve field information stored in a table; ***unbound text boxes*** gather from the user information that's not related to a specific field in a specific record. For example, you can use a text box to gather information about report criteria from a user.

Access automatically adds text boxes to a form when you click and drag a field from the field list to the form. The **Display Control** property for the field must be set to **Text Box**. Another way to add a text box is to select the **Text Box** tool from the toolbox and then click and drag to place the text box on the form. This process adds an unbound text box to the form. If you want to bind the text box to data, you must set its **Control Source** property

Combo Boxes

Combo boxes allow users to select from a list of appropriate choices. Access offers several easy ways to add a combo box to a form. If you have set a field's **Display Control** property to **Combo Box**, Access adds a combo box to a form when you add the field to the form. The combo box automatically knows the source of its data as well as all its other important properties. Combo boxes are covered in detail in **63** **Work with Combo Boxes and List Boxes**.

List Boxes

List boxes are similar to combo boxes, but they differ from them in three major ways:

- They consume more screen space.

- They allow the user to select only from the list that's displayed. This means the user can't type new values into a list box (as you can with a combo box).

- They can be configured to let the user select multiple items.

KEY TERMS

Bound text box—Displays and retrieves field information stored in a table.

Unbound text box— Gathers from the user information that's not related to a specific field in a specific record.

If you set the **Display Control** property of a field to **List Box**, Access adds a list box to the form when the field is clicked and dragged from the field list to the form.

Check Boxes

You use check boxes when you want to limit the user to entering one of two values, such as **yes/no**, **true/false**, or **on/off**. You can add a check box to a form in several ways:

- Set the **Display Control** property of the underlying field to **Check Box** and then click and drag the field from the field list to the form.

- Click the **Check Box** tool in the toolbox; then click and drag a field from the field list to the form. This method adds a check box to the form even if the **Display Control** property of the underlying field isn't set to **Check Box**.

- Click the **Check Box** tool in the toolbox and then click and drag to add a check box to the form. The check box you have added is unbound. To bind the check box to data, you must set the control's **Control Source** property.

TIP

Use the **Triple State** property of a check box to add a third value, **Null**, to the possible choices for the check box value. **Null** refers to the absence of a value, which is different from the explicit value **False**.

Option and Toggle Buttons

You can use option buttons and toggle buttons alone or as part of an option group. You can use an option button or toggle button alone to display a **true/false** value, but this isn't a standard use of an option or toggle button. (Check boxes are standard for this purpose.) As part of an option group, option buttons and toggle buttons force the user to select from a mutually exclusive set of options, such as choosing among American Express, MasterCard, Visa, and Discover for a payment type. This use of option buttons and toggle buttons is covered in the next section, "Option Groups." In summary, although you can use option and toggle buttons outside an option group, you will almost always associate them with an option group.

The difference between option buttons and toggle buttons is in their appearance. Personally, I find toggle buttons confusing to users. I find that option buttons provide a much more intuitive interface (see the following figure).

Option Groups

Option groups allow the user to select from a mutually exclusive set of options. They can include check boxes, toggle buttons, or option buttons, but the most common implementation of an option group is option buttons.

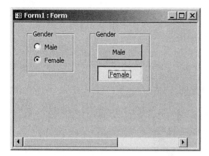

Option buttons (left) versus toggle buttons (right).

The easiest way to add an option group to a form is to use the **Option Group Wizard**. To do so, you select the **Control Wizards** button in the toolbox, click **Option Group** in the toolbox, and then click and drag to add the option group to the form. This launches the **Option Group Wizard**.

The first step of the **Option Group Wizard**, shown in the following figure, allows you to type the text associated with each item in the option group.

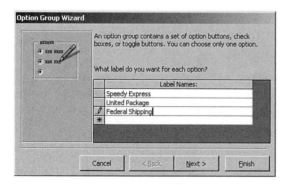

The first step of the Option Group Wizard: adding text to options.

The second step of the wizard gives you the option of selecting a default choice for the option group. This choice goes into effect when the user adds a new record to the table underlying the form.

The third step of the wizard lets you select values associated with each option button (see the following figure). The text displayed with the option button isn't stored in the record; instead, Access stores the underlying numeric value in the record. In the following figure, Access stores the number 1 in the field if the user selects Speedy Express.

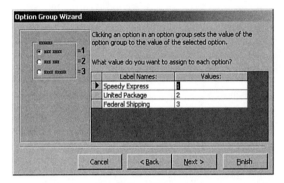

The third step of the Option Group Wizard: selecting values for options.

The fourth step of the **Option Group Wizard** asks whether you want to remember the option group value for later use or store the value in a field. In the following figure, for example, the option group value is stored in the **ShipVia** field.

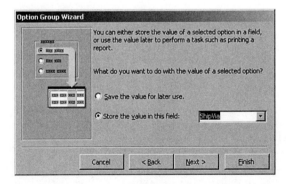

The fourth step of the Option Group Wizard: tying the group to data.

In the fifth step of the wizard, you can select from a variety of styles for the option group buttons, including option buttons, check boxes, and toggle buttons. You can also select from etched, flat, raised, shadowed, or sunken effects for the buttons. The wizard lets you preview each option.

The sixth and final step of the wizard allows you to add an appropriate caption to the option group. The completed group of option buttons created in this section is shown in the following figure.

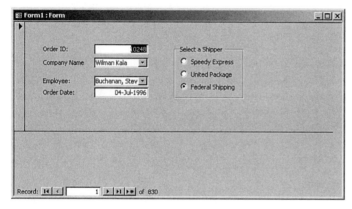

The results of running the Option Group Wizard.

It's important to understand that the **Option Group Wizard** sets properties of the frame, the option buttons within the frame, and the labels attached to the option buttons. The following figure shows the properties of the frame. The **Option Group Wizard** sets the control source of the frame and the default value of the option group. Each individual option button is assigned a value, and the caption of the attached label associated with each button is set.

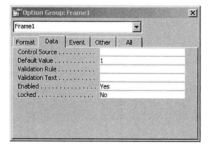

An option group frame, showing the properties of the selected button.

61 Change the Tab Order of Controls

Before You Begin

✔ **17** Open a Form

✔ **55** Create a Form in
Design View

✔ **56** Add Controls

See Also

→ **62** About Form
Properties

Access bases the tab order for the objects on a form on the order in which you add the objects to the form. However, this order isn't necessarily appropriate for the user. You might need to modify the tab order of the objects on a form yourself.

1 Select View, Tab Order

Select **View, Tab Order**. The **Tab Order** dialog box appears.

2 Click Auto Order

Click **Auto Order**, or opt to manually set the tab order for each object.

If you want to customize the order of the objects, you click and drag the gray buttons to the left of the object names listed under the **Custom Order** heading to specify the objects' tab order.

You must set the tab order for the objects in each section of a form (header, detail, and footer) separately. To do this, you select the appropriate section from the **Tab Order** dialog box and then set the order of the objects in the section. If the selected form doesn't have a header or footer, the **Form Header** and **Form Footer** sections are unavailable.

Click **OK** to apply your changes. Access applies your changes.

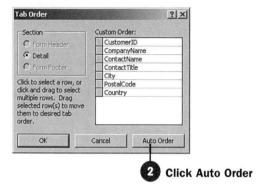

2 Click Auto Order

---

62 **About Form Properties**

Forms have many properties that you can use to affect their look and behavior. The properties are broken down into categories: **Format**, **Data**, **Event**, and **Other**.

To view a form's properties, you must select the form in one of two ways:

- Click the **form selector** (the small gray button at the intersection of the horizontal and vertical rulers).

- Choose **Edit**, **Select Form**.

It is important that you understand how to work with form properties. The sections that follow begin by focusing on the **Properties** window. They then hone in on a discussion of important form properties.

Working with the Properties Window

After you have selected a form, you can click the **Properties** button on the toolbar to view its properties. The **Properties** window, shown in the following figure, consists of five tabs: **Format**, **Data**, **Event**, **Other**, and **All**.

Before You Begin

✔ **17** Open a Form

✔ **55** Create a Form in Design View

✔ **56** Add Controls

✔ **57** About Selecting Controls

See Also

→ **63** Work with Combo Boxes and List Boxes

Viewing the Format properties of a form.

Many developers prefer to view all properties at once on the **All** tab, but a form can have a total of 107 properties! Rather than view all 107 properties at once, you should try viewing the properties by category. The **Format** category includes all the physical attributes of the form— the ones that affect the form's appearance, such as background color. The **Data** category includes all the properties of the data that the form is bound to, such as the form's underlying record source. The **Event** category contains all the Windows events to which a form can respond. For example, you can write code that executes in response to the form being loaded, becoming active, displaying a different record, and so on. The **Other** category holds a few properties that don't fit into the other three categories.

Working with the Important Form Properties

As mentioned in the preceding section, a form has 107 properties. Of those 107 properties, 52 are **Event** properties, and they are covered in most books focused on Access programming. The following sections cover the **Format** and **Data** properties of forms.

The Format Properties of a Form

The **Format** properties of a form affect its physical appearance. A form has 31 **Format** properties; the most commonly used are the following:

- **Caption**—The **Caption** property sets the text that appears on the form's title bar.

- **Default View**—The **Default View** property allows you to select from five available options:

  - **Single Form**—Allows only one record to be viewed at a time.

  - **Continuous Forms**—Displays as many records as will fit within the form window at one time, presenting each as the detail section of a single form.

  - **Datasheet**—Displays the records in a spreadsheet-like format, with the rows representing records and the columns representing fields.

  - **PivotTable**—Displays the records in a Microsoft Excel–type PivotTable format.

  - **PivotChart**—Displays the records in a Microsoft Excel–type PivotChart format.

  The selected option becomes the default view for the form.

- **Scroll Bars**—The **Scroll Bars** property determines whether scrollbars appear if the controls on a form don't fit within the form's display area. You can select from both vertical and horizontal scrollbars, neither vertical nor horizontal scrollbars, just vertical scrollbars, or just horizontal scrollbars.

- **Record Selectors**—A *record selector* is the gray bar to the left of a record in **Form** view, or the gray box to the left of each record in **Datasheet** view. It's used to select a record to be copied or deleted. The **Record Selectors** property determines whether the record selectors appear. If you give the user a custom menu, you can opt to remove the record selector to make sure the user copies or deletes records using only the features specifically built into the application.

- **Navigation Buttons**—*Navigation buttons* are the controls that appear at the bottom of a form; they allow the user to move from record to record within a form. The **Navigation Buttons** property

KEY TERMS

Record selector—The gray bar to the left of a record in **Form** view, or the gray box to the left of each record in **Datasheet** view. It's used to select a record to be copied or deleted.

Navigation buttons—the controls that appear at the bottom of a form; they allow the user to move from record to record within a form.

determines whether the navigation buttons are visible. You should set it to **No** for any dialog box forms, and you might want to set it to **No** for data entry forms, too, and add your own toolbar or command buttons to enhance or limit the functionality of the standard buttons. For example, in a client/server environment, you might not want to give users the ability to move to the first or last record because that type of record movement can be inefficient in a client/server architecture.

- **Dividing Lines**—The **Dividing Lines** property indicates whether you want a line to appear between records when the default view of the form is set to **Continuous Forms**. It also determines whether Access places dividing lines between the form's sections (that is, header, detail, and footer).

- **Auto Resize**—The **Auto Resize** property determines whether Access automatically sizes a form to display a complete record.

- **Auto Center**—The **Auto Center** property specifies whether a form should automatically be centered within the **Application** window whenever it's opened.

- **SubdatasheetHeight**—The **SubdatasheetHeight** property is used to designate the maximum height for a subdatasheet.

- **SubdatasheetExpanded**—The **SubdatasheetExpanded** property allows you to designate whether a subdatasheet is initially displayed in an expanded format. When this property is set to **False**, the subdatasheet appears collapsed. When it is set to **True**, the subdatasheet appears in expanded format.

- **Moveable**—The **Moveable** property determines whether the user can move the form window around the screen by clicking and dragging the form by its title bar.

The Data Properties of a Form
You use the **Data** properties of a form to control the source for the form's data, what sort of actions the user can take on the data in the form, and how the data in the form is locked in a multiuser environment. A form has 11 **Data** properties (8 of which are covered here).

- **Record Source**—The **Record Source** property indicates the table, stored query, or SQL statement on which the form's records are based. After you have selected a record source for a form, the controls on the form can be bound to the fields in the record source.

- **Filter**—You use the **Filter** property to automatically load a stored filter along with the form. I prefer to base a form on a query that limits the data displayed on the form. You can pass the query parameters at runtime to customize exactly what data Access displays.

- **Order By**—The **Order By** property specifies in what order the records on a form appear. You can modify this property at runtime.

- **Allow Filters**—The **Allow Filters** property controls whether you can filter records at runtime. When this option is set to **No**, all filtering options become disabled to the user.

- **Allow Edits, Allow Deletions, and Allow Additions**—The **Allow Edits**, **Allow Deletions**, and **Allow Additions** properties let you specify whether the user can edit data, delete records, or add records from within a form.

- **Data Entry**—The **Data Entry** property determines whether users can only add records within a form. You should set this property to **Yes** if you don't want users to view or modify existing records but want them to be able to add new records.

NOTE

The **Field List** window is unavailable until you have set the **Record Source** property of the form.

63 Work with Combo Boxes and List Boxes

If a field's **Display Control** property hasn't been set to **Combo Box**, the easiest way to add a combo box to a form is to use the **Control Wizards** tool. The **Control Wizards** tool helps you add combo boxes, list boxes, option groups, and subforms to forms. Although you can manually set all the properties set by the **Combo Box Wizard**, using the wizard saves both time and energy.

Although the **Combo Box Wizard** is a helpful tool, it's important that you understand the properties it sets. We're going to take a moment to go over the properties set by the **Combo Box Wizard**.

Before You Begin

✔ **17** Open a Form
✔ **55** Create a Form in Design View
✔ **56** Add Controls

Work with Combo Boxes and List Boxes

1 Click the Control Wizards Tool

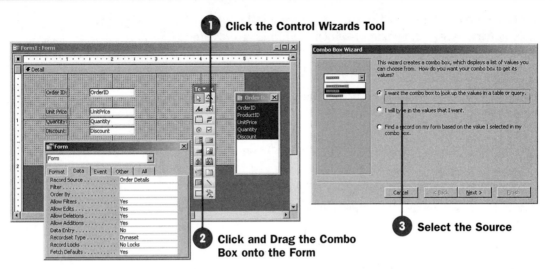

3 Select the Source

2 Click and Drag the Combo Box onto the Form

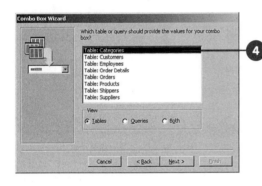

4 Select the Table or Query for the Record Source

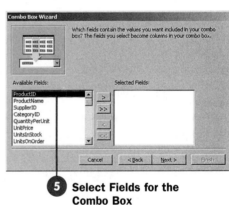

5 Select Fields for the Combo Box

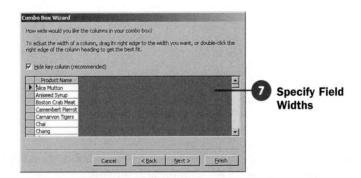

7 Specify Field Widths

The **Control Source** property indicates the field in which the selected entry is stored. For example, the **ProductID** of the selected entry can be stored in the **ProductID** field of the **Order Details** table. The **Row Source Type** property specifies whether the source used to populate the combo box is a table/query, value list, or field list. For our example, the **Row Source Type** property is set to **Table/Query**. The **Row Source** property is the name of the actual table or query used to populate the combo box. In our example, the **Row Source** property is a SQL SELECT statement that selects the **ProductID** and **ProductName** from the **Products** table. The **Column Count** property designates how many columns are in the combo box, and the **Column Widths** property indicates the width of each column. In our example, the width of the first column is zero, which renders the column invisible. Finally, the **Bound Column** property is used to specify which column in the combo box is being used to store data in the control source.

The first step of the **Combo Box Wizard** gives you three choices for the source of the combo box's data. You use the first option if the combo box will select the data that's stored in a field, such as the state associated with a particular customer. I rarely, if ever, use the second option, which requires that you type the values for the combo box. Populating a combo box this way makes it difficult to maintain. Every time you want to add an entry to the combo box, you must modify the application. You use the third option when you want to use the combo box as a tool to search for a specific record. For example, a combo box can be placed in a form's header to display a list of valid customers. After you select a customer, the user is moved to the appropriate record. This option is available only when the form is bound to a record source.

The **List Box Wizard** is almost identical to the **Combo Box Wizard**. After you run the **List Box Wizard**, the list box properties affected by the wizard are the same as the combo box properties.

❶ Click the Control Wizards Tool

If you want Access to launch the **Combo Box Wizard** when you add a combo box to the form, you need to make sure you click the **Control Wizards** tool in the toolbox before you add the combo box.

❷ Click and Drag the Combo Box onto the Form

Select the **Combo Box** tool in the toolbox and then click and drag to place the combo box on the form. This launches the **Combo Box Wizard**.

3 Select the Data Source

Indicate whether the source of the data will be a field in a table, a list of values that you type, or if you want to use the combo box as a tool to look up records on a form. The third option is available only if the form is bound to data.

4 Select the Table or Query for the RecordSource

If you select to have the combo box look up the values in a table or query, in the second step of the **Combo Box Wizard**, select a table or query to populate the combo box and then click **Next**.

5 Select Fields for the Combo Box

In the third step of the wizard, select the fields that appear in the combo box.

6 Designate a Sort Order

The fourth step of the wizard allows you to designate the sort order for the data in the combo box. You can opt to sort on as many as four fields.

7 Specify Field Widths

The fifth step of the wizard lets you specify the width of each field in the combo box. Access recommends that you hide the key column. The idea is that the user will see the meaningful English description, while Access worries about storing the appropriate key value in the record.

8 Specify What to Do with the Value

In the wizard's sixth step, specify whether you want Access to simply remember the selected value or store it in a particular field in a table.

9 Enter the Label Text

The seventh and final step of the **Combo Box Wizard** prompts for the text that will become the attached label for the combo box. Enter the text and click the **Finish** button. Access completes the process, building the combo box and filling in all its properties with the appropriate values.

11

Create Your Own Reports

IN THIS CHAPTER:

Although forms provide an excellent means for data entry, reports are the primary output device in Access. You can preview reports onscreen, output them to a printer, display them in a browser, and more. They are relatively easy to create, and they are extremely powerful.

64 Create a Report in Design View

Before You Begin

✔ **25** Open and View a Report

✔ **37** Using the Report Wizard

See Also

→ **65** About Working with Report Sections

→ **66** About Working with Controls

→ **67** Create Groups and Totals Reports

Although it is generally most efficient to get started with most reports by using the Report Wizard, you should understand how to create a new report in Design view. This is because there are times when you will need to build a report that does not look or behave like any of the reports that the Report Wizard provides.

1 Click Reports in the Objects List

Click **Reports** in the **Objects List**. A list of reports contained in the database appears.

2 Double-click Create Report in Design View

Double-click the **Create Report in Design View** icon or click **New** on the **Database** window toolbar to open the **New Report** dialog box. Select **Design View** (the default choice).

3 Select Table or Query for Report's Foundation

If you clicked **New** to open the **New Report** dialog box and your report will be bound to data, use the drop-down list in the **New Report** dialog box to select the table or query that will serve as the form's foundation.

Click **OK**. The **Report Design** window appears. Now you are ready to create your report.

> **NOTE**
>
> If you double-click the **Create Report in Design View** icon, your report will not be bound to data. You must then set the Record Source property of the report. **68** About Working with Report Properties covers the process of working with report properties.

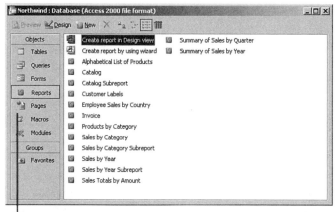

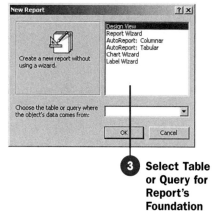

3 Select Table or Query for Report's Foundation

2 Double-click Create Report in Design View

65 About Working with Report Sections

Reports can have many parts, referred to as *sections* of the report. A new report is automatically made up of the following three sections, as shown in the following figure:

- Page Header section
- Detail section
- Page Footer section

The Detail section is the main section of the report; it's used to display the detailed data of the table or query underlying the report. Certain reports, such as Summary reports, have nothing in the Detail section. Instead, Summary reports contain data in group headers and footers.

The Page Header section automatically prints at the top of every page of the report. It often includes information such as the report's title. The Page Footer section automatically prints at the bottom of every page of the report and usually contains information such as the page number and date. Each report can have only one page header and one page footer.

Before You Begin

✔ **25** Open and View a Report

✔ **37** Using the Report Wizard

✔ **64** Create a Report in Design View

See Also

→ **66** About Working with Controls

→ **67** Create Groups and Totals Reports

→ **68** About Working with Report Properties

KEY TERM

Section—The parts of a report. A new report comprises the Page Header section, Detail section, and Page Footer section.

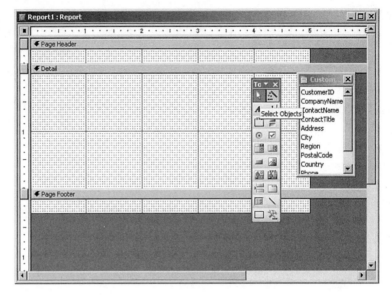

Sections of a report.

In addition to the three sections that Access automatically adds to every report, a report can have the following sections:

- Report Header section

- Report Footer section

- Group Headers section

- Group Footers section

A report header prints once, at the beginning of the report; the report footer prints once, at the end of the report. Each Access report can have only one report header and one report footer. The report header is often used to create a cover sheet for a report. It can include graphics or other fancy effects to add a professional look to a report. The most common use of the report footer is for grand totals, but it can also include any other summary information for a report.

In addition to report and page headers and footers, an Access report can have up to 10 group headers and footers. Report groupings separate data logically and physically. The group header prints before the detail for the group, and the group footer prints after the detail for the group. For example, you can group customer sales by country and city, printing the name of the country or city for each related group of records. If you total the sales for each country and city, you can place the country and city names in the country and city group headers and the totals in the country and city group footers.

66 About Working with Controls

Microsoft Access offers several techniques to help you select, move, align, and size report objects. Different techniques are most effective in different situations. Experience will tell you which technique you should use and when. Selecting, moving, aligning, and sizing report objects are quite similar to performing the same tasks with form objects.

Selecting Report Objects

To select a single report object, you click it; selection handles appear around the selected object. After you have selected the object, you can modify any of its attributes (properties), or you can size, move, or align it.

To select multiple objects so that you can manipulate them as a unit, you can use any of the following techniques:

- Hold down the **Shift** key as you click multiple objects. Each object you click is then added to the selection.

- Place the mouse pointer in a blank area of the report. Click and drag to lasso the objects you want to select. When you let go of the mouse button, any objects completely or even partially within the lasso are selected.

- Click and drag within the horizontal or vertical ruler. As you click and drag, lines appear, indicating the potential selection area. When you release the mouse button, all objects within the lines are selected.

Before You Begin

✔ **64** Create a Report in Design View

✔ **65** About Working with Report Sections

See Also

➜ **67** Create Groups and Totals Reports

➜ **68** About Working with Report Properties

You need to make sure you understand which objects are actually selected; attached labels can cause some confusion. The following figure shows a report with four objects selected: the **Summary of Sales by Quarter** label, the **Year** label, the **Sales** label, and the **Page Number** expression within the Page Footer. If you were to modify the properties of the selected objects, they would be the only objects affected.

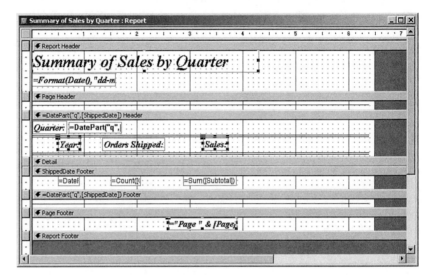

Selecting objects in an Access report.

Moving Report Objects

If you want to move a single control along with its attached label, you click the object and drag it to a new location. The object and the attached label move as a unit. To move multiple objects, you use one of the methods described in the previous section to select the objects you want to move. After you have selected the objects, you click and drag any of them; the selected objects and their attached labels move as a unit.

Moving an object without its attached label is a trickier process. When the mouse pointer is placed over the center or border of a selected object (not on a sizing handle), the cursor looks like a hand with all five fingers pointing upward. This indicates that the selected object and its attached label move as a unit, maintaining their relationship to one another. However, if you place the mouse pointer directly over the selection handle in the object's upper-left corner, the cursor looks like a hand with only the index finger pointing upward. This indicates that the object and the attached label move independently of one another so that you can alter the distance between them.

Aligning Objects with One Another

To align objects with one another, you must select them first. To do so, you choose **Format**, **Align** and then select **Left**, **Right**, **Top**, **Bottom**, or **To Grid**. The selected objects align themselves in relationship to each other.

You need to watch out for a few "gotchas" when you're aligning report objects. If you select several text boxes and their attached labels and align them, Access tries to align the left sides of the text boxes with the left sides of the labels. To prevent this from happening, you have to align the text boxes separately from their attached labels.

During the alignment process, Access never overlaps objects. Therefore, if the objects you're aligning don't fit, Access can't align them. For example, if you try to align the bottoms of several objects horizontally and they don't fit across the report, Access aligns only the objects that fit on the line.

Using Snap to Grid

The **Snap to Grid** feature is a toggle found under the **Format** menu. When you select **Snap to Grid**, all objects that you're moving or sizing snap to the report's gridlines. To temporarily disable the **Snap to Grid** feature, you hold down the **Ctrl** key while sizing or moving an object.

Using Power-Sizing Techniques

Access offers many techniques to help you size report objects. A selected object has eight sizing handles, and you can use any of them, except for the upper-left handle, to size the object. You simply click and drag one of the sizing handles. If you selected multiple objects to size at once, Access sizes them by the same percentage.

To size objects, you can also select **Format**, **Size** and then **To Fit**, **To Grid**, **To Tallest**, **To Shortest**, **To Widest**, or **To Narrowest**. Chapter 10 discusses these options in detail.

 TIP

Access offers a great trick that can help you size labels to fit. You simply double-click any of the four corner sizing handles, and Access automatically sizes the object to fit the text within it.

Controlling Object Spacing

Access makes it easy to control object spacing. You can make both the horizontal and vertical distances between selected objects equal. To do so, you select the objects and then choose **Format**, **Horizontal Spacing**, **Make Equal** or **Format**, **Vertical Spacing**, **Make Equal**. You can also maintain the relative relationship between selected objects while increasing or decreasing the space between them. To do this, you choose **Format**, **Horizontal Spacing**, **Increase/Decrease** or **Format**, **Vertical Spacing**, **Increase/Decrease**.

Selecting the Correct Control for the Job

Reports usually contain labels, text boxes, lines, rectangles, image controls, and bound and unbound object frames (see the following figure). The other types of controls (such as combo boxes and list boxes) are generally used for reports that emulate data-entry forms. The different controls that you can place on a report, as well as their uses, are discussed briefly in the following sections.

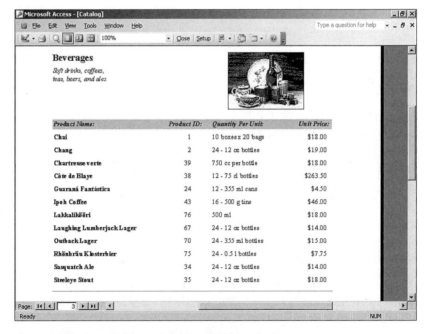

A report that contains various types of controls.

PART III: Create Your Own Database and Objects

Labels

You use labels to display information to users. Labels are commonly used as report headings, column headings, or group headings for a report. Although you can modify the text labels display at runtime by using Visual Basic for Applications (VBA) code, you cannot bind them directly to data.

To add a label to a report, you select the **Label** tool in the toolbox and then click and drag to place the label on the report.

Text Boxes

You use text boxes to display field information or the result of an expression. You can use them throughout a report's different sections. For example, in a page header, a text box might contain an expression showing the date range that's the criterion for the report. In a group header, a text box might be used to display a heading for the group. The possibilities are endless because a text box can hold any valid expression.

To add a text box to a report, you select the **Text Box** tool from the toolbox and then you click and drag the text box to place it on the report. You can also add a text box to a report by dragging a field from the field list to a report. This works as long as the field's **Display Control** property is a text box.

Lines

You can use lines to visually separate objects on a report. For example, you can place a line at the bottom of a section or under a subtotal. To add a line to a report, you click the **Line** tool in the toolbox to select it and then you click and drag to place the line on the report. When you add a line, it has several properties that you can modify to customize its look.

Rectangles

You can use rectangles to visually group items that logically belong together on a report. You can also use them to make certain controls on a report stand out. For example, you can draw rectangles around important subtotal or grand total information that you want to make sure the report's readers notice.

To add a rectangle to a report, you select the **Rectangle** tool from the toolbox and then click and drag to place the rectangle on the report.

NOTE

Alison Balter's Mastering Microsoft Office Access 2003, published by Sams, covers the ins and outs of Visual Basic for Applications.

TIPS

To make sure that a line you draw is perfectly straight, you can hold down the **Shift** key while you click and drag to draw the line.

A rectangle might obscure objects you already added to the report. To rectify this problem, set the rectangle's **Back Style** property to **Transparent**. If you want the rectangle to have a background color, choose **Format**, **Send to Back** to layer the objects so that the rectangle lies behind the other objects on the report.

Bound Object Frames

Bound object frames let you display the data in OLE fields, which contain objects from other applications, such as pictures, spreadsheets, and word processing documents.

To add a bound object frame to a report, you click the **Bound Object Frame** tool in the toolbox and then click and drag the frame onto the report. You need to then set the **Control Source** property of the frame to the appropriate field. You can also add a bound object frame to a report by dragging and dropping an OLE field from the field list onto the report.

Unbound Object Frames

You can use unbound object frames to add logos and other pictures to a report. Unlike bound object frames, however, unbound object frames aren't tied to underlying data.

To add an unbound object frame to a report, you click the **Unbound Object Frame** tool in the toolbox and then click and drag the object frame to place it on the report. An **Insert Object** dialog box, shown in the following figure, appears, and you use this dialog box to create a new OLE object or to insert an existing OLE object from a file on disk.

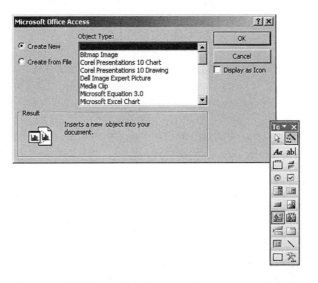

The **Insert Object** dialog box, where you insert a new or existing object into an unbound object frame.

If you select the **Create from File** option, the **Insert Object** dialog box changes to look like the figure that follows. You can click **Browse** to locate the file you want to include in the report. The Insert Object dialog box gives you the option of linking to or embedding an OLE object. If you select **Link**, a reference is created to the OLE object. Access stores only the bitmap of the object in the report, and the report continues to refer to the original file on disk. If you don't select **Link**, Access copies the object you select and embeds it in the report so that it becomes part of the Access .MDB file; no link to the original object is maintained.

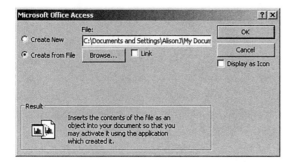

The Insert Object dialog box with Create from File selected.

Image Controls

Image controls are the best option for displaying static images, such as logos, on a report. An unbound object can be modified after it is placed on a report, but you can't open the object application and modify an image when it's placed on a report. This limitation, however, means far fewer resources are needed with the image control, so performance improves noticeably. The following figure shows a report with an image control.

 TIP

It's usually preferable to use an image control rather than an unbound object frame for static information such as a logo, because the image control requires far fewer resources than does an unbound object frame.

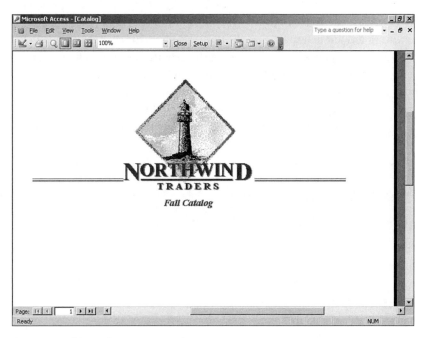

A report with an image control.

Other Controls

As mentioned earlier in this chapter, it's standard to include mostly labels and text boxes on reports, but you can add other controls, such as combo boxes, when appropriate. To add any other type of control, you click to select the control in the toolbox and then click and drag to place it on the report.

67 Create Groups and Totals Reports

Before You Begin

✔ **64** Create a Report in Design View

✔ **65** About Working with Report Sections

✔ **66** About Working with Controls

See Also

→ **68** About Working with Report Properties

Unlike sorting data within a form, sorting data within a report isn't determined by the underlying query. In fact, the underlying query affects the report's sort order only when you have not specified a sort order for the report. Any sort order specified in the query is completely overwritten by the report's sort order, which is determined in the report's **Sorting and Grouping** window. The sorting and grouping of a report is affected by what options you select when you run the **Report Wizard**. You can use the **Sorting and Grouping** window to add, remove, or modify sorting and grouping options for a report. Sorting simply affects the order of the records in the report. Grouping adds group headers and footers to the report.

1 Click Sorting and Grouping Button

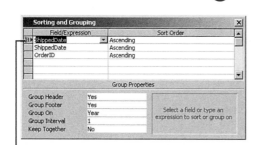

4 Click in the Field/Expression Column

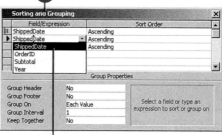

2 Click the Appropriate Selector

5 Select the Field on Which to Group

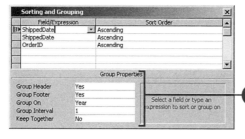

6 Set the Appropriate Properties

---

1 **Click Sorting and Grouping Button**

Click **Sorting and Grouping** on the **Report Design** toolbar to open the **Sorting and Grouping** window.

2 **Click the Appropriate Selector**

Click the selector of the line above where you want to insert the sorting and grouping level.

3 **Press the Insert Key**

Press the **Insert** key on the keyboard to insert a blank line in the **Sorting and Grouping** window.

---

4 **Click in the Field/Expression Column**

Click in the **Field/Expression** column.

5 **Select the Field on Which to Group**

Use the drop-down list to select the field on which you want to sort and group.

6 **Set the Appropriate Properties**

Set the properties to determine the nature of the sorting and grouping.

Each grouping in a report has properties that define the group's attributes. Each group has five properties that determine whether the field or expression is used for sorting, grouping, or both. They are also used to specify details about the grouping options.

The **Group Header** property specifies whether the selected group contains a header band. When you set the **Group Header** property to **Yes**, an additional band appears in the report that you can use to display information about the group. For example, if you're grouping by country, you can use the **Group Header** property to display the name of the country you're about to print. If the **Group Header** and **Group Footer** properties are both set to **No**, the field is used only to determine the sort order of the records in the report.

The **Group Footer** property specifies whether the selected group contains a footer band. When you set the **Group Footer** property to **Yes**, an additional band appears in the report. You can use this band to display summary information about the group; it's often used to display subtotals for a group.

The **Group On** property specifies what constitutes a new group. It is often used for situations such as departmental roll-ups where you roll several subdepartments into a summary department. Rather than group on the entire department number, you might want to group on the first three digits, for example.

The **Group On** settings for Text fields are **Each Value** and **Prefix Characters**. For Date fields, the settings are much more complex. They include **Each Value**, **Year**, **Qtr**, **Month**, **Week**, **Day**, **Hour**, and **Minute**. This means you could group by a Date field and have Access subtotal and begin a new group each time the week changes in the field. For AutoNumber, Currency, and Number fields, the settings are **Each Value** and **Interval**.

You use the **Group Interval** property with the **Group On** property to specify an interval value by which data is grouped. If, for example, the **Group On** property for a Text field is set to **Prefix Characters**, and the **Group Interval** property is set to **3**, the field's data is grouped on the first three characters.

The **Keep Together** property determines whether Access tries to keep an entire group together on one page. The three settings for the property are **No**, **Whole Group**, and **With First Detail**. Setting this property to **Whole Group** causes Access to try to keep the entire group together on one page. This includes the group header, the group footer, and the Detail section. Setting this property to **With First Detail** causes Access to print the group header on a page only if it can also print the first detail record on the same page.

NOTE

If you set the **Keep Together** property to **Whole Group** and the group is too large to fit on a page, Access ignores the property setting. If you set **Keep Together** to **With First Detail** and either the group header or the detail record is too large to fit on one page, that setting is ignored, too.

68 About Working with Report Properties

You can modify many different properties on reports to change how the report looks and performs. Like form properties, report properties are divided into categories: Format, Data, Event, and Other. To view a report's properties, you first select the report, rather than a section of the report, in one of three ways:

- Click the **report selector**, which is the small gray button at the intersection of the horizontal and vertical rulers (see the following figure).

Before You Begin

✔ **64** Create a Report in Design View

✔ **65** About Working with Report Sections

✔ **66** About Working with Controls

See Also

→ **69** Create Reports Based on Multiple Tables

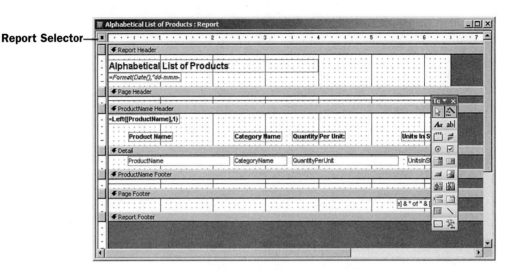

Report Selector—

The report selector allows you to select the report.

- Select **Report** from the drop-down list box in the **Properties** window.

- Choose **Edit, Select Report**.

After you have selected a report, you can view and modify its properties.

Working with the Properties Window

To select a report and open the **Properties** window at the same time, you double-click the **report selector**. When you select a report, the **Properties** window appears, showing all the properties associated with the report. A report has 47 properties available on the property sheet (there are additional properties available only from code), broken down into the appropriate categories in the **Properties** window. Forty of the properties relate to the report's Format, Data, and the properties on the **Other** tab; the remaining seven relate to the events that occur when a report is run. The sections that follow cover the Format and Data properties. Programming books such as *Alison Balter's Mastering Access 2003 Desktop Development* cover the Other properties and the seven event properties.

The Format Properties of a Report

A report has the 23 **Format** properties, the most commonly used which are described in the following text, for changing the report's physical appearance.

- **Caption**—The **Caption** property of a report is the text that appears in the **Report** window's title bar when the user is previewing the report. You can modify it at runtime to customize it for a particular situation.

- **Auto Resize**—The **Auto Resize** property determines whether a report is resized automatically to display all the data on the report.

- **Auto Center**—You use the **Auto Center** property to designate whether you want the Report window to automatically be centered on the screen.

- **Page Header** and **Page Footer**—The **Page Header** and **Page Footer** properties determine on what pages the Page Header and Page Footer sections appear. The options are **All Pages**, **Not with Rpt Hdr**, **Not with Rpt Ftr**, and **Not with Rpt Hdr/Ftr**. You might not want the page header or page footer to print on the report header or report footer pages, and these properties give you control over where those sections print.

- **Grp Keep Together**—In Access, you can keep a group of data together on the same page by using the **Grp Keep Together** property. The **Per Page** setting forces the group of data to remain on the same page, and the **Per Column** setting forces the group of data to remain within a column. A group of data refers to all the data within a report grouping (for example, all the customers in a city).

- **Moveable**—The **Moveable** property determines whether the user can move the **Report** window around the screen by clicking and dragging the report by its title bar.

The Data Properties of a Report

A report has five **Data** properties, described in the following text, which are used to supply information about the data underlying a report.

- **Record Source**—The **Record Source** property specifies the table or query whose data underlies the report. You can modify the record source of a report at runtime. This feature of the **Record Source** property makes it easy for you to create generic reports that use different record sources in different situations.

- **Filter**—The **Filter** property allows you to open a report with a specific filter set. I usually prefer to base a report on a query rather than apply a filter to it. Sometimes, however, it's more appropriate to base the report on a query and then apply and remove a filter as required, based on the report's runtime conditions.

- **Filter On**—The **Filter On** property determines whether a report filter is applied. If the **Filter On** property is set to **No**, the **Filter** property of the report is ignored.

- **Order By**—The **Order By** property determines how the records in a report are sorted when the report is opened.

- **Order By On**—The **Order By On** property determines whether the **Order By** property of the report is used. If the **Order By On** property is set to **No**, the report's **Order By** property is ignored.

69 Create Reports Based on Multiple Tables

69 Create Reports Based on Multiple Tables

Before You Begin

✔ **64** Create a Report in Design View

✔ **65** About Working with Report Sections

✔ **66** About Working with Controls

✔ **67** Create Groups and Totals Reports

The majority of reports you create will probably be based on data from more than one table. This is because a properly normalized database usually requires that you bring table data back together to give users valuable information. For example, a report that combines data from a **Customers** table, an **Orders** table, an **Order Details** table, and a **Product** table can supply the following information:

- Customer information, such as company name and address

- Order information, such as order date and shipping method

- Order detail information, such as quantity ordered and price

- A product table, including a product description

You can base a multitable report directly on the tables whose data it displays, or you can base it on a query that has already joined the tables, providing a flat table structure.

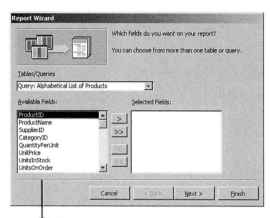

3 Select Tables, Queries, and Fields to Include on the Report

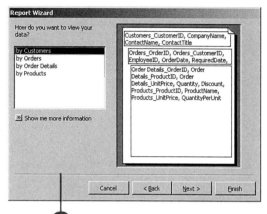

4 Designate How You Want to View Data

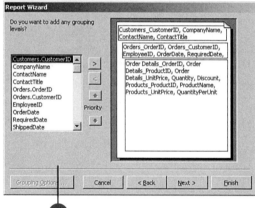

5 Add Any Grouping Levels

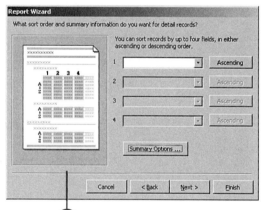

6 Designate Sorting

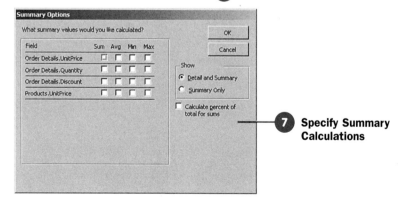

7 Specify Summary Calculations

1 Click Reports

Click **Reports** in the **Objects** list. A list of reports contained in the database appears.

2 Double-click Create Report by Using Wizard

Double-click **Create Report by Using Wizard**. The Report Wizard appears.

3 Select Tables, Queries, and Fields to Include on the Report

From the **Tables/Queries** drop-down list box, select the first table or query whose data will appear on the report.

Select the fields you want to include from that table.

Select each additional table or query you want to include on the report, selecting the fields you need from each. Click **Next**.

4 Designate How You Want to View the Data

Determine how you want to view the data. You can accept Access's suggestion (**By Orders**), or you can choose from any of the available options (for example, **By Customers**, **By Orders**, **By Order Details**, or **By Products**). Click **Next**.

5 Add Any Grouping Levels

Determine whether you want to add any grouping levels. You can use grouping levels to visually separate data and to provide subtotals. After you select grouping levels, click **Next**.

6 Designate Sorting

Select how you want the records in the report's Detail section to be sorted. Then click the **Summary Options** button to specify the summary calculations.

7 Specify Summary Calculations

By clicking the **Summary Options** button, you can opt to include the percentage of total calculations. Click **OK** when you're done adding the summary options. Then click **Next**.

8 Select the Layout and Orientation

Select the layout and orientation of the report. Layout options include **Stepped, Blocked, Outline 1, Outline 2, Align Left 1**, and **Align Left 2**. You can click the different option buttons to preview how each of the reports will look. Click **Next**.

9 Select a Style

Select from predefined styles for the report, including **Bold, Casual, Compact, Corporate, Formal**, and **Soft Gray**. You can preview each style to see what it looks like. Click **Next**.

10 Select a Title

Select a title for the report. The title also becomes the name of the report. I like to select an appropriate name and change the title after the wizard is finished. When you are ready to complete the process, click **Finish**. The report appears in Preview mode unless you designated that you wanted to modify the report's design.

PART IV

Power Access Techniques

12

Power Table Techniques

IN THIS CHAPTER:

Working with the design of tables is not as simple as adding a field, naming it, and selecting the field type. You can do a lot more than that to customize what you store in a table and how it behaves. This chapter delves into the techniques that allow you to take full advantage of the power of Access tables.

70 About Working with Field Properties

Before You Begin

✓ **42** Build a New Table

✓ **43** About Selecting the Appropriate Field Type for Your Data

See Also

→ **71** Look Up Values in a Table or Query

→ **72** About Working with Table Properties

→ **73** Improve Performance with Indexes

After you have added fields to a table, you need to customize their properties. Field properties let you control how Access stores data as well as what data the user can enter into a field. The available properties differ depending on which field type you select. You can find a comprehensive list of properties under the Text data type (see the following figure). The following sections describe the various field properties. Notice that the lower portion of the Design view window in the figure is the Field Properties pane. This is where you can set properties for the fields in a table.

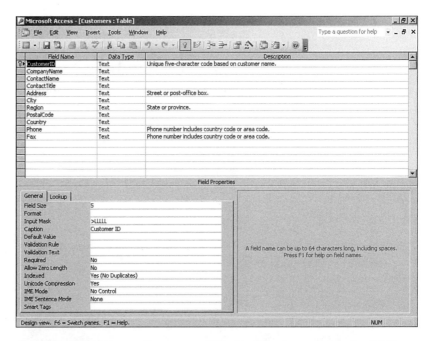

Using the Field Properties pane of the Design view window to set the properties of a field.

The Field Size Property

The **Field Size** property limits what the user enters into a field. The **Field Size** property is available for **Text** and **Number** fields only. It's best to set the **Field Size** property to the smallest value possible. For **Number** fields, a small size means lower storage requirements and faster performance. The same is true for **Text** fields. To modify the **Field Size** property, first you select the desired field name from the top pane of the **Design view** window. Then you click the **Field Size** property text box in the **Field Properties** pane. Finally, you type the desired field size. The preceding figure shows 5 as the field size of the **CustomerID** field.

The Format Property

The **Format** property determines how access displays data. It allows you to customize the way Access displays and prints numbers, dates, times, and text. You can select a predefined format or create a custom format.

To select a predefined display format (from Design view), first you select the desired field, and then you click the **Format** property text box in the Field Properties pane. Click the drop-down arrow that appears, and select the desired format based on the type of field you are formatting.

You create a custom format by using a combination of the special characters, called *placeholders*, listed in the following table:

Placeholders That Allow You to Build a Custom Format

Placeholder	Function
0	Displays a digit if one exists in the position; otherwise, displays a zero. You can use the 0 placeholder to display leading zeros for whole numbers and trailing zeros for decimals.
#	Displays a digit if one exists in the position; otherwise, displays a blank space.
$	Displays a dollar sign in the position.
. % ,	Displays a decimal point, percent sign, or comma at the indicated position.
/	Separates the day, month, and year to format date values.
M	Used as a month placeholder: m displays 1, mm displays 01, mmm displays Jan, mmmm displays January.
D	Used as a day placeholder: d displays 1, dd displays 01, ddd displays Mon, dddd displays Monday.

NOTE

For **Number** fields, you should select the smallest **Field Size** property value that can store the values you will be entering. Limiting the **Field Size** property of **Number** fields saves disk space.

TIP

You can move between the two panes of the Design view window by pressing **F6**. Also, to get help with a field property, you click the property line in the Field Properties pane and press **F1**.

KEY TERM

Placeholders—Special characters you use in combination to create a custom format.

Placeholder	Function
Y	Used as a year placeholder: yy displays 95, yyyy displays 1995.
:	Separates hours and minutes.
h, n, s	Used as time placeholders for h hours, n minutes, and s seconds.
AM/PM	Displays time in 12-hour format, with AM or PM appended.
@	Indicates that a character is required in the position in a text or memo field.
&	Indicates that a character is optional.
>	Changes all the text characters to uppercase.
<	Changes all the text characters to lowercase.

To create a custom display format while in Design view of a form, first you select the desired field and then you click the **Format** text box in the **Field Properties** pane. Now simply type the desired format, using the placeholders listed in the table.

The Caption Property

The **Caption** property provides alternatives to the field name. The text you place in the **Caption** property becomes the caption for fields in the **Datasheet** view. Access also uses the contents of the **Caption** property as the caption for the *attached label* it adds to *data bound controls* when you add them to forms and reports. The **Caption** property becomes important whenever you name fields without spaces. Whatever is in the **Caption** property overrides the field name for use in **Datasheet** view, on forms, and on reports.

To set the **Caption** property (from Design view), select the desired field name from the top pane of the **Design view** window and click the **Caption** text box in the **Field Properties** pane. Then simply type the desired caption.

The Default Value Property

The **Default Value** property saves you data-entry time. Assigning a **Default Value** property to a field causes a specified value to be filled in for the field in new records. Setting a commonly used value as the **Default Value** property facilitates the data entry process. When you add data, you can accept the default entry or replace it with another value.

NOTES

Generally, field names should be short and should not contain spaces. You can, however, assign to the field a **Caption** property that describes the field's contents. Access displays the **Caption** property as the field label on forms and reports. For example, you can assign "Fax Number" to the **Caption** property for a field named **FaxNum**.

It's important to set the **Caption** property for fields before you build forms or reports that use those fields. When you produce a form or report, Access looks at the current caption. Access doesn't modify captions for a field on existing forms and reports, so if you add or modify the caption later, the change won't be made.

KEY TERMS

Data bound control—A control that is bound to a field in a table or query.

Attached label—Refers to the label that is attached to a data bound control.

For example, if most of your customers are in California, you can assign a default value of CA. When you're doing data entry, if the customer is in California, you do not need to change the value for the state. If the customer is in another state, you simply replace CA with the appropriate state value.

To set a Default Value property (from Design view), select the desired field from the top pane of the **Design view** window and click the **Default Value** property text box in the **Field Properties** pane. Then type the desired value.

The data users enter in tables must be accurate if the database is to be valuable to you or your organization. You can use the **Validation Rule** property (covered next) to add data entry rules to the fields in tables.

The Validation Rule and Validation Text Properties

The **Default Value** property suggests a value to the user, but the **Validation Rule** property actually limits what the user can place in the field. Validation rules can't be violated; the database engine strictly enforces them. As with the **Default Value** property, this property can contain either text or a valid Access expression, but you cannot include user-defined functions in the **Validation Rule** property. You also can't include references to forms, queries, or tables in the **Validation Rule** property.

You can use operators to compare two values; the less than (<) and greater than (>) symbols are examples of *comparison operators*. **And, Or, Is, Not, Between,** and **Like** are called *logical operators*. The table that follows provides a few examples of validation rules.

NOTE

A **Default Value** property can be constant, such as CA for California, or a function that returns a value, such as **Date()**, which displays the current date.

KEY TERMS

Comparison operator—A symbol that allows you to compare two values.

Logical operator—An operator that allows you to create logical criteria.

Examples of Validation Rules

Validation Rule	Validation Text Examples
>0	Please enter a valid Employee ID Number.
"H" or "S" or "Q"	Only H or S or Q codes will be accepted.
Between Date()-365 and Date()+365	Date cannot be later than one year ago today or later than one year from today.
>0 or is Null	Enter a valid ID number or leave blank if not approved.
Between 0 and 9 or is Null	Rating range is 0 through 9 or is blank.
>Date()	Date must be after today.

If you set the **Validation Rule** property but do not set the **Validation Text** property, Access automatically displays a standard error message whenever the user violates the validation rule. To display a custom message, you must enter message text in the **Validation Text** property.

You can require users of a database to enter a valid value in selected fields when editing or adding records. For example, you can require a user to enter a date for each record in an **Invoice** table.

Whereas the **Validation Rule** property limits what the user can enter into the table, the **Validation Text** property provides the error message that appears when the user violates the validation rule.

To establish a field-level validation rule (from Design view), select the desired field name from the top pane of the **Design view** window and click the **Validation Rule** property text box in the **Field Properties** pane. Then type the desired validation rule (for example, **Between 0 and 120**).

To add validation text, click the **Validation Text** property text box in the **Field Properties** pane and type the desired text (for example, **Age Must Be Between 0 and 120**).

The Required Property

The **Required** property is very important: It determines whether you require a user to enter a value in a field. This property is useful for *foreign key fields*, when you want to make sure the user enters data into the field. For example, in the case of a Customers table and an Orders table, both might contain a CustomerID field. In the Customers table, the CustomerID field is the primary key field. In the Orders table, the CustomerID field is the foreign key field because its value is looked up in the Customers table.

It's also useful for any field containing information that's needed for business reasons (company name, for example).

To designate a field as required (from Design view), first select the desired field and click the **Required** property text box in the **Field Properties** pane. Then type **Yes**.

The Allow Zero Length Property

The **Allow Zero Length** property lets you accommodate for situations with nonexistent data. You can use the **Allow Zero Length** property to allow a string of no characters. You enter a zero-length string by typing a pair of quotation marks with no space between them ("")). You use the **Allow Zero Length** property to indicate that you know there is no value for a field.

To allow a zero-length field (from Design view), select the desired field and click the **Allow Zero Length** property text box in the **Field Properties** pane. Then select **Yes** from the drop-down list box.

The Input Mask Property

An *input mask* controls data the user enters into a field. For instance, a short date input mask appears as --/--/---- when the field is active. You can then simply type **07042005** to display or print **7/4/2005**. Based on the input mask, you can ensure that the user enters only valid characters into the field.

The table that follows lists some of the placeholders that you can use in character strings for input masks in fields of the **Text** data type.

Placeholders That Can Be Included in an Input Mask

Placeholder	Description
0	A number (0–9) is required.
9	A number (0–9) is optional.
#	A number (0–9), a space, or a plus or minus sign is optional; a space is used if no number is entered.
L	A letter (A–Z) is required.
?	A letter (A–Z) is not required; a space is used if no letter is entered.
A	A letter (A–Z) or number (0–9) is required.
a	A letter (A–Z) or number (0–9) is optional.
&	Any character or space is required.
C	Any character or space is optional.
>	Any characters to the right are converted to uppercase.
<	All the text characters to the right are changed to lowercase.

To create an input mask (from Design view), first you select the desired field and click the **Input Mask** property text box. Then you type the desired format, using the placeholders listed in the table.

Access includes an **Input Mask Wizard** that appears when you place the cursor in the **Input Mask** text box and click the ellipsis (...) button to the right of the text box. The wizard, shown in the following figure, provides common input mask formats from which to choose. To start the **Input Mask Wizard**, you click the button to the right of the **Input Mask** property.

NOTE

The **Input Mask Wizard** is available only if you selected the **Additional Wizards** component during Access setup. If you did not select this component and then you try to open the **Input Mask Wizard**, Access prompts you to install the option on-the-fly the first time you use it.

Entering an input mask with the Input Mask Wizard.

For example, the input mask **000-00-0000;;_** (converted to **000\-00\-0000;;_** as soon as you tab away from the property) forces the entry of a valid Social Security number. Everything that precedes the first semicolon designates the actual mask. The zeros force the entry of the digits 0 through 9. The dashes are literals that appear within the control as the user enters data. The character you enter between the first and second semicolon determines whether literal characters (the dashes, in this case) are stored in the field. If you enter a 0 in this position, literal characters are stored in the field; if you enter 1 or leave this position blank, the literal characters aren't stored. The final position (after the second semicolon) indicates what character is displayed to denote the space where the user types the next character (in this case, the underscore).

Here's a more detailed example: In the mask \(999") "000\-0000;;_, the first backslash causes the character that follows it (the open parenthesis) to be displayed as a literal. The three nines allow the user to enter optional numbers or spaces. Access displays the close parenthesis and space within the quotation marks as literals. The first three zeros require values 0 through 9. The dash that follows the next backslash is displayed as a literal. Four additional numbers are then required. The two semicolons have nothing between them, so the literal characters aren't stored in the field. The second semicolon is followed by an underscore, so an underscore is displayed to indicate the space where the user types the next character. This sounds pretty complicated, but here's how it works. The user types 8054857632. What appears is (805) 485-7632. What is actually stored is 8054857632. Because the input mask contains three 9s for the area code, the area code is not required. The remaining characters are all required numbers.

71 Look Up Values in a Table or Query

You can select **Lookup Wizard** as a field's data type. The Lookup Wizard guides you through the steps to create a list of values from which you can choose. You can select the values from a table or a query, or you can create a list of your own values.

1 Select the Field

Select the desired field.

2 Choose Lookup Wizard

Choose **Lookup Wizard** as the data type.

3 Select the Source of Values

Select the desired source of the values and click **Next**.

4 Select a Table or Query

Select the table or query to provide the values and click **Next**.

5 Double-click the Field(s)

Double-click the field(s) that contains the desired values and then click **Next**.

6 Select a Sort Order

Select the sort order you want for your list.

7 Drag the Lookup Column to the Desired Width

Drag the **Lookup** column to the desired width and then click **Next**.

8 Type a Name for the Lookup Column

Type a name for the **Lookup** column. Click **Finish** when you're done.

Before You Begin

✔ **42** Build a New Table

✔ **43** About Selecting the Appropriate Field Type for Your Data

✔ **70** About Working with Field Properties

See Also

→ **72** About Working with Table Properties

→ **73** Improve Performance with Indexes

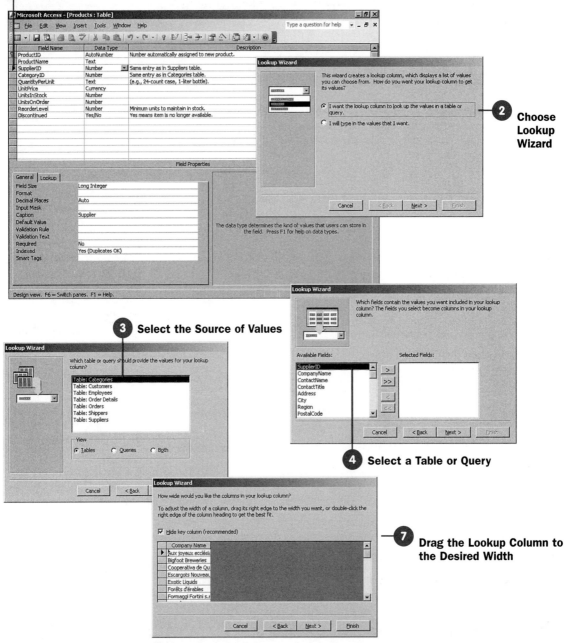

1 Select the Field

2 Choose Lookup Wizard

3 Select the Source of Values

4 Select a Table or Query

7 Drag the Lookup Column to the Desired Width

72 About Working with Table Properties

In addition to field properties, you can specify properties that apply to a table as a whole. To access the table properties, you click the **Properties** button on the toolbar while in a table's **Design view**. The available table properties are shown in the following figure.

Before You Begin

✔ **42** Build a New Table

✔ **43** About Selecting the Appropriate Field Type for Your Data

✔ **70** About Working with Field Properties

See Also

→ **73** Improve Performance with Indexes

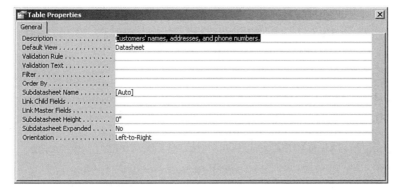

Viewing the available table properties.

The **Description** property is used mainly for documentation purposes. The **Default View** property designates the view in which the table appears when the user first opens it. The **Validation Rule** property specifies validations that must occur at a record level instead of a field level. For example, credit limits might differ depending on what state a customer is in. In that case, what's entered in one field depends on the value in another field. If you enter a table-level validation rule, it doesn't matter in what order the user enters the data. A table-level validation rule ensures that Access enforces the proper dependency between fields. The validation rule might look something like this:

> [State] In ("AZ","NV") And [IntroDate]<=#12/31/2003# Or _
>
> [State] In ("CA","UT") And [IntroDate]<=#12/31/2004# Or _
>
> [State] Not In ("AZ", "NV", "CA", "UT")

This validation rule requires an intro date of December 31, 2003 or earlier for customers in Arizona and Nevada and an intro date of December

31, 2004 or earlier for customers in California and Utah, but it doesn't specify an intro date for residents of any other states. Table-level validation rules can't be in conflict with field-level validation rules. If they are in conflict, you will not be able to enter data into the table.

The **Validation Text** property determines what message appears when a user violates the validation rule. If this property is left blank, a default message appears.

The **Filter** property is used to indicate a subset of records that appears in a datasheet, form, or query. The **Order By** property is used to specify a default order for the records. The **Filter** and **Order By** properties aren't generally applied as properties of a table.

The **Subdatasheet Name** property identifies the name of a table that is used as a drill-down. If this property is set to [**Auto**], Access automatically detects the drill-down table, based on relationships established in the database. The **Link Child Fields** and **Link Master Fields** properties are implemented to designate the fields that are used to link the current table with the table specified in the **Subdatasheet Name** property. These properties should be left blank when you select [**Auto**] for the **Subdatasheet Name**. You use the **Subdatasheet Height** property to specify the maximum height of the subdatasheet and the **Subdatasheet Expanded** property to designate whether Access automatically displays the subdatasheet in an expanded state.

The **Orientation** property determines the layout direction for a table when it is displayed. The default setting for USA English is **Left-to-Right**. The **Orientation** property is language specific, and the **Right-to-Left** setting is available only if you are using a language version of Microsoft Access that supports right-to-left language displays. Arabic and Hebrew are examples of right-to-left languages. You must run a 32-bit Microsoft operating system that offers right-to-left support, such as the Arabic version of Windows 2000, to take advantage of this feature in Access. By installing the Microsoft Office Multilanguage Pack and the Microsoft Office Proofing Tools for a specific language, and by enabling the specific right-to-left language under the Microsoft Office language settings, you can also turn on right-to-left support.

73 Improve Performance with Indexes

Indexes improve performance when you're searching, sorting, or grouping on a field or fields. Primary key indexes are used to maintain unique values for records. For example, you can create a single-field index that does not allow a duplicate order number or a multiple-field index that does not allow records with the same first and last names.

1 Select a Field

Select the field to be indexed.

2 Click the Indexed Row

Click the **Indexed** row of the **Field** properties pane.

3 Select the Index Type

Select the desired index type—**No, Yes (Duplicates OK)**, or **Yes (No Duplicates)**. The **Yes (Duplicates OK)** option means that you are creating an index and that you will allow duplicates within that field. The **Yes (No Duplicates)** option means that you are creating an index and you will not allow duplicate values within the index. If the index is based on company name and you select **Yes (Duplicates OK)**, you can enter two companies with the same name. If you select **Yes (No Duplicates)**, you cannot enter two companies with the same name.

4 Click the Indexes Tool

To create a multi-field index, choose **View, Indexes**. The **Indexes** window appears.

5 Type the Index Name

Type the desired index name in the **Index Name** column.

6 Select the Desired Fields

From the **Field Name** column, select the desired fields to include in the index.

Before You Begin

✔ **42** Build a New Table

✔ **43** About Selecting the Appropriate Field Type for Your Data

✔ **70** About Working with Field Properties

See Also

→ **78** Refine Your Queries with Field, Field List, and Query Properties

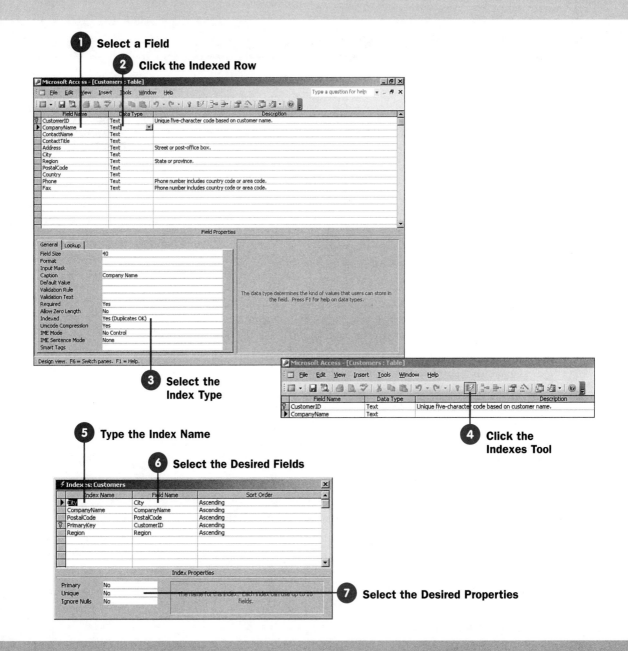

① **Select a Field**

② **Click the Indexed Row**

③ **Select the Index Type**

④ **Click the Indexes Tool**

⑤ **Type the Index Name**

⑥ **Select the Desired Fields**

⑦ **Select the Desired Properties**

⑦ **Select the Desired Properties**

Select the desired index properties. Click **Close** to close the **Indexes** dialog box.

13

Power Query Techniques

IN THIS CHAPTER:

74 **Apply Advanced Filters**

Before You Begin

✔ **48** Create Queries

✔ **52** About Building Queries Based on Multiple Tables

✔ **53** Create Calculated Fields

See Also

→ **75** Create and Run Parameter Queries

→ **77** Incorporate Aggregate Functions

Using advanced filters, you can further refine the data that appears in a query result. You can apply advanced filters to tables or queries while in **Datasheet** view.

1 **Open a Query or Table**

In **Datasheet** view, open the query or table whose data you want to filter.

2 **Select Records, Filter, Advanced Filter/Sort**

Select **Records, Filter, Advanced Filter/Sort**. The filter design grid appears.

3 **Add Fields to the Design Grid**

Add to the design grid the fields on which you want to filter.

4 **Enter Criteria**

For each field on the grid, enter the value or expression that you want to use as a filter in the **Criteria** cell for the fields you have included.

5 **Select Filter, Apply Filter/Sort**

Click **Apply Filter** or select **Filter, Apply Filter/Sort**. Access applies the filter that you created.

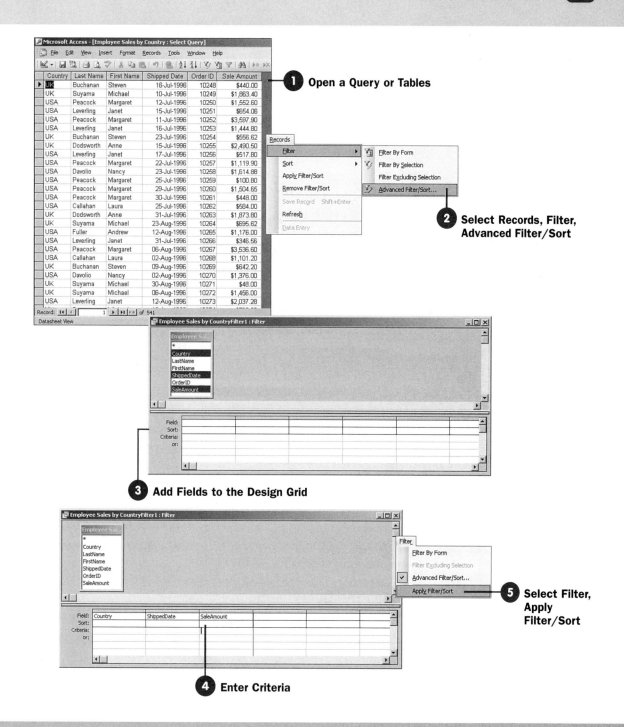

1 Open a Query or Tables

2 Select Records, Filter, Advanced Filter/Sort

3 Add Fields to the Design Grid

5 Select Filter, Apply Filter/Sort

4 Enter Criteria

75 Create and Run Parameter Queries

Before You Begin

✔ **48** Create Queries

✔ **52** About Building Queries Based on Multiple Tables

✔ **53** Create Calculated Fields

See Also

→ **76** Create and Run Action Queries

→ **77** Incorporate Aggregate Functions

You might not always know the parameters for the query output when you're designing a query—and your application's users also might not know the parameters. *Parameter queries* let you specify specific criteria at runtime so that you don't have to modify the query each time you want to change the criteria.

1 Open Query in Design View

Open a query in **Design** view.

2 Click the Criteria Cell

Click the criteria cell.

3 Enter the Parameters

Rather than typing the parameters as you usually do, instead surround the "variables" with square brackets.

For example, imagine you have a query for which you want users to specify the date range they want to view each time they run the query. You have entered the following clause as the criterion for the **OrderDate** field:

Between [Enter Start Date] And [Enter End Date]

This criterion causes two dialog boxes to appear when the user runs the query. The first one prompts the user with the text in the first set of brackets. Access substitutes the text the user types for the bracketed text. A second dialog box appears, prompting the user for whatever is in the second set of brackets. Access uses the user's responses as criteria for the query.

4 Open the Query Parameters Dialog

To make sure Access understands what type of data the user should place in these parameters, you must define the parameters. You do this by selecting **Query**, **Parameters** to open the **Query Parameters** dialog box. Another way to display the **Query Parameters** dialog box is to right-click a gray area in the top half of the query grid and then select **Parameters** from the context menu.

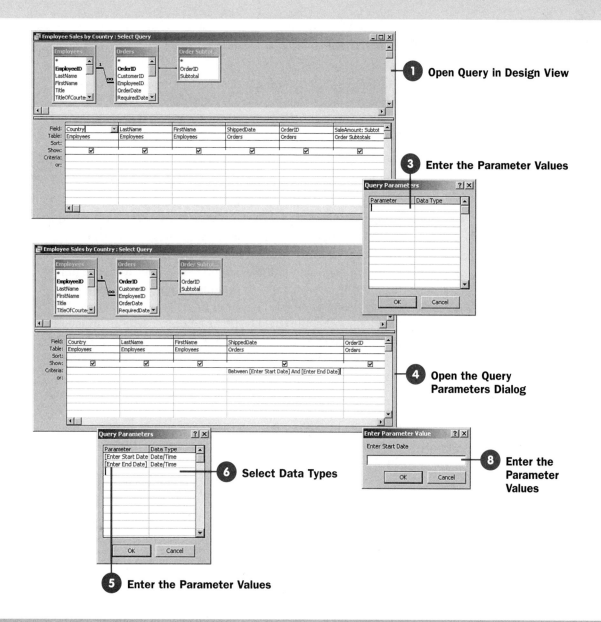

1 Open Query in Design View

3 Enter the Parameter Values

4 Open the Query Parameters Dialog

6 Select Data Types

8 Enter the Parameter Values

5 Enter the Parameter Values

5 **Enter the Parameter Values**

You must enter the text that appears within the brackets for each parameter in the **Parameter** field of the **Query Parameters** dialog box.

6 **Select Data Types**

You must define the type of data in the brackets in the **Data Type** column.

You can easily create parameters for as many fields as you want. You add additional parameters just as you would add more criteria. For example, you could enter parameters for the **Title**, **HireDate**, and **City** fields in the **Employees** table from the Northwind database. All the criteria would appear on one line of the query grid, which means that all the parameters entered must be satisfied in order for the records to appear in the output. The criterion for the title could be [**Please Enter a Title**]. This means that the records in the result must match the title the user enters when he or she runs the query. The criterion for the **HireDate** field could be >=[**Please Enter a Hire Date**]. Only records with a hire date on or after the hire date the user enters when he or she runs the query appear in the output. Finally, the criterion for the **City** field could be [**Please Enter a City**]. This means that only records with City containing the value the user enters when he or she runs the query will appear in the output.

When you are finished entering the parameters, click **OK**. This closes the **Parameters** dialog.

NOTE

Parameter queries offer significant flexibility because they allow the user to enter specific criteria at runtime. What you type in the **Query Parameters** dialog box must exactly match what you type within the brackets; otherwise, Access prompts the user with additional dialog boxes.

7 **Click Run**

Click **Run** to run the Parameter query.

8 **Enter the Parameter Values**

Access prompts you with an **Enter Parameter Value** dialog. Enter the first parameter, and click **OK**.

9 **Repeat Step 8 as Necessary**

Repeat step 8 as Access prompts you with additional **Enter Parameter Value** dialogs.

76 Create and Run Action Queries

With Action queries, you can easily modify data without writing any code. In fact, using Action queries is often a more efficient method of modifying data than using code. Four types of Action queries are available: Update, Delete, Append, and Make Table.

You use *Update* queries to modify all records or any records that meet specific criteria. You can use an Update query to modify the data in one field or several fields (or even tables) at one time. For example, you could create a query that increases the salary of everyone in California by 10%. As mentioned previously, using Action queries, including Update queries, is usually more efficient than performing the same task with Visual Basic for Applications (VBA) code, so you can consider Update queries a respectable way to modify table data.

Rather than simply modifying table data, *Delete* queries permanently remove from a table any records that meet specific criteria; they're often used to remove old records. You might want to use a Delete query to delete all orders from the previous year, for example.

You can use *Append* queries to add records to existing tables. You often perform this function during an archive process. First, you append the records that need to be archived to the history table by using an Append query. Next, you remove the records from the master table by using a Delete query.

Whereas an Append query adds records to an existing table, a *Make Table* query creates a new table, which is often a temporary table used for intermediary processing. You might want to create a temporary table, for example, to freeze data while you are running a report. By building temporary tables and running a report from those tables, you make sure users can't modify the data underlying the report during the reporting process. Another common use of a Make Table query is to supply a subset of fields or records to another user.

1 Click Queries

In the Database window, Click **Queries** in the **Objects** list.

2 Double-click Create Query in Design View

Double-click the **Create Query in Design View** icon. The **Show Table** dialog box appears.

Before You Begin

✔ **48** Create Queries
✔ **52** About Building Queries Based on Multiple Tables
✔ **53** Create Calculated Fields

See Also

→ **77** Incorporate Aggregate Functions

KEY TERMS

Update query—A query that updates all data in a table that meets the specified criteria.

Delete query—A query that deletes all data in a table that meets the specified criteria.

Append query—A query that appends data meeting specified criteria in the source table to a destination table.

Make Table query—A query that makes a new table containing all records meeting the specified criteria in the source table.

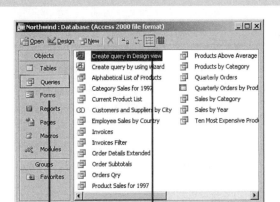

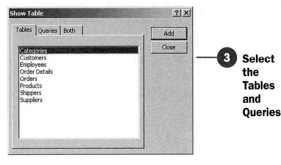

3 Select the Tables and Queries

1 Click Queries **2** Double-click Create Query in Design View

5 Add Fields

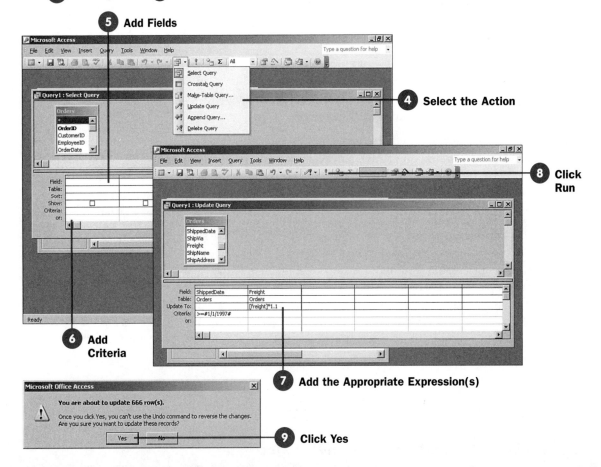

4 Select the Action

8 Click Run

6 Add Criteria

7 Add the Appropriate Expression(s)

9 Click Yes

❸ Select the Tables and Queries

In the **Show Table** dialog box, select the tables or queries that will participate in the action query and click **Add**. Click **Close** when you're ready to continue.

❹ Select the Action

To let Access know you're building an action query, open the **Query Type** drop-down list on the toolbar and select the appropriate query type. You can also choose **Query**, **Update Query**.

❺ Add Fields

Add to the query fields that you will use for criteria or that Access will update, delete, or insert as a result of the query.

❻ Add Criteria

Add the appropriate criteria to the query.

❼ Add the Appropriate Expression(s)

Add the appropriate expressions, if any. For example, with an Update query you may enter an expression that increases the Credit Limit by 10%.

❽ Click Run

Click **Run** on the toolbar. A message box appears, verifying that you want to proceed.

❾ Click Yes

Click **Yes** to continue. Access updates, deletes, or inserts all records that meet the selected criteria.

77 Incorporate Aggregate Functions

Before You Begin

✔ **48** Create Queries

✔ **52** About Building Queries Based on Multiple Tables

✔ **53** Create Calculated Fields

See Also

→ **78** Refine Your Queries with Field, Field List, and Query Properties

By using aggregate functions, you can easily summarize numeric data. You can use aggregate functions to calculate the sum, average, count, minimum, maximum, and other types of summary calculations for the data in a query result. These functions let you calculate one value for all the records in a query result or group the calculations as desired. For example, you could determine the total sales for every record in the query result, or you could output the total sales by country and city. You could also calculate the total, average, minimum, and maximum sales amounts for all customers in the United States. The possibilities are endless.

1 Create a Query

Create a new query based on data that you want to summarize.

2 Add the Fields to Summarize

Add to the query grid the fields or expressions you want to summarize. It's important that you add the fields in the order in which you want them grouped. For example, you can create a query grouped by country and then by city.

3 Click Totals

Click **Totals** on the toolbar or select **View**, **Totals** to add a **Total** row to the query. By default, each field in the query has **Group By** in the **Total** row.

4 Click the Total Row

Click the **Total** row on the design grid.

5 Select a Calculation

Open the combo box and choose the calculation you want.

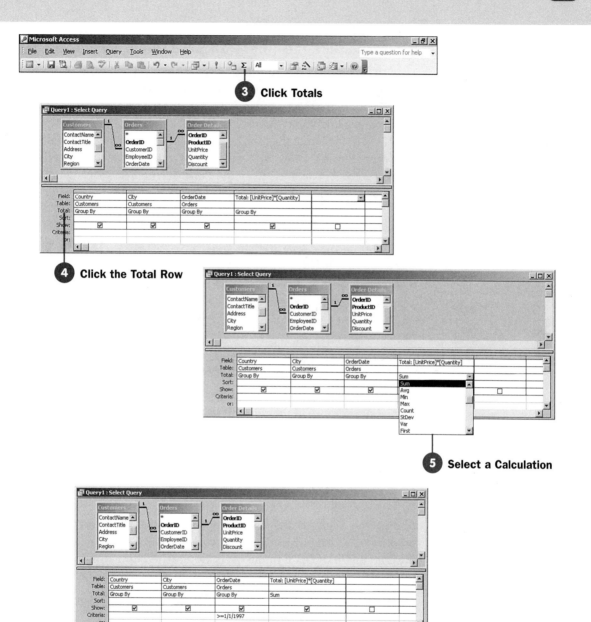

3 Click Totals

4 Click the Total Row

5 Select a Calculation

6 Make Sure the Total Row Says Group By

Leave **Group By** in the **Total** row for any field you want to group by. Remember to place the fields in the order in which you want them grouped. For example, if you want the records grouped by country and then by contact title, you must place the **Country** field to the left of the **ContactTitle** field on the query grid. On the other hand, if you want records grouped by contact title and then by country, you must place the **ContactTitle** field to the left of the **Country** field on the query grid.

7 Add Criteria

Add the appropriate criteria to the query.

8 Click Run

Click **Run** on the toolbar.

---

78 Refine Your Queries with Field, Field List, and Query Properties

Before You Begin

✔ **48** Creating Queries

✔ **52** About Building Queries Based on Multiple Tables

✔ **53** Create Calculated Fields

You can use field and query properties to refine and control the behavior and appearance of the columns in a query and of the query itself.

The properties of a field in a query include the **Description**, **Format**, **Input Mask**, and **Caption** properties of the column. The **Description** property documents the use of the field and controls what appears on the status bar when the user is in that column in the query result. The **Format** property is the same as the **Format** property in a table's field: It controls the display of the field in the query result. The **Input Mask** property, like its table counterpart, actually controls how the user enters the data and modifies it in the query result. The **Caption** property in the query does the same thing as a **Caption** property of a field: It sets the caption for the column in **Datasheet** view and the default label for forms and reports.

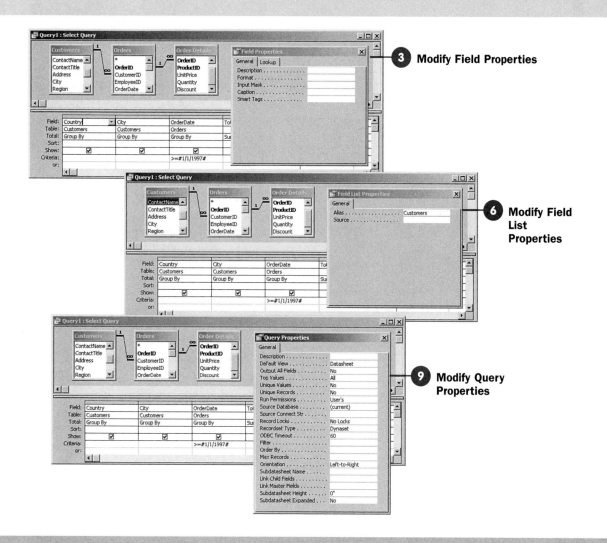

3 Modify Field Properties

6 Modify Field List Properties

9 Modify Query Properties

NOTE

You can use the **Input Mask** property of the query to further restrict the **Input Mask** property of the table, but not to override it. If the query's **Input Mask** property conflicts with the table's **Input Mask** property, the user will not be able to enter data into the table.

You might be wondering how the properties of the fields in a query interact with the same properties of a table. For example, how does the **Caption** property of a table's field interact with the **Caption** property of the same field in a query? All properties of a table's field are automatically inherited in queries. Properties you explicitly modify in a query override those same properties of a table's fields. Any objects based on the query inherit the properties of the query, not those of the original table.

Field list properties specify attributes of each table participating in a query. The two field list properties are **Alias** and **Source**. You most often use the **Alias** property when you use the same table more than once in the same query. You do this in self-joins. The **Source** property specifies a connection string or database name when you're dealing with external tables that aren't linked to the current database.

Microsoft offers many properties that allow you to affect the behavior of a query. The **Description** property documents what the query does. Access 2002 introduced the **Default View** property. This property determines which view displays by default whenever the user runs the query. **Datasheet** is the default setting; **PivotTable** and **PivotChart** are the other two **Default View** property settings that are available. **Output All Fields** shows all the fields in the query results, regardless of the contents of the **Show** check box in each field. **Top Values** lets you specify the top x number or x percentage of values in the query result. You use the **Unique Values** and **Unique Records** properties to determine whether Access displays only unique values or unique records in the query's output. The **Top Values**, **Unique Values**, and **Unique Records** properties are covered in more detail later in this section.

The **Subdatasheet Name** property allows you to specify the name of the table or query that will appear as a subdatasheet within the current query. After you set the **Subdatasheet Name** property, the **Link Child Fields** and **Link Master Fields** properties designate the fields from the child and parent tables or queries that Access uses to link the current query to its subdatasheet. Finally, the **Subdatasheet Height** property sets the maximum height for a subdatasheet, and the **Subdatasheet Expanded** property determines whether the subdatasheet automatically appears in an expanded state.

The **Top Values** property enables you to specify a certain percentage or a specific number of records that the user wants to view in the query result. For example, you can build a query that outputs the country/city combinations with the top 10 sales amounts. You can also build a query that shows the country/city combinations whose sales rank in the top 50%. You can specify the **Top Values** property in a few different ways. Here are two examples:

- Click the **Top Values** combo box on the toolbar and choose from the predefined list of choices. (Note that this combo box is not available for certain field types.)

- Type a number or a number with a percent sign directly into the **Top Values** property in the Query Properties window, or select one of the predefined entries from the drop-down list for the property.

Remember that the field(s) Access uses to determine the top values must appear as the left-most field(s) in the query's sort order.

Also, you might be surprised to discover that the **Top Values** property doesn't always seem to accurately display the correct number of records in the query result. All records with values that match the value in the last record are returned as part of the query result. In a table with 100 records, for example, the query asks for the top 10 values. Twelve records appear in the query result if the 10th, 11th, and 12th records all have the same value in the field being used to determine the top value.

When it is set to **Yes**, the **Unique Values** property causes the query output to contain no duplicates for the combination of fields included in it. For example, if you create a query that includes only the **Country** and **City** fields from **tblClients**, and the **Unique Values** property is set to **No** (its default value), many combinations of countries and cities appear more than once. This happens whenever more than one client is found in a particular country and city. When the **Unique Values** property is set to **Yes**, each combination of country and city appears only once.

The default value for the **Unique Records** property is **No**. Setting it to **Yes** causes Access to include the **DISTINCTROW** statement in the SQL statement underlying the query. When set to **Yes**, the **Unique Records** property denotes that Access includes only unique rows in the recordset underlying the query in the query result—and not just unique rows based on the fields in the query result. The **Unique Records** property applies only to multitable queries; Access ignores it for any query that includes only one table.

Several other more advanced properties exist. These are covered in programming texts such as *Alison Balter's Mastering Access 2003 Desktop Development*.

❶ Click a Field

While in **Design view**, click to select a field within the query.

❷ Select Properties

Click the **Properties** tool to open the **Properties** window.

❸ Modify Field Properties

Modify the desired field properties.

❹ Click the Field List

While in **Design view**, click to select the **Field List**.

❺ Select Properties

If not already open, click the **Properties** tool to open the **Properties** window.

❻ Modify Field List Properties

Modify the desired **Field List** properties.

❼ Click a Blank Area in the Query Design Window

Click a blank area in the **Query Design** window. This selects the query.

❽ Select Properties

If not already open, click the **Properties** tool to open the **Properties** window.

❾ Modify Query Properties

Modify the desired **Query** properties. When you run the query, Access will apply the new property values.

14

Access and the Internet

IN THIS CHAPTER:

79 Export to HTML

Before You Begin

✔ **42** Build a New Table

✔ **43** About Selecting the
Appropriate Field
Type for Your Data

✔ **48** Create Queries

See Also

→ **80** Export to XML

→ **81** Import from HTML

→ **82** Import from XML

Probably one of the most basic but powerful features in Access is the capability to save database objects as HTML documents. You can publish table data, query results, form datasheets, forms, and reports as HTML. This allows users that do not have Access to update the tables in your database using a browser.

1 Click Tables in the Objects List

Click **Tables** in the **Objects** list of the **Database** window. The list of tables contained in the database appears.

2 Select the Appropriate Table

Select the table whose data you want to save as HTML.

3 Choose File, Export

Choose **File, Export** to open the **Export Table** dialog box.

4 Open the Save as Type Drop-Down

Click to open the **Save as type** drop-down.

5 Select HTML Documents

From the **Save as type** drop-down list, select **HTML Documents**. The list of existing HTML documents appears.

6 Select a Filename and Location

Select a filename and a location for the HTML document.

7 Click Export

Click **Export** to finish the process. Access exports the file to HTML so that you can view it from any Web browser. You can also view the HTML source. To view the HTML file in a browser, you simply locate the file on your hard disk in Explorer or My Computer and double-click the file. The file then launches in Internet Explorer (or your default browser). To view the source, you select **View, Source** while in Internet Explorer.

NOTE

The capability to save query results as HTML means you don't need to save all fields and all records to an HTML file. You can even save the results of Totals queries and other complex queries as HTML. You can also save form datasheets and reports (including formatting) as HTML.

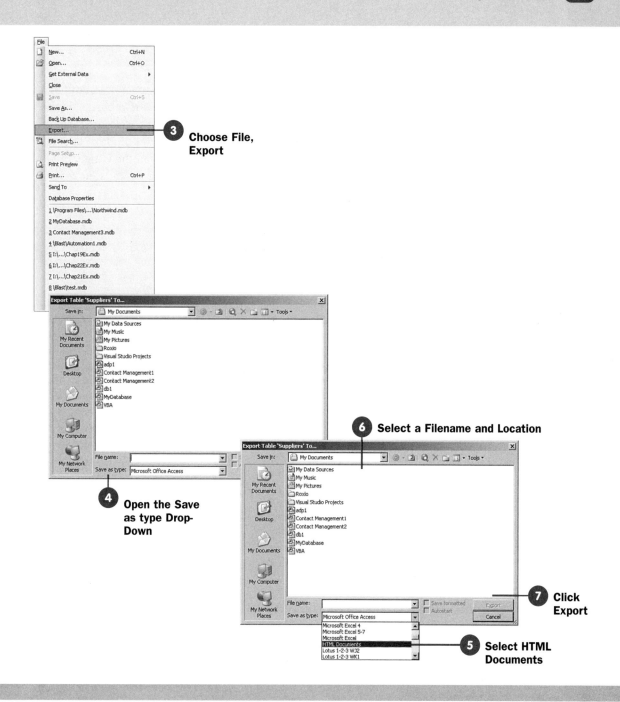

3 Choose File, Export

4 Open the Save as type Drop-Down

6 Select a Filename and Location

7 Click Export

5 Select HTML Documents

80 Export to XML

Before You Begin

✔ **42** Build a New Table

✔ **43** About Selecting
the Appropriate
Field Type for Your
Data

✔ **48** Create Queries

✔ **79** Export to HTML

See Also

→ **81** Import from HTML

→ **82** Import from XML

HTML has one major limitation: HTML inextricably combines data and its presentation. XML, on the other hand, allows you to separate data from its presentation. Furthermore, it provides a universal data format that can be read by a multitude of machines on a multitude of operating systems and platforms. It bridges the gap between the variety of systems that store data in a variety of disparate formats. Access makes it easy for you to export data to XML.

1 Right-click the Object to Export

Right-click the object you want to export. A list of available options appears.

2 Select Export

Select **Export** from the context menu. The **Export** dialog box appears.

3 Open the Save As Type Drop-down

Click to open the **Save as type** drop-down.

4 Select XML

Select **XML** from the drop-down.

5 Select a Folder to Export To

Select the folder where you want Access to save the XML file.

6 Click Export

Click **Export**. The **XML** dialog box appears.

7 Select What to Export

Select what to export: the data, the schema of the data, the presentation of the data, or any combination of the three.

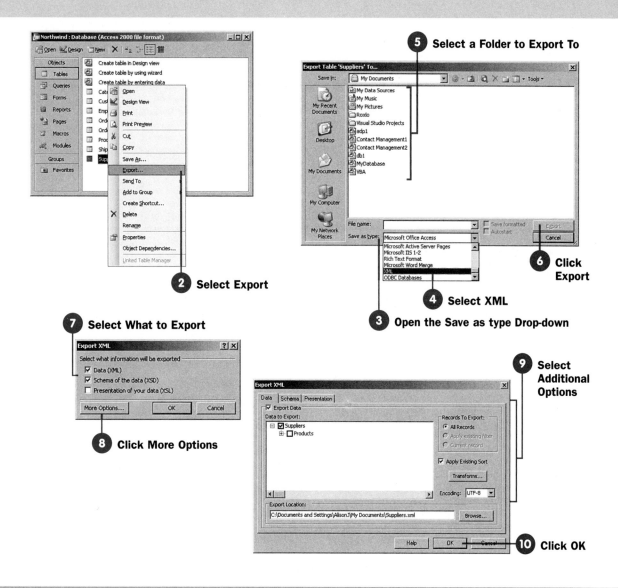

5 Select a Folder to Export To

2 Select Export

3 Open the Save as type Drop-down

4 Select XML

6 Click Export

7 Select What to Export

8 Click More Options

9 Select Additional Options

10 Click OK

8 ## Click More Options

Click the **More Options** button to designate additional options. Once you have clicked the **More Options** button, numerous sophisticated options are available. For example, you can select the encoding type, a filter for the records to export, whether you want to export related tables, and much, much more!

9 Select Additional Options

Select options such as including data from related tables.

10 Click OK

Click **OK** to create the XML document.

81 Import from HTML

81 Import from HTML

Before You Begin

✔ **42** Build a New Table

✔ **43** About Selecting the Appropriate Field Type for Your Data

✔ **48** Create Queries

✔ **79** Export to HTML

See Also

→ **82** Import from XML

→ **83** Create and Modify Data Access Pages

You can import the data from an HTML file so that it becomes exactly like any other Access table.

1 Right-click in the Database Window

Right-click anywhere in the **Database** window. A list of available options appears.

2 Select Import

Select **Import** from the context-sensitive menu. The **Import** dialog box appears.

3 Open the File of Type Drop-down

Open the **File of Type** drop-down.

4 Select HTML Documents

Select **HTML Documents**.

5 Select the HTML File to Import

Select the HTML file you want to import.

6 Click Import

Click **Import** to open the **Import HTML** wizard.

2 Select Import

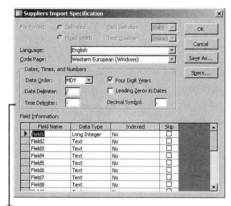

9 Designate Specifics About the Import

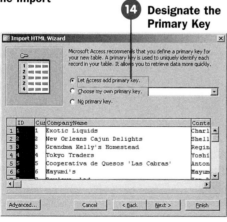

14 Designate the Primary Key

7 Indicate Whether First Row Contains Column Headings

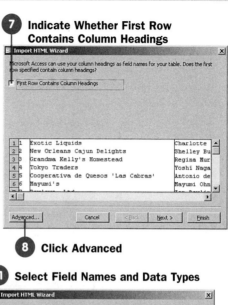

8 Click Advanced

11 Select Field Names and Data Types

13 Select Fields to Exclude

12 Select Fields to Index

CHAPTER 14: Access and the Internet

7 Indicate Whether First Row Contains Column Headings

Indicate whether the first row of data contains column headings. You can see Access's proposed layout for the imported table.

8 Click Advanced

Click **Advanced**. The **Import Specification** dialog box opens.

9 Designate Specifics About the Import

Select which fields you want to include in the imported table, date delimiters, and other specifics of the imported file. Make the appropriate selections and then click **OK**. Click **Next** to advance to the next step of the wizard.

10 Select New or Existing Table

You have the choice of importing the data into a new table or adding it to an existing table. Designate the appropriate option. Click **Next** to proceed to the next step of the wizard.

11 Select Field Names and Data Types

Select a field name and a data type for each field in the HTML file.

12 Select Fields to Index

Designate whether you want Access to create an index for each field.

13 Select Fields to Exclude

Designate which fields you want Access to exclude from the import. Click **Next** to continue with the wizard.

14 Designate the Primary Key

Designate a primary key for the imported table. If you prefer, you can have Access supply the primary key. Click **Next** to proceed to the final step of the wizard.

15 Supply a Table Name

Supply a table name for the imported table. If you're concerned about whether the imported table is normalized, you can have Access launch the **Table Analyzer** after it completes the import process.

16 Click Finish

Click **Finish** to perform the import.

82 Import from XML

You can import an XML file into Access. The process is very simple but is also somewhat limited in that it does not provide you with very many import options. For example, it strictly limits the format for the XML file that you are importing.

1 Open the Destination Database

Open the database that is to contain the XML file.

2 Right-click the Database Window

Right-click anywhere in the **Database** window. A list of available options appears.

3 Click Import

Click **Import**. The **Import** dialog box appears.

4 Open the Files of Type Drop-down

Click to open the **Files of Type** drop-down.

5 Select XML

Select **XML**.

6 Select the Appropriate Folder

Select the folder where the XML file is located.

Before You Begin

✔ **42** Build a New Table

✔ **43** About Selecting the Appropriate Field Type for Your Data

✔ **48** Create Queries

✔ **80** Export to XML

✔ **81** Import from HTML

See Also

→ **83** Create and Modify Data Access Pages

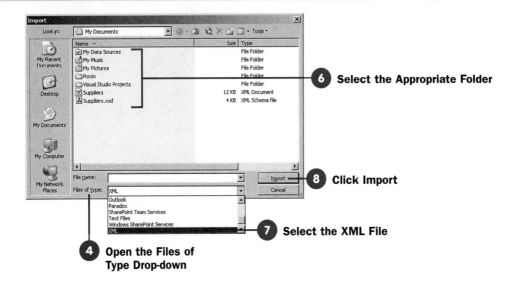

6 Select the Appropriate Folder

8 Click Import

7 Select the XML File

4 Open the Files of Type Drop-down

The only type of Schema Definition (XSD) files that Access can read are Access-generated XSD files. This means that unless an Access-generated XSD file is available to you to use during the import process, you have little control over the structure of the imported table.

If the XML file is not syntactically correct, the import process fails. In that case, Access generates an **ImportErrors** table.

7 **Select the XML File**

Select the XML file.

8 **Click Import**

Click **Import**. The **Import XML** dialog box appears. Click **OK**. A message appears indicating that the file was imported successfully.

83 Create and Modify Data Access Pages

Data access pages are similar to forms. Access stores them as dynamic HTML files with the .HTM extension. Users can view and update data access pages in Internet Explorer 5.0 and above.

1 **Click Pages**

Click **Pages** in the list of objects in the **Database** window. A list of existing data access pages appears.

2 **Double-click Create Data Access Page By Using Wizard**

Double-click the **Create Data Access Page By Using Wizard** option. The **Page Wizard** appears.

3 **Select a Table or Query**

Select the table or query on which you want to base the data access page.

4 **Select Fields**

Select the fields that you want to appear on the data access page. Click **Next** to continue.

5 **Select Grouping Levels**

Add any desired grouping levels to the page. In Access 2000 the created page is rendered not editable when you apply grouping. Fortunately, that is not the case in Access 2002 and 2003. Click **Next** to continue.

6 **Select a Sort Order**

Select a sort order for the records included on the page. You can select either ascending or descending order. Click **Next** to proceed to the next step of the wizard.

7 **Enter a Title**

Enter a title for the page.

Before You Begin

✔ **42** Build a New Table

✔ **43** About Selecting the Appropriate Field Type for Your Data

✔ **48** Create Queries

✔ **81** Import from HTML

✔ **82** Import from XML

See Also

➔ **84** Save PivotTables and PivotCharts to Data Access Pages

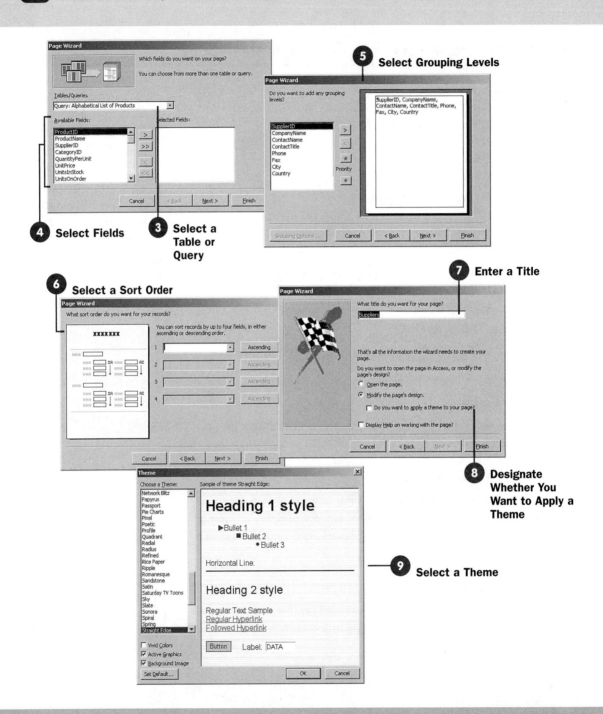

5 Select Grouping Levels

4 Select Fields

3 Select a Table or Query

7 Enter a Title

6 Select a Sort Order

8 Designate Whether You Want to Apply a Theme

9 Select a Theme

⑧ Designate Whether You Want to Apply a Theme

Designate whether you want to apply a theme to the page. Click **Finish** to complete the process.

⑨ Select a Theme

If you elected to apply a theme to the page, the **Theme** dialog box appears. Select a theme. Click **OK** to apply the theme. The page appears in Design view. Click **Save** to save the page. The **Save As** dialog appears.

⑩ Name the Page

Enter a name and location for the page. Click **Save** to save the .HTM file to the designated location.

⑪ Click Form view

Click **Form** view to view the page.

NOTE

Access does not store data access pages in a database file or project. Instead, it saves data access pages as HTML files.

84 Save PivotTables and PivotCharts to Data Access Pages

Access allows you to easily add **PivotTables** and **PivotCharts** to the data access pages that you create.

① Click Pages

From the **Database** window, click **Pages** in the list of objects. A list of existing data access pages appears.

② Double-click Create Data Access Page in Design View

Double-click the **Create Data Access Page in Design View** item. A new data access page appears in Design view.

③ Activate the Field List

Activate the field list.

Before You Begin

✔ **81** Import from HTML
✔ **82** Import from XML
✔ **83** Create and Modify Data Access Pages

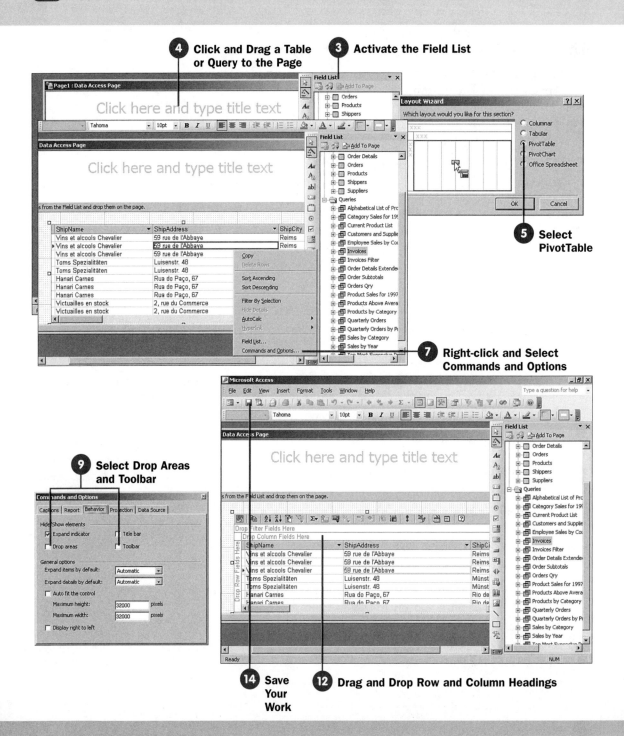

4 Click and Drag a Table or Query to the Page

3 Activate the Field List

5 Select PivotTable

7 Right-click and Select Commands and Options

9 Select Drop Areas and Toolbar

14 Save Your Work

12 Drag and Drop Row and Column Headings

4 Click and Drag a Table or Query to the Page

Click and drag a table or query to the data access page. The **Layout Wizard** appears.

5 Select PivotTable or PivotChart

Select **PivotTable** or **PivotChart**. Click **OK**. If you based the data access page on a query and the query required parameters, the **Enter Parameters** dialog box appears.

6 Enter Any Required Parameters

Enter any parameters required by the query.

Click **OK** to accept the parameter value. Access adds the PivotTable or PivotChart to the data access page. The PivotTable or PivotChart appears as a control on the page.

7 Right-click and Select Commands and Options

Right-click the control and select **Commands and Options** from the context menu. The **Commands and Options** dialog box appears.

8 Click the Behavior Tab

Click to select the **Behavior** tab. A list of available behavior options appears. Such options include whether the pivot table will contain an expand indicator and whether it will contain a toolbar.

9 Select Drop Areas and Toolbar

Click to select the **Drop Areas** and **Toolbar** check boxes. Close the **Commands and Options** window.

10 Switch to Form View

Switch to **Form** view.

11 Enter Necessary Parameters

Enter any parameters required by the underlying query.

12 Drag and Drop Row and Column Headings

Drag and drop row and column headings to the **Drop Filter Fields Here** and **Drop Column Fields Here** drop zones, as desired.

13 Use the Filter Drop-downs

Use the filter drop-downs to apply desired filters. For example, you can filter to show just the customers whose contact title is Owner.

14 Save Your Work

Click **Save** to save your work.

NOTE

The process of creating a PivotChart is almost identical to that of a PivotTable.

15

Database Administration

IN THIS CHAPTER:

85 Back Up and Restore a Database

New to Access 2003 is the ability to back up a database right from within Microsoft Access. Access databases can become corrupt. Many times, if you don't have a backup, you will lose all of your data. You also can lose your data if your system crashes—for instance, if you have a hard-disk crash. This further emphasizes the need for a backup.

I recommend backing up your database at least once a day. I also recommend iterative backups. This means that you back up to a different file name or location each day for seven days. Only after seven days do you overwrite the file from the previous week. Finally, it is very important that you back up to a physical drive different from the drive on which your source database is stored. This is so that in the case of a hard-disk failure, you can still recover your database.

1 Open the Database

Open the database that you want to back up.

2 Select Tools, Database Utilities, Back Up Database

Select **Tools, Database Utilities, Back Up Database**. The **Save Backup As** dialog box appears.

3 Supply a Filename and Location

Supply a filename and location for the database that you are backing up. Click **Save**. Access creates a backup that has the name and location that you designated.

NOTE

Because the backup process simply creates a copy of the open database with a name and in a location that you specify, restoring the database involves moving and/or renaming the backup database file to the production location and with the original name. You can then simply open the backup database and continue working as usual.

PART IV: Power Access Techniques

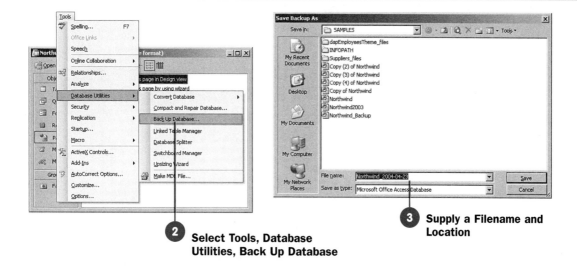

2 Select Tools, Database Utilities, Back Up Database

3 Supply a Filename and Location

86 Compact and Repair a Database

As you and the users of an application work with a database, the database grows in size. In order to maintain a high state of performance, Access defers the removal of discarded pages from the database until you explicitly compact the database file. This means that as you add data and other objects to a database and remove data and objects from the database, Access does not reclaim the disk space that the deleted objects occupied. This not only results in a very large database file, but it also ultimately degrades performance as the physical file becomes fragmented on disk. Compacting a database accomplishes the following tasks:

- It reclaims all the space occupied by deleted data and database objects.

- It reorganizes the database file so that the pages of each table in the database are contiguous. This improves performance because as the user works with the table, the data in the table is located contiguously on the disk.

Before You Begin

✔ **85** Back Up and Restore a Database

See Also

→ **87** Encode and Decode a Database

→ **88** Convert a Database to Another Version

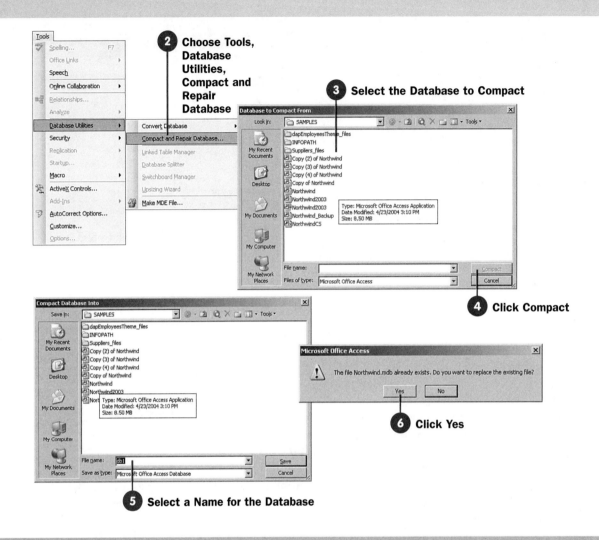

2 Choose Tools, Database Utilities, Compact and Repair Database

3 Select the Database to Compact

4 Click Compact

5 Select a Name for the Database

6 Click Yes

- It resets autonumber fields so that the next value will be one greater than the last undeleted counter value. If, while testing, you add many records that you delete just prior to placing the application in production, compacting the database resets all the counter values back to **1**.

- It re-creates the table statistics used by the Jet Engine when it executes queries, and it marks all queries so that Jet recompiles them the next time they are run. These are two very important related benefits of the compacting process. If you have added indexes to a table or if the volume of data in the table has changed dramatically, the query won't execute efficiently. This is because Jet bases the stored query plan it uses to execute the query on inaccurate information. When you compact the database, Jet updates all table statistics and the plan for each query to reflect the current state of the tables in the database.

To compact a database, you can use one of three techniques:

- Use commands provided in the user interface.

- Click an icon you set up.

- Set up the database so that Access compacts it whenever you close it.

Regardless of which method you select for the compacting procedure, the following conditions must be true:

- The user performing the procedure must have the rights to open the database exclusively.

- The user performing the procedure must have Modify Design permission for all tables in the database.

- The database must be available so that you or the user can open it for exclusive use. This means that no other users can be using the database.

- The drive or network share that the database is located on cannot be read-only.

- You cannot set the file attribute of the database to read-only.

- Enough disk space must be available for both the original database and the compacted version of the database. This is true even if you compact the database to a database with the same name as the original.

It is a good idea to back up a database before you attempt to compact it. It is possible for the compacting process to damage the database, such as when a power failure occurs during the compacting process. Also, you should not use the compacting process as a substitute for carefully

TIP

You should defragment the hard drive that a database is stored on before performing the compacting process. The disk defragmentation process ensures that as much contiguous disk space as possible is available for the compacted database. The compaction process is a defragmentation of the database. By defragmenting the disk drive and then the database, you increase database performance.

following backup procedures. The compacting process is not always successful. Nothing is as foolproof as a fastidiously executed routine backup process.

If, at any time, Access detects that something has damaged a database, it prompts you to repair the database. This occurs when you attempt to open, encode, or decode a damaged database. At other times, Access might not detect the damage. Instead, you might suspect that damage has occurred because the database behaves unpredictably. If you suspect damage, you should first back up and then perform the compacting process, using one of the methods covered in this chapter. The text that follows covers compacting a database *other* than the open database.

1 Close the Open Database

Close the currently open database.

2 Choose Tools, Database Utilities, Compact and Repair Database

Choose **Tools, Database Utilities, Compact and Repair Database**. The **Database to Compact From** dialog box appears.

3 Select the Database to Compact

Select the database that you want to compact.

4 Click Compact

Click **Compact**. The **Compact Database Into** dialog box appears.

5 Select a Name for the Database

Select a name for the compacted database. You can make it the same name as the original database name, or you can create a new name. (If you are compacting a database to the same name, make sure that it is backed up.) Click **Save**.

6 Click Yes

If you select the same name for the compacted database as for the original, Access prompts you to replace the existing file. Click **Yes**.

NOTE

To compact and repair the currently open database, simply select **Tools, Database Utilities, Compact and Repair Database**. Access will close the database, compact and repair it, and then reopen it.

87 Encode and Decode a Database

Even after you secure a database, someone with a disk editor can view the contents of the file. Although the data in the file will not appear in an easy-to-read format, the data is there and available for unauthorized individuals to see.

You might be feeling discouraged and asking why you should bother with security. Do not despair! Access enables you to encode a database, rendering the data in the database indecipherable in word processors, disk utilities, and other products that are capable of reading text. When a database is encoded, it is difficult to decipher any of its data.

When you encode a database, Access encodes the entire database—not just the data. As you access the data and the objects in the database, Access needs to decode the objects so that users can use them. When users are finished accessing the objects, Access encodes them again. Regardless of the encoding method you use, the encoded database degrades performance by about 15%. Furthermore, encoded databases usually cannot be compressed by most disk-compression software utilities because compression software usually relies on repeated patterns of data. The encoding process is so effective at removing any patterns that it renders most compression utilities ineffective. You need to decide whether this decrease in performance and the inability to compress the database file is worth the extra security that the encoding process provides.

1 Select Tools, Security, Encode/Decode Database

Select **Tools, Security, Encode/Decode Database**. The **Encode/Decode Database** dialog box appears.

2 Select the File to Encode

In the **Encode/Decode Database** dialog box, select the file you want to encode. Click **OK**. Access prompts you for the name of the encoded database.

3 Select a Name

Select a name for the encoded database. If you select the same name as the existing file, Access deletes the original decoded file after it determines that the encode process is successful.

Before You Begin

✔ **85** Back Up and Restore a Database

✔ **86** Compact and Repair a Database

See Also

→ **88** Convert a Database to Another Version

→ **89** Create an MDE File

→ **90** Use the Database Splitter

NOTE

You cannot encode a database to itself if it is open. You must first close the database and then select **Tools, Security, Encode/Decode Database**.

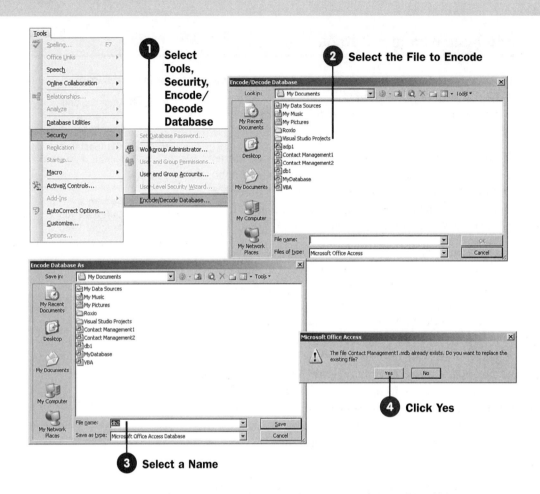

Select Tools, Security, Encode/Decode Database

2 Select the File to Encode

3 Select a Name

4 Click Yes

 TIP

It is always a good idea to back up the original database before you begin the encode process. This ensures that if something goes awry during the encode process, you won't lose data.

4 Click Yes

If you are encoding the database into a database of the same name, Access will prompt you to replace the file. Click **Yes**.

88 Convert a Database to Another Version

Access 2002 and 2003 make it easy to interact with other versions of Access. Access 2002 and 2003 allow you to open, read, and update Access databases stored in the Access 2000 file format without converting the files to the Access 2002-2003 file format. Furthermore, Access 2002 and 2003 allow you to easily convert files stored in the Access 2002-2003 file format to either the Access 97 or the Access 2000 file format. In this way you can share data with users who are still using Access 97 or Access 2000.

In versions of Access prior to Access 2002, when problems occur during the conversion process, users are left wondering exactly what has gone awry. Access 2002 and Access 2003 address this problem. If errors occur while converting from earlier versions of Access to the Access 2002-2003 file format, Access creates a table that lists each error. You can easily use the data in that table to handle the conversion problem gracefully.

Before You Begin

✔ **85** Back Up and Restore a Database

✔ **86** Compact and Repair a Database

✔ **87** Encode and Decode a Database

See Also

→ **89** Create an MDE File

→ **90** Use the Database Splitter

1 Open the Source Database

Open the database that you wish to convert.

2 Select Tools, Database Utilities, Convert Database

Select **Tools, Database Utilities, Convert Database**.

3 Select the Destination Format

Select the destination format. The options are **To Access 97 File Format**, **To Access 2000 File Format**, and **To Access 2002-2003 File Format**. Depending on the version of the current database, one of the options will be unavailable. Once you make your selection, the **Convert Database Into** dialog appears.

4 Enter a Name and Location

Enter a name and location for the converted file.

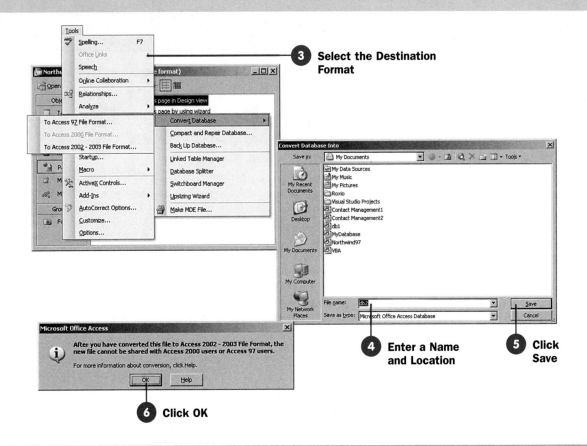

③ Select the Destination Format

④ Enter a Name and Location

⑤ Click Save

⑥ Click OK

⑤ Click Save

Select **Save**. A warning message appears regarding compatibility of the new version of the database. The message differs depending on the version that you are converting from and to.

⑥ Click OK

Click **OK** to close the dialog.

NOTE

After converting a database to another format, you remain in the original database. If you wish to work with the converted database, you must first open it.

Access 2003 offers an additional level of security through the creation of MDE files. An *MDE (compiled database) file* is a database file that has all editable source code removed. This means that Access eliminates all the source code behind the forms, reports, and modules contained in the database. The forms, reports, and modules still run as usual. It is just that they contain only compiled code. An MDE file offers additional security because the forms, reports, and modules in an MDE file cannot be modified. Other benefits of an MDE file include reduced size and optimized memory usage.

Before you begin creating and using MDE files, you need to be aware of the restrictions they impose. If you plan ahead, these restrictions probably will not cause you too many problems. On the other hand, if you enter the world of MDE files unaware, they can cause you much grief. You should consider these restrictions:

- No one can view or modify the design of the forms, reports, and modules in an MDE file. In fact, no one can add new forms, reports, and modules to an MDE file. It is therefore important that you keep the original database when you create an MDE file: That is where you will make changes to existing forms, reports, and modules and add new forms, reports, and modules. When you are finished making changes to the database, you simply rebuild the MDE file.

- Because you must rebuild the MDE file every time you make changes to the application, the front-end/back-end approach is a good approach to take: You place the tables in a standard Access database and store the other objects in the MDE file. You can therefore rebuild the MDE file without worrying about the reconciliation of data.

- You cannot import or export forms, reports, or modules to or from an MDE file.

- You cannot convert an MDE file to later versions of Access. It is necessary to convert the original database and then rebuild the MDE file with the new version.

Before You Begin

✔ **85** Back Up and Restore a Database

✔ **86** Compact and Repair a Database

✔ **87** Encode and Decode a Database

✔ **88** Convert a Database to Another Version

See Also

→ **90** Use the Database Splitter

KEY TERM

MDE file—A database file that has all editable source code removed.

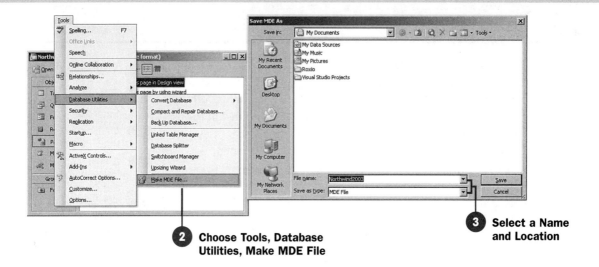

2 Choose Tools, Database Utilities, Make MDE File

3 Select a Name and Location

- You cannot add or remove references to object libraries and databases from an MDE file. Also, you cannot change references to object libraries and databases.

- Every library database that an MDE references also must be an MDE file. This means that if Database1 references Database2, which references Database3, all three databases must be stored as MDE files. You first must save Database3 as an MDE file, reference it from Database2, and then save Database2 as an MDE file. You can then reference Database2 from Database1, and finally, you can save Database1 as an MDE file.

- A replicated database cannot be saved as an MDE file. The replication must first be removed from the database. You accomplish this by removing the replication system tables and properties from the database. The database can then be saved as an MDE file, and the MDE file can be replicated and distributed as a replica set. Any time changes must be made to the database, they must be made to the original database, resaved as an MDE file, and then redistributed as a new replica set.

- Any security that applies to a database follows through to an MDE file that is created from it. To create an MDE file from a database

that is already secured, you must first join the workgroup information file associated with the database. You must have Open/Run
and Open Exclusive permissions to the database. You must also
have Modify Design and Administer permissions to all tables in
the database, or you must own all tables in the database. Finally,
you must have Read Design permissions on all objects contained
in the database.

- If you want to remove security from the database, you must
remove the security from the original database and rebuild the
MDE file.

As long as you are aware of the restrictions associated with MDE files,
they can offer many benefits. In addition to the natural security they
provide, the size and performance benefits MDE files offer are significant.

1 Open the Source Database

Open the database on which you will base the MDE file.

2 Choose Tools, Database Utilities, Make MDE File

Choose **Tools, Database Utilities, Make MDE File**. The **Save MDE
As** dialog appears.

3 Select a Name and Location

Enter a name and location for the newly created MDE file. Click
Save to complete the process.

NOTE

A great use for MDE files is
for demo versions of applications. Performance of
MDE files is excellent, but
more importantly, if you
use Visual Basic for
Applications (VBA) code,
MDE files can easily be rendered both time- and data-
limited.

TIP

Other programmatic limita-
tions exist regarding MDE
files that are beyond the
scope of this book. To learn
more about these restric-
tions, please consult a programming text such as
*Alison Balter's Mastering
Access 2003 Desktop
Development.*

---

90 Use the Database Splitter

When you're designing an application, you should split the application
objects into two separate .MDB files. One .MDB file should contain the
tables, and the other should contain the application queries, forms,
reports, data access pages, macros, and modules. This allows you and
others to enter data while you continue to refine the other application
objects. When you need to make changes to the application, you simply
copy the application database. When you have made the appropriate
changes, you can copy the application database over the production
copy without overwriting the data in the database.

Before You Begin

✔ **85** Back Up and
Restore a
Database

✔ **86** Compact and
Repair a Database

✔ **87** Encode and
Decode a
Database

✔ **89** Create an MDE File

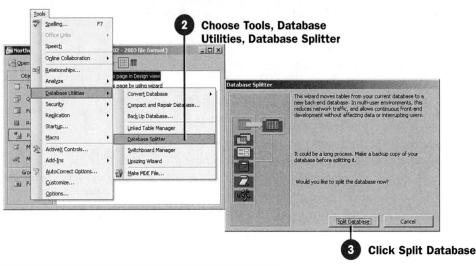

2 Choose Tools, Database Utilities, Database Splitter

3 Click Split Database

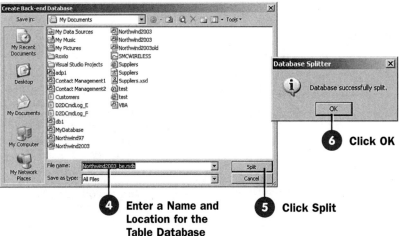

4 Enter a Name and Location for the Table Database

5 Click Split

6 Click OK

① Open the Database

Open the database whose objects you want to split.

② Choose Tools, Database Utilities, Database Splitter

Choose **Tools, Database Utilities, Database Splitter**. The **Database Splitter Wizard** appears.

3 **Click Split Database**

Click **Split Database**. The **Create Back-end Database** dialog box appears.

4 **Enter a Name and Location for the Table Database**

Enter a name and location for the database that will contain all the tables.

5 **Click Split**

Click **Split**. The **Database Splitter Wizard** creates a new database that holds all the tables. It creates links between the current database and the database that contains the tables.

6 **Click OK**

Click **OK** to complete the process.

16

Finishing Touches

IN THIS CHAPTER:

91 Add Toolbars

See Also

→ **92** Add Menu Bars
→ **93** Build Switchboards

KEY TERM

Command bars—Custom menu bars, toolbars, and pop-up menus.

You can create custom menus, toolbars, and shortcut menus to display with forms and reports. There's no limit to how many custom menu bars, toolbars, and shortcut menus you can use. You can attach each menu bar, toolbar, and shortcut menu to one or more forms or reports. Quite often, you need to restrict what users can do while they're working with a form or report. By creating a custom menu, toolbar, or shortcut menu, you can restrict and customize what users are allowed to do.

In Access, custom menu bars, toolbars, and pop-up menus are called *command bars*. To create any of these three objects, you choose **View**, **Toolbars** and then select **Customize**. After you have created a custom command bar, you can easily associate it with forms and reports by using the **MenuBar**, **Toolbar**, and **Shortcut MenuBar** properties.

1 **Choose View, Toolbars, and Click Customize**

Choose **View**, **Toolbars** and click **Customize** or right-click any command bar and select **Customize**. The **Customize** dialog appears.

2 **Click the Toolbars Tab**

Click the **Toolbars** tab.

3 **Click New**

Click **New**. The **New Toolbar** dialog appears.

4 **Assign a Name**

Assign a name for the toolbar. Click **OK** to close the dialog. The new toolbar appears.

5 **Click the Properties Button**

Click the **Properties** button on the **Customize** dialog box to view the properties for the newly created command bar. In the **Toolbar Properties** dialog box that appears, you name the toolbar, select the type, indicate the type of docking that's allowed, and set other options for the command bar.

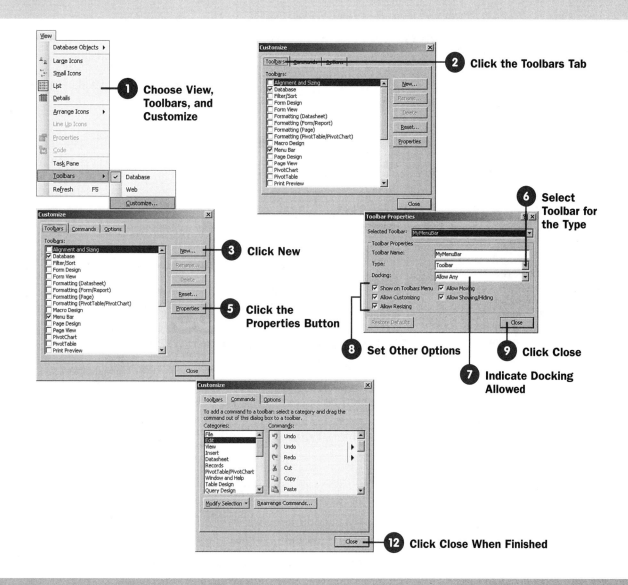

Select Toolbar for the Type

The **Type** drop-down list box allows you to select **Menu Bar**,
Toolbar, or **Pop-up**. Select **Toolbar** for the **Type**.

7 **Indicate Docking Allowed**

The options in the **Docking** drop-down list box are **Allow Any**, **Can't Change**, **No Vertical**, and **No Horizontal**. Indicate the docking that you would like to allow.

8 **Set Other Options**

You can also choose whether you will allow the user to customize or move the command bar. Select the appropriate options.

NOTES

Menu bars, toolbars, and pop-up menus are all referred to generically as *command bars*. The process you use to create each of these objects is very similar. You use the **Type** property of the command bar to designate the type of object you want to create.

To associate a toolbar with a form or report, set the **Toolbar** property of the form or report to the name of the appropriate toolbar.

9 **Click Close**

Click **Close** to close the **Toolbar Properties** dialog. Access returns you to the **Customize** dialog.

10 **Click the Commands Tab**

Click the **Commands** tab of the **Toolbars** dialog.

11 **Click and Drag Commands to the Toolbar**

Select the appropriate category in the list box on the left-hand side of the dialog. Then click and drag the appropriate command to the toolbar.

12 **Click Close When Finished**

Click **Close** to close the **Customize** dialog. You may now use your toolbar.

---

92 **Add Menu Bars**

Before You Begin

✔ **91** Add Toolbars

See Also

→ **93** Build Switchboards

→ **94** About Setting Startup Options

The process of adding menu bars to your application is quite similar to that of adding toolbars. There are some differences involved, which is why the discussion of menu bars warrants its own section.

1 **Choose View, Toolbars, and Click Customize**

Choose **View**, **Toolbars** and click **Customize** or right-click any command bar and select **Customize**. The **Customize** dialog appears.

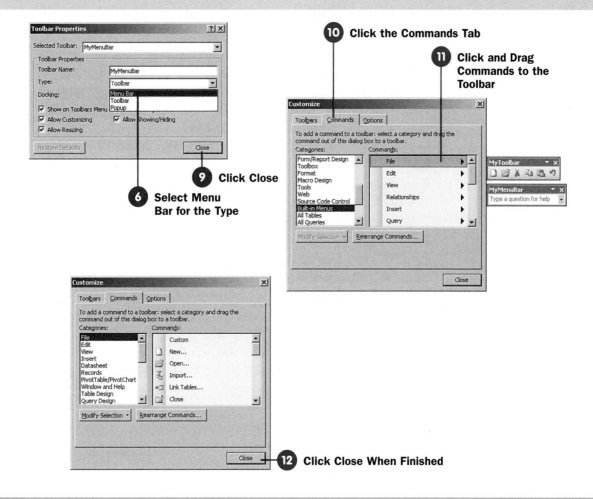

10 Click the Commands Tab

11 Click and Drag Commands to the Toolbar

9 Click Close

6 Select Menu Bar for the Type

12 Click Close When Finished

② Click the Toolbars Tab

Click the **Toolbars** tab.

③ Click New

Click **New**. The **New Toolbar** dialog appears.

④ Assign a Name

Assign a name for the menu. Click **OK** to close the dialog. The new menu bar appears.

---

5 Click the Properties Button

Click the **Properties** button on the **Customize** dialog box to view the properties for the newly created command bar. In the **Toolbar Properties** dialog box that appears, you name the menu bar, select the type, indicate the type of docking that's allowed, and set other options for the command bar.

6 Select Menu Bar for the Type

The **Type** drop-down list box allows you to select **Menu Bar**, **Toolbar**, or **Pop-up**. Select **Menu Bar** for the **Type**.

7 Indicate Docking Allowed

The options in the **Docking** drop-down list box are **Allow Any**, **Can't Change**, **No Vertical**, and **No Horizontal**. Indicate the docking that you would like to allow.

8 Set Other Options

You can also choose whether you will allow the user to customize or move the command bar. Select the appropriate options.

9 Click Close

Click **Close** to close the **Toolbar Properties** dialog. Access returns you to the **Customize** dialog.

10 Click the Commands Tab

Click the **Commands** tab of the **Toolbars** dialog. A list of available categories and commands appears.

11 Click and Drag Commands to the Toolbar

Select the appropriate category in the list box on the left side of the dialog. Then click and drag the appropriate command to the toolbar.

Here are some tips to help you to create custom menu bars, toolbars, and pop-up menus:

- To add an entire built-in menu to a menu bar, select **Built-in Menus** from the **Categories** list box on the **Commands** tab of the **Customize** dialog box. Click and drag a menu pad from the **Commands** list box over to the menu bar to add the entire built-in menu pad to the custom menu.

- To create a custom menu pad, select **New Menu** from the **Categories** list box. Click and drag the **New Menu** option to the menu bar. To modify the text on the menu pad, right-click the menu pad and type a new value in the **Name** text box.

- To add a built-in command to the menu, select a category from the **Categories** list box and then click and drag the appropriate command to the menu pad. The new item appears underneath the menu pad.

- To add a separator bar to a menu, right-click the menu item that will follow the separator bar and select **Begin a Group**. To remove the separator bar, again select **Begin a Group**.

- Menu items can contain text only or images and text. To select one of these options, right-click a menu item and select **Default Style**, **Text Only (Always)**, **Text Only (in Menus)**, or **Image and Text**. To customize an image, right-click a menu item and select **Change Button Image** and choose one of the available images. To modify the button image, right-click a menu item and select **Edit Button Image**; the **Button Editor** dialog box appears. If you want to reset the button to its original image, right-click the menu item and select **Reset Button Image**.

- If you want to modify several properties of a menu item at once, you can right-click the menu item and select **Properties** (while viewing the design of the menu) to open the **File Control Properties** dialog box. In this dialog box you can select properties for the menu item, such as **Caption**, **Screen Tip**, **Style**, **Help File**, and **Help ContextID**.

12 Click Close When Finished

Click **Close** to close the **Customize** dialog. You may now use your menu bar.

 NOTE

To associate a menu bar with a form or report, set the **Menu Bar** property of the form or report to the name of the appropriate menu bar.

93 Build Switchboards

Before You Begin

✔ **91** Add Toolbars

✔ **92** Add Menu Bars

See Also

→ **94** About Setting
Startup Options

When you're creating an application with distribution to users in mind, you need to build the application around forms. This means that everything in the application needs to be form-driven. The application generally should begin by displaying a Main switchboard. The Main switchboard can then navigate the user to additional switchboards, such as a Data Entry switchboard, Reports switchboard, Maintenance switchboard, and so on. The easiest way to create such a switchboard is by using the **Switchboard Manager**.

1 Choose Tools, Database Utilities, Switchboard Manager

Choose **Tools**, **Database Utilities**, **Switchboard Manager**. If you have not yet created a switchboard for the application, the **Switchboard Manager** message box appears, asking if you would like to create one.

2 Click Yes

Click **Yes**. The **Switchboard Manager** dialog box appears. Notice that Access automatically creates a Main Switchboard.

3 Click New

You must add additional switchboard pages. To do this, click **New**. The **Create New** dialog box appears.

4 Type a Name

Type a name for the new switchboard page.

5 Click OK

Click **OK**.

6 Repeat Steps 3 Through 5

Repeat steps 3 through 5 for each switchboard page you want to add.

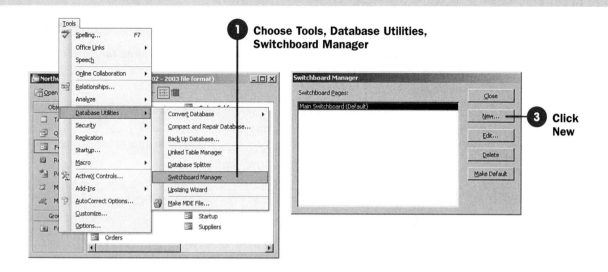

1 Choose Tools, Database Utilities, Switchboard Manager

3 Click New

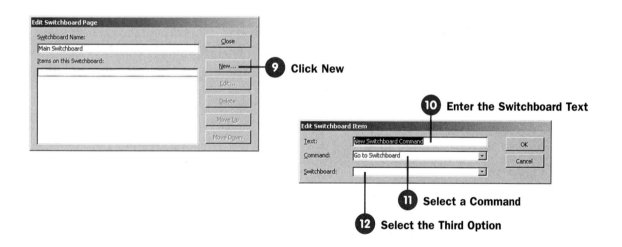

9 Click New

10 Enter the Switchboard Text

11 Select a Command

12 Select the Third Option

7 **Click the Switchboard Entry**

You now are ready to add items to each switchboard page. To add items to a page, click the page entry.

8 Click Edit

Click **Edit**. The **Edit Switchboard Page** dialog box appears.

9 Click New

Click **New** to add a new item to the switchboard page. The **Edit Switchboard Item** dialog box appears.

10 Enter the Switchboard Text

In the **Text** text box, enter the text for the new switchboard item.

11 Select a Command

Select an appropriate command from the **Command** drop-down list box. The commands that are available in this list box control the capability to go to another switchboard, open a form, and open a report.

12 Select the Third Option

The third item in the **Edit Switchboard Item** dialog box varies, depending on which command you select from the **Command** drop-down list box. If you select **Go to Switchboard** from the **Command** drop-down list box, for example, the third option enables you to select from available switchboards. If you select **Open Form in Edit Mode**, the third option enables you to select from available forms. If you select **Open Report**, the third option enables you to select from available reports. Select an appropriate value for the third option.

13 Click OK

Click **OK** to close the **Edit Switchboard Item** dialog.

14 Repeat Steps 9 Through 13

Repeat steps 9 through 13 for each item that you want to add to the selected switchboard.

15 Click Close

Click **Close** to close the **Edit Switchboard Page** dialog.

16 Repeat Steps 3 Through 14

Repeat steps 3 through 14 for all of the switchboard pages and
items that you want to add.

17 Click Close

Click **Close** to close the **Switchboard Manager**. Access generates
the switchboard.

NOTE

To add, remove, or edit
items from an existing
switchboard, choose **Tools**,
Database Utilities,
Switchboard Manager. The
Switchboard Manager dialog appears. Click **Delete**
to delete the page, click
Edit to make changes to
the page, or click **Add** to
add a new page.

94 About Setting Startup Options

Access provides several startup options that enable you to control what
happens to an application when it is loaded. The following figure shows
the **Startup** dialog box, and the following table lists each option in the
Startup dialog box.

Before You Begin

✔ 91 Add Toolbars

✔ 92 Add Menu Bars

✔ 93 Build Switchboards

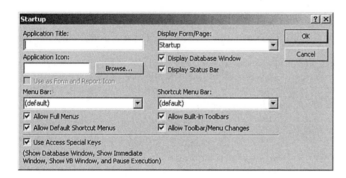

The Startup dialog box.

Startup Dialog Box Options

Option	Function
Application Title	Sets the **AppTitle** property, which displays a cus-tom title in the application title bar.
Application Icon	Sets the **AppIcon** property, which displays a cus-tom icon in the application title bar.
Menu Bar	Sets the **StartupMenuBar** property, which speci-fies the custom menu bar displayed by default when the application is loaded.

Option	Function
Allow Full Menus	Sets the **AllowFullMenus** property, which allows or restricts the use of Access menus.
Allow Default Shortcut Menus	Sets the **AllowShortcutMenus** property, which allows or restricts the use of standard Access shortcut menus (that is, menus accessed with a right-click).
Display Form/Page	Sets the **StartupForm** property, which specifies the form displayed when the application is loaded.
Display Database Window	Sets the **StartupShowDBWindow** property, which determines whether the **Database** window is visible when the application is opened.
Display Status Bar	Sets the **StartupShowStatusBar** property, which determines whether the status bar is visible when the application is opened.
Shortcut Menu Bar	Sets the **StartupShortcutMenuBar** property, which specifies that a menu bar should be displayed by default as the shortcut (that is, right-click) menu bar.
Allow Built-in Toolbars	Sets the **AllowBuiltInToolbars** property, which indicates whether built-in toolbars are available to users.
Allow Toolbar/Menu Changes	Sets the **AllowToolbarChanges** property, which determines whether users can customize toolbars in the application.
Use Access Special Keys	Sets the **AllowSpecialKeys** property, which determines whether users can use keys such as **F11** to display the **Database** window, **Ctrl+F11** to toggle between custom and built-in toolbars, and so on.

Notice that the **Use as Form and Report Icon** option that is available in the following figure is grayed out *before* you designate an application icon. When you check this option, Access uses the icon you designate as the application icon as the icon for forms and reports.

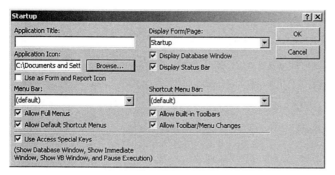

Using the application icon for forms and reports.

As you might have guessed, many of the options in the **Startup** dialog box apply only when you are running the application under the full version of Access (as opposed to the runtime version). You do not need to set the **Display Database Window** option, for example, if the application will be running only under the runtime version of Access. The **Database** window is never available under the runtime version of Access, so Access ignores this property when the application is run under the runtime version. Nevertheless, I like to set these properties to ensure that the application behaves as I want it to under *both* the retail and runtime versions of Access.

 NOTE

Only users with Administrator permission for the database can modify the **Startup** dialog box options. If you want to ensure that certain users cannot modify these options of the database, you must make sure that they do not have Administrator permission.

Index

Symbols

A

B

C

How can we make this index more useful? Email us at indexes@samspublishing.com

303

D

How can we make this index more useful? Email us at indexes@samspublishing.com

305

How can we make this index more useful? Email us at indexes@samspublishing.com

307

G-H

I

J-K

L

How can we make this index more useful? Email us at indexes@samspublishing.com

309

M

N

O

P

S

T

How can we make this index more useful? Email us at indexes@samspublishing.com

315

tables

U

V

W

X-Z

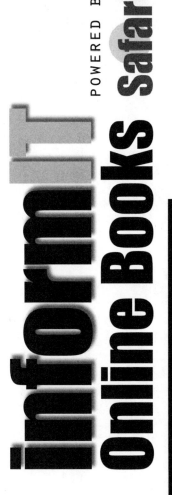

Your Guide
to Computer
Technology

Key Terms

Don't let unfamiliar terms discourage you from learning all you can about Microsoft Office Access 2003. If you don't completely understand what one of these words means, flip to the indicated page, read the full definition there, and find techniques related to that term.

Action query   *Lets you add to, update, and delete table data.*   **Page 16**

And condition   *Used to indicate that two or more conditions must be met in order for the row to be included in the resulting recordset.*   **65**

Append query   *A query that appends data meeting specified criteria in the source table to a destination table.*   **245**

Attached label   *Refers to the label that is attached to a data-bound control.*   **228**

AutoCorrect   *A feature shared with the rest of Microsoft Office that is designed to automatically correct common spelling errors as you type.*   **52**

Bound text box   *Displays and retrieves field information stored in a table.*   **187**

Column or field   *A single piece of information about an object (for example, a company name).*   **122**

Command bars   *Custom menu bars, toolbars, and pop-up menus.*   **288**

Comparison operator   *A symbol that allows you to compare two values.*   **229**

Composite key field   *A primary key field comprising more than one field in a table (for example, LastName and FirstName fields).*   **123**

Continuous Forms view   *Allows you to view multiple rows of data in a form at a time.*   **77**

Control   *An object that you add to a form or report.*   **178**

Data access pages   *Hypertext Markup Language (HTML) documents that are bound directly to data in a database.*   **7**

Data bound control   *A control that is bound to a field in a table or query.*   **228**

Database   *A collection of all the tables, queries, forms, data access pages, reports, macros, and modules that compose a complete system.*   **3**

Data normalization   *The process of eliminating duplicate information from a system by splitting information into several tables, each containing a unique value (that is, a primary key).*   **140**

Datasheet view   *Reflects any criteria, sort order, and other parameters defined for the query.*   **56**

Delete query   *A query that deletes all data in a table that meets the specified criteria.*   **Page 245**

Display format   *The format in which Access displays data.*   **43**

Dynamic HTML pages   *Pages that are published by the Web server each time that they are rendered.*   **7**

Dynaset   *A dynamic set of records, based on table data, that results from a query.*   **16**

Enforced referential integrity   *A rule by which Access looks up key values on the "many" side of a one-to-many relationship in a multitable query as you fill in those key values. The value entered on the "many" side must exist on the "one" side of the relationship.*   **169**

Filter   *Something you apply to fields in a table to allow you to hone in on the data that is important to you at a particular moment in time.*   **45**

Foreign key field   *A field on the many side of the relationship in a one-to-many relationship. Whereas the table on the one side of the relationship is related by the primary key field, the table on the many side of the relationship is related by the foreign key field.*   **123**

Form   *Allows you to display table data, or the results of a query.*   **72**

Input mask   *Controls data the user enters into a field.*   **231**

Logical operator   *An operator that allows you to create logical criteria.*   **229**

Macro   *Allows you to build logic into your application flow.*   **24**

Make Table query   *A query that makes a new table containing all records meeting the specified criteria in the source table.*   **245**

Many-to-many relationship   *Records in two tables have matching records.*   **143**

MDE file   *A database file that has all editable source code removed.*   **281**

Module   *Lets you create libraries of functions that you can use throughout an application.*   **25**

Natural key field   *A primary key field that is naturally part of the data contained within the table (for example, a Social Security number).*   **123**